A

Fishing Guide
to
Kentucky's
Major Lakes

A
Fishing Guide
to
Kentucky's
Major Lakes

Second Edition

Arthur B. Lander Jr.

THE UNIVERSITY PRESS OF KENTUCKY

Scholarly publisher for the Commonwealth,
serving Bellarmine College, Berea College, Centre
College of Kentucky, Eastern Kentucky University,
The Filson Club Historical Society, Georgetown College,
Kentucky Historical Society, Kentucky State University,
Morehead State University, Murray State University,
Northern Kentucky University, Transylvania University,
University of Kentucky, University of Louisville,
and Western Kentucky University.

Editorial and Sales Offices: The University Press of Kentucky
663 South Limestone Street, Lexington, Kentucky 40508-4008

02 01 00 99 98   5 4 3 2 1

Frontispiece: Fishing for largemouth bass in Taylorsville Lake
in early April. Photograph by Ron Garrison.

Library of Congress Cataloging-in-Publication Data

Lander, Arthur B.
   A fishing guide to Kentucky's major lakes / Arthur B. Lander, Jr.
— 2nd ed.
      p.   cm.
   Includes index.
   ISBN 0-8131-0946-9 (paper : alk. paper)
   1. Fishing—Kentucky—Guidebooks. 2. Freshwater fishes
—Kentucky. 3. Lakes—Kentucky—Guidebooks. I. Title.
SH499.L36   1998
799.1'1'09769—dc21   97-44130

This book is printed on acid-free recycled paper meeting
the requirements of the American National Standard
for Permanence of Paper for Printed Library Materials.

Manufactured in the United States of America

To Laura,
John,
and Maggie

CONTENTS

Additional Information

Major Lakes
of
Kentucky

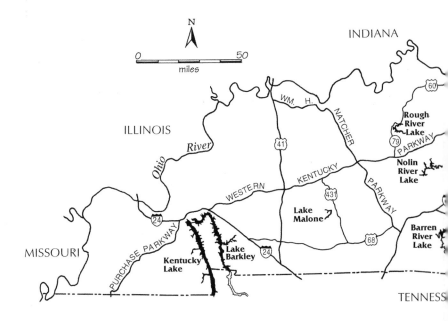

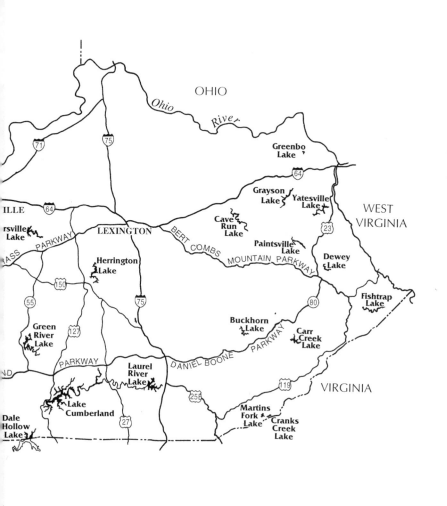

WHY WE FISH

There is no better place to be on a warm spring afternoon than relaxing with a fishing pole in your hand. Fishing is something anyone—regardless of age, gender, or previous outdoors experience—can learn. To children, fishing is magic. Like planting a row of seeds in the garden, what happens next is hard to comprehend. It does not take long to discover how much there is to appreciate about fishing—the scenery, spending time with family and friends, but most of all those beautiful finned creatures. Hold a shiny, green bass in your hands and that is all the proof you need that nature is infinitely more wondrous than the works of man.

Rising before the sun comes up and going fishing is a celebration of life. The air is so fresh and clean at sunrise. Fishing rejuvenates your spirit and sets your mind at ease. Fishing wipes the slate clean. The mystique of dawn has never lost its appeal. When I was very young my mom and dad would bundle me up in a blanket in the bottom of the boat on foggy mornings. The rock of the boat and the hum of our Johnson Sea Horse outboard motor would put me back to sleep every time.

We spent our vacations fishing. Many a night we would fish for white bass and crappie, with the warm glow of a Coleman lantern fending off the chilly night air. I feel lucky to have been raised by fishermen. Some of the best memories of my parents are from fishing trips we took together as a family. I liked to fish with my parents even when I was a teenager, although we didn't agree on much during those years. When we got out on the lake, the disagreements and arguments didn't seem important anymore. Fishing soothed the tension. Fishing was proof we enjoyed each other's company.

Now that I have a family, I'm trying hard to make learning to fish as much fun for my children as it was for me. When you take children fishing, your own kids or those of a friend or relative, you can't help but relive some of your childhood fishing memories in the process. Fishing teaches patience and self-confidence, but more importantly it fosters an understanding of how nature can provide for us, if we manage resources competently, with a vision for the future.

Children are eager to learn about nature, especially those who have little if any contact with the outdoors. America has become an urban society, and population experts predict that by the year 2000 almost 50 percent of Americans will live in big cities and the surrounding metropolitan areas. More and more of our youth are growing up completely out of touch with nature at a time when we all need to be more attuned to the complex interrelationships of plants and animals, air and water. When you introduce children to fishing, you are teaching them more than how to bait a hook, run the boat, or carve out fish fillets—you are showing them by example that to love is to teach and share.

Professional bass angler Denny Brauer is an expert at fishing jig and pork rind combinations when bass are shallow and located in heavy cover. This fishing technique is called flippin'.

PREFACE

Many changes have occurred in the decade since *A Fishing Guide to Kentucky's Major Lakes* was first published. Several new lakes have opened, and at others there have been significant changes in fishery management programs. The lakes are being managed on an individual basis today. This reflects a more realistic picture of their biological potential, and allows managers to fine-tune fish populations as never before.

In the last decade there has been a rise in the popularity of predator fish—striped bass, hybrid striped bass, and muskie. These fish have been stocked to take advantage of abundant forage and to decrease the numbers of adult gizzard shad, which compete for food (plankton) with young-of-the-year largemouth bass and other game fish. The obvious secondary benefit is an increase in fishing opportunities. Hybrid striped bass populations have been established in five major Kentucky lakes, in some cases to supplement declining white bass populations.

To prevent overharvest and increase the average size of fish taken by anglers, daily creel limits have been reduced, and minimum size limits have been lengthened at many reservoirs. These regulation changes, which affect black bass species and crappie more than other species, reflect angler preferences for higher quality fishing experiences in the face of increasing fishing pressure.

As of March 1, 1996, Dale Hollow, Green, Herrington, Laurel, and Martins Fork were the only major lakes in Kentucky that still had a 12-inch minimum size limit on largemouth bass. All of our major lakes likely will have a 15-inch minimum size limit on largemouth and smallmouth bass within the next few years.

Readers will notice that this second edition is much more comprehensive and better organized for quicker access. There are fewer details on marinas and facilities at the lakes, but more emphasis on the current status of fisheries and the fishing tackle and techniques that have been proven successful. Introductions have been added to the book's two major units—The Fish and The Lakes—to provide overviews and perspective. Additionally, about twenty sections have been added which will help anglers find answers when questions arise. Some of the topics addressed in these new sections include who manages Kentucky's major lakes, district fishery biologists, fishing regulations, fishing licenses, U.S. Army Corps of Engineers district offices, how to obtain lake maps, how to report fish and game law violations, illegal fishing methods, catch-and-release, how to fillet fish, zebra mussels, and the Kentucky Department of Travel Development.

This second edition profiles fifteen sport fish species and twenty-two lakes, an increase of three fish and six lakes over the first edition. These additions were made to expand the scope of the book and make it as comprehensive as possible.

I would like to thank past and present staff members of the Kentucky Department of Fish and Wildlife Resources, in particular, Pete Pfeiffer, Ted Crowell, Benjy Kinman, Jim Axon, B.D. Laflin, Betty Gardner, Kimberly M. Hermes, Gerry Buynak, Dan Wilson, Lew Kornman, Doug Stephens, Al Surmont, Jeff Preston, Tom Culton, Roy Harris, Tim Abney, Kerry Prather, Dick Hudson, Paul Rister, Bill McLemore, John Williams, Robert Rold, Steve Reeser, David Bell, Norm Minch, Steve Votaw, Steve Curry, and creel clerks Ronnie Mosley and Richard Mehlbauer.

My thanks to the following fishing guides who were willing to share information: David "Crash" Mullins, James Baker, Hagan Wonn, Brad Weakley, Fletcher Wise, Bill Jarboe, Randell Gibson, Bobby Leidecker, Tommy Hall, Bill Craig, Tim Tarter, and Rick Holt.

These knowledgeable anglers were also unselfish with tips on tackle and techniques: Al Lindner, Denny Brauer, Randy Fite, Kevin Van Dam, Ronnie Grant, Kevin Mullins, Johnny Crase, Gary Nelson, Chris Haley, Billy Westmorland, Willard Parnell, Hugh Glasscock, Alex Thomasson, Kirk W. Robinson, Steve Woodring, Rick Markesbery, Gerald Baker, Tim McDonald, Dwight "Nightcrawler" Stambaugh, Ben Trail, and Bob Kise. Lexington taxidermist Harry Whitehead and Scott King, president of the Kentucky Bass Federation, were also very helpful. Thanks.

I also wish to thank Danny Scott, Wayne Pollock, Reed Tatum, Anders Myhr, and John Mayer of the Tennessee Wildlife Resources Agency and all the resource managers of the U.S. Army Corps of Engineers at the lakes, especially John McGinn.

All these people helped to make this book possible by providing me with up-to-date factual information, astute observations, and candid opinions. I hope this book is an accurate reflection of what you have shared with me through the years.

Also, I would like to thank the Lexington *Herald-Leader* for giving me the opportunity to cover the outdoors as a staff writer since 1986, and in particular, President and Publisher Timothy M. Kelly for giving me permission to include previously published fishing information in this book.

And last, but certainly not least, I wish to thank my wife, Bonnie, for sharing the hardships of creativity and giving me the time and space needed to get this project done.

Art Lander Jr.
January 14, 1998
Bethlehem, Kentucky

INTRODUCTION

A Fishing Guide to Kentucky's Major Lakes is the definitive source of information on the top twenty-two reservoirs in Kentucky and the fifteen sport fish species found in these impoundments. It is a valuable tool for anglers of all skill levels. Fishery biologists assess the current status of important fisheries, and there are where-to and how-to recommendations from local experts and guides who fish regularly and know the lakes intimately. The book is especially useful to anglers planning weekend trips or family vacations to unfamiliar waters.

The fish and lakes profiled are listed in alphabetical order, and each profile includes quick information boxes to help anglers easily find the best fishing possible. Each quick information box ranks the fish species or lakes on a scale of one (⤙) to four (⤙ ⤙ ⤙ ⤙) fish, four being highest. More life history information was added to the profiles of fish species, as well as basic fishing tackle and techniques. Chapters on each lake detail its location, size, trophic state index (relative fertility), lake manager's office, managing fishery biologist, lake level/fishing report hot line, marinas, boat launching ramps, local tourism information sources, fishing overview, important fish species, and tailwater fishing opportunities. The lakes are owned and operated by various state or federal agencies, with one exception—Herrington Lake, which was built in 1925 and is owned by Kentucky Utilities, a Lexington-based power company.

The addresses and telephone numbers for lake managers, district fishery biologists, and local tourism officials have been added to help anglers find information more easily. Persons who live and work on the lakes are valuable sources of current, accurate information on water conditions, fishing activity, and recreational facilities. Making a few calls is worth the time and expense to get specific questions answered before heading out to an unfamiliar lake. Local tourism agencies can be especially helpful because they can provide brochures and answer questions about restaurants, shopping areas, and local attractions so that nonfishing family members will enjoy their visits to lakes too.

Anglers are reminded that fees charged for boat launching and other services, as well as the use of facilities, are subject to change without notice.

Who Manages Kentucky's Major Lakes

Fishery biologists of the Kentucky Department of Fish and Wildlife Resources (KDFWR) manage the fish in Kentucky's public waters, which include 158 small lakes in sixty-five Kentucky counties, fifteen major reservoirs, and about 13,000 miles of streams.

The KDFWR division of fisheries has an annual budget of about $3.2 million, which includes $2 million in federal matching funds. The division operates two fish hatcheries (in Frankfort and Morehead) and has a total of seventy biologists, fishery technicians, hatchery personnel, researchers, and administrative personnel on staff.

Questions about fishing opportunities across Kentucky should be addressed to the Kentucky Department of Fish and Wildlife Resources, Information and Education Division, 1 Game Farm Road, Frankfort, KY 40601, telephone (502) 564-4336. The direct line to the Division of Fisheries is (502) 564-3596. The telephone number of the fisheries laboratory, where many of the department's fishery biologists have their offices, is (502) 564-5448.

The Tennessee Wildlife Resources Agency manages the fisheries in the waters of Dale Hollow Lake, Kentucky Lake, and Lake Barkley, which extend into Tennessee. Questions about fishing opportunities in the Tennessee waters of these lakes should be addressed to the Tennessee Wildlife Resources Agency, Box 40747, Nashville, TN 37204, telephone (615) 781-6575.

Kentucky District Fishery Biologists and the Lakes They Manage

Central Fishery District, Kerry Prather, District Biologist, 1 Game Farm Road, Frankfort, KY 40601, telephone (502) 564-5448.
Herrington Lake and Taylorsville Lake.

Western Fishery District, Paul Rister, District Biologist, Route 4, Box 785, Murray, KY 42071, telephone (502) 753-3886.
Kentucky Lake and Lake Barkley.

Northwestern Fishery District, David Bell, District Biologist, 1398 Highway 81 North, Calhoun, KY 42327, telephone (502) 273-3117.
Lake Malone, Nolin River Lake, and Rough River Lake.

Southwestern Fishery District, B.D. Laflin, District Biologist, 4800 Nashville Road, Bowling Green, KY 42101, telephone (502) 842-3677.
Barren River Lake and Green River Lake.

Northeastern Fishery District, Lewis Kornman, District Biologist, Minor Clark Fish Hatchery, 120 Fish Hatchery Road, Morehead, KY 40351, telephone (606) 784-6872.
Cave Run Lake, Grayson Lake, and Greenbo Lake.

Southeastern Fishery District, Doug Stephens, District Biologist, 2073 N. Highway 25 West, Williamsburg, KY 40769, telephone (606) 549-1332.
Dale Hollow Lake, Lake Cumberland, and Laurel River Lake.

Eastern Fishery District, Steve Reeser, District Biologist, 2744 Lake Road, Prestonsburg, KY 41653, telephone (606) 886-9575.
Buckhorn Lake, Carr Creek Lake, Dewey Lake, Fishtrap Lake, Martins Fork Lake, Paintsville Lake, and Yatesville Lake.

Kentucky Fishing Regulations

Kentucky fishing regulations are established by the Kentucky Fish and Wildlife Commission, a nine-member citizens board. Commission meetings, which are open to the public, are held quarterly (December, March, June, and August) at the central office of the Kentucky Department of Fish and Wildlife Resources, three miles west of Frankfort, Kentucky, on U.S. 60. For more information telephone (502) 564-3400.

Detailed fishing regulations are published annually in the *Kentucky Sport Fishing and Boating Guide*, a brochure that is available free to the public. For a copy send a self-addressed, stamped envelope to *Kentucky Sport Fishing and Boating Guide*, Kentucky Department of Fish and Wildlife Resources, 1 Game Farm Road, Frankfort, KY 40601.

Anglers are reminded that many of Kentucky's major lakes have more restrictive size and creel limits than the statewide limits, which apply to all Kentucky waters, public and private (including streams, farm ponds, and small lakes). Anglers should consult the *Kentucky Sport Fishing and Boating Guide* to familiarize themselves with regulation differences across the state.

Kentucky Fishing Licenses

In 1994-95 there were 447,589 fishing licenses sold to Kentucky residents, including 115,383 combination hunting and fishing licenses and 30,780 joint husband/wife fishing licenses. By comparison, nonresidents purchased 123,620 fishing licenses. A total of 38,580 trout permits were sold. All licenses, tags, and permits are printed on Tyvek, a durable, waterproof paper.

Kentucky's sport fishing and hunting licenses are sold through an automated, on-line, statewide computer system which links about 935 agents to the Kentucky Department of Fish and Wildlife Resources in Frankfort. Only sport licenses are sold on-line. Commercial licenses must be purchased in Frankfort. Automated license sales started December 1, 1995. Each year the department sells about 1 million licenses, generating about $16 million in revenue, which is combined with federal matching funds to finance agency operation and management programs. The Kentucky Department of Fish and Wildlife Resources receives no general fund tax dollars.

From the 75-cent issuing fee, now included in every license's cost, the license agent gets 25 cents, and the inventory agent (usually the county clerk) gets 15 cents. The remaining 35 cents is used to pay for the automated system, which cost about $2 million.

Identification is required to buy licenses. Purchasers are required to provide their driver's license number and date of birth. If a person does not have a driver's license, a social security number will be accepted. Annual Kentucky resident fishing and hunting licenses are $12.50 each; combination hunting/fishing licenses, $20; and joint husband/wife fishing licenses, $22.50. Nonresident annual fishing licenses are $30. The cost of a fifteen-day license is $20, and $12.50 for a three-day license. A state trout permit is $5. Trout stamps are no longer valid, and are produced for sales to collectors only. Trout stamps are $5 each. For information about sport fishing license sales, telephone (502) 564-4224.

THE FISH

The gods do not subtract from the alloted span of men's lives the hours spent fishing.

—Assyrian Tablet (2000 B.C.)

INTRODUCTION

Because of its climate and geography, Kentucky has always been a fisherman's paradise. The fish fauna of Kentucky is as diverse as anywhere in inland North America. Only two states, Tennessee and Alabama, have more species. There are 242 fish species in Kentucky, 226 of which are native. About forty fish species are important to anglers, and fifteen species are common in Kentucky's major lakes, all of which are manmade impoundments. Three black bass species, the largemouth, smallmouth, and spotted bass, are Kentucky's most popular game fish. Other popular and widely distributed game fish are crappie, catfish, bluegill, and white bass, all of which are native, warm-water species. The rainbow trout, brown trout, striped bass, and hybrid striped bass are nonnative species that have been introduced into Kentucky's major lakes and their tailwaters. The walleye, muskie, and sauger are native fisheries that have been restored through restocking and intensive management.

Each profile in this chapter includes the fish's scientific name (genus and species), family, description, distinguishing characteristics, food/

sport value, range in Kentucky and North America, and any significant information relating to where and when the fish spawns. Also listed is the Kentucky state record and International Game Fish Association all-tackle world record for the species. Finally, there are basic fishing tackle and technique recommendations. Readers can find additional details on fishing tackle and techniques in the lake profiles.

Not only are Kentucky's major lakes able to support a wide variety of fish species, they also are capable of producing lunkers. Every year hundreds of anglers receive certificates, decals, and plaques for catching trophy-size fish, documented through the Angler Awards Program of the Kentucky Department of Fish and Wildlife Resources.

Weight records are kept by the department on forty fish species. Several Kentucky state records are close to being all-tackle world records, and the potential exists for new state records for brown trout, hybrid striped bass, muskie, striped bass, and catfish (flathead) to be taken from our lakes.

Anyone who needs help with fish identification should get a copy of *Kentucky Fish*, a free brochure distributed by the Kentucky Department of Fish and Wildlife Resources. The thirty-eight-page, color brochure, which measures 5 3/8 X 8 3/8 inches, just the right size to fit in almost any tackle box, has photographs and life history information for fifty-six fish species.

The spotted bass (*Micropterus punctulatus*), identified as a separate species from the largemouth bass (*M. salmoides*) in 1927, is Kentucky's state fish. Because of its abundance in the Bluegrass State the spotted bass is often called the Kentucky bass.

State Record/World Record Fish

Kentucky's state record fish list dates back to 1943. "To be listed as a Kentucky state record, a fish must tie or break an existing record. The department keeps records on forty species," said Kim Hermes, who administers the state record fish program for the Kentucky Department of Fish and Wildlife Resources.

Kentucky's list of state record fish includes some rough fish species not actively pursued by anglers, some sunfish species found almost exclusively in streams, and a few game species not commonly found in Kentucky's major lakes. This includes the yellow perch, a fugitive from Ohio lakes that now is found in the Ohio River; the northern pike, stocked in strip mine lakes and Herrington Lake decades ago; and the tiger

Taxidermist Ray Brown (*left*) and Roger Foster with Foster's 58-pound, 4-ounce state record striped bass, which was caught on December 11, 1985, from Lake Cumberland.

muskie, which was once stocked in Dewey Lake but may not exist in Kentucky anymore.

An updated list of Kentucky state record fish is published annually in the July-August issue of *Kentucky Afield* magazine, produced by the Kentucky Department of Fish and Wildlife Resources. An annual subscription to the bimonthly full-color magazine is $5. For information, write to *Kentucky Afield,* Kentucky Department of Fish and Wildlife Resources, 1 Game Farm Road, Frankfort, KY 40601, or telephone (502) 564-4336.

To qualify for a Kentucky state record, a fish must have been caught by sportfishing methods only, a species verification must be made by a department fishery biologist, and the fish must be weighed on a certified scale. Hermes said two state records were established in 1995, and three in 1994. Both of the records broken in 1995 were for rough fish— a 4-pound, 8-ounce blue sucker caught from the Kentucky River in June, and a 10.49-pound big head carp taken from Ledbetter Creek of Kentucky Lake in November.

"Some of our records haven't been beaten since the 1950s," observed Hermes. "And it doesn't look like they'll be broken anytime soon."

The International Game Fish Association (IGFA) compiles line class (including fly fishing) and all-tackle world records for the world's game fish—both freshwater and saltwater species. Current world records for all species are listed in their annual publication, *World Record Game Fishes.* Annual membership in IGFA is $25 and includes a current copy of *World Record Game Fishes.* For information write to IGFA, 1301 East Atlantic Boulevard, Pompano Beach, FL 33060, or telephone (954) 941-3474, or fax (954) 941-5868.

Angler Awards Program

Each year hundreds of fishermen gain recognition for their catches through Kentucky's Angler Awards Program. Awards are based on the length of the catch, not its weight. "We figure we've received about 1,500 applications [for awards] since the program began in 1987," said Betty Gardner, who coordinates the program for the Kentucky Department of Fish and Wildlife Resources.

Anglers receive Trophy Fish certificates and decals for each single catch that exceeds the trophy fish length for the species, and Master Angler plaques and decals if they catch three different fish species that exceed trophy fish length. "We also give out annual awards," said Gardner, "for the longest fish caught that year for each of the twenty-five species [in the program]." In 1995, 208 certificate awards were issued to anglers, eighteen master angler plaques, plus thirty-three annual awards (there were eight ties).

The trophy fish lengths were determined by a panel of department fishery biologists. Some trophy fish lengths include largemouth bass, 23 inches; smallmouth bass, 20 inches; muskie, 40 inches; striped bass, 36 inches; walleye, 25 inches; bluegill, 10 inches; and crappie, 15 inches.

Anglers under the age of sixteen are placed in a special junior division. "That way youngsters don't have to compete against adults," said Gardner. "And they can keep on fishing for the enjoyment of the sport."

Gardner said the program is conducted on the honor system. "In no way is it as strict as our state record fish program," explained Gardner. "We're taking their word they made the catch." Anglers submit photographs of their catches, along with other pertinent information. This includes the angler's name, address, and telephone number, the fish's length, and where and when it was caught. A witness is required. Include the witness's address and telephone number. "Our program is ideal for catch-and-release," said Gardner. "All you need to do is get the measurements and take a good picture before you put the fish back."

For information on Kentucky Angler Awards or for an application, write to Trophy Fish/Master Angler Coordinator, Kentucky Department of Fish and Wildlife Resources, 1 Game Farm Road, Frankfort, KY 40601, or telephone (502) 564-3596.

Forage Fish

Forage fish are eaten—preyed upon—by game fish. In Kentucky's major lakes, forage fish include shad, herring, minnows, shiners, and sunfish. Forage fish may be collected for bait with cast nets, dipped from water swirling around bridge abutments in tailwaters, or netted under bright lights at night. Anglers are reminded that the stocking of any fish (including forage fish) without permission in public water is strictly prohibited.

Gizzard Shad The gizzard shad (*Dorosoma cepedianum*) is a member of family Clupeidae, the herrings and shads, which includes the skipjack herring and threadfin shad. The Clupeidae are extremely important because they are the primary forage in Kentucky's major lakes. The gizzard shad has a silvery-blue back, silvery sides (sometimes with a yellow sheen), and a white belly. The young have a dark spot behind the gill plate, similar to its cousin, the threadfin shad. This native species may reach 12 to 15 inches in length in five years of growth, and rarely 20 inches. The snout is rounded, with a small mouth below the snout.

The gizzard shad is found primarily in rivers and large impoundments, but it can adapt to small lakes. Shad eat algae and organic debris strained from mud by fine gill rakers. They often feed around boat docks, nibbling algae off drums and foam flotation. The young consume insect larvae and small crustaceans.

Spawning occurs along the shoreline in April or early May when adults swim side by side, spewing eggs and milt. There is no parental care of the young. Sometimes there are multiple spawns throughout the summer in large impoundments.

Along the coast, gizzard shad live in brackish water and migrate up freshwater rivers. In Kentucky, the gizzard shad is found statewide in all river basins.

Threadfin Shad The threadfin shad (*Dorosoma petenense*) rarely exceeds 6 inches in length and has a more slender body and pointed snout. They have been stocked with varying success in the deeper lakes, since they are prone to winter kill when water temperatures fall below 40 degrees. Lake Barkley, Lake Cumberland, Herrington Lake, Kentucky Lake, Laurel River Lake, Barren River Lake, and Green River Lake support populations of threadfin shad. In June, gizzard and threadfin shad school up in open water, where they are preyed upon by white bass, hybrid striped bass, and other game fish.

Shad are found in larger rivers of the Mississippi and Ohio River basin, from the Gulf Coast and northeastern Mexico north to South Dakota and Minnesota, to the southern Great Lakes, New York, and the St. Lawrence River, and into New England.

Skipjack Herring The skipjack herring (*Alosa chrysochloris*) is a slender, bluish-green fish with a deeply forked, yellowish caudal fin. Adults are commonly 12 to 15 inches, and occasionlly 18 to 20 inches. Found in most large rivers of Kentucky, skipjacks are especially prolific in the Ohio and lower Cumberland and Tennessee Rivers, where they gather below dams in great numbers during runs.

Skipjack herring are taken with dip nets and cast nets in boils and swift water below dams, then cut up for use as catfish bait. Since skipjack herring feed on small minnows, they also can be caught by anglers, and are game fighters on ultralight tackle. They are usually taken by casting tiny hair jigs or plastic curlytail grubs.

Alewife   Alewives have been present in Dale Hollow Lake (and other Tennessee reservoirs) for over ten years but only became established in Lake Cumberland in the early 1990s. Biologists aren't sure what effects the presence of alewives, a nonnative forage fish, will have on Lake Cumberland's striped bass fishery. Anglers have noticed that since alewives prefer the deepest, coolest water which holds oxygen, striped bass are staying in deeper water and don't seem to feed on the surface as often as they do when shad is their primary forage.

The alewife (*Alosa pseudoharengus*) was apparently brought to Lake Cumberland by anglers for use as bait. "There's too many Johnny Appleseeds out there," said Ted Crowell, assistant director of fisheries for the Kentucky Department of Fish and Wildlife Resources. . . . Our biggest concern with exotic forage is how it competes with gizzard and threadfin shad. It could suppress their numbers."

Brook Silverside   The brook silverside is a translucent, greenish minnow with a long, flattened head and silvery lateral stripe, edged with black. It is found in major lakes statewide, but is less abundant in the western third of the state. The fish prefers clear, clean water. It spawns in the late spring, attaching its eggs to rocks and brush using sticky filaments. A surface swimmer, its common name is skipjack because it "skips" out of the water. Very attracted to light, skipjacks intended for use as bait are often netted at night over lights.

Bluntnose Minnow   The bluntnose minnow is a 3-inch minnow found in all stream drainages in Kentucky, hence in every major lake. A prolific fish, females can carry more than 2,000 eggs, and the developmental rate is so rapid that minnows spawned in April or May can mature and breed by August or September of the same year. Eggs are deposited under a rock by the female and fiercely protected by the male, two reasons for the species' high survival rate. The bluntnose minnow is a very successful native species that is often raised as a bait minnow.

Emerald Shiner   The emerald shiner (*Notropis atherinoides*) is a slender, 4-inch minnow found in every river and large creek in Kentucky, and therefore in every major lake. The whitish, almost transparent minnow, which has no prominent markings on its fins or body, has an emerald-green, silvery belly and a short, rounded snout. It prefers gravel and rock substrate and lives close to the surface.

Rough Fish

Rough fish are ignored by most sport fish anglers, but nonetheless they are found in large numbers in Kentucky's major lakes. They may be fun to catch (especially on light tackle) but are generally less palatable. Excluding catfish (which I consider game fish), the rough fish species include:

Carp (*Cyprinus carpio*). This nonnative exotic from Asia was introduced into American waters in the late 1800s.

Bigmouth buffalo (*Ictiobus cyprinellus*). A dark, chunky fish, it can weigh up to 30 pounds and is abundant in the turbid waters of the Ohio River and its lower tributaries.

Golden redhorse (*Moxostoma erythrurum*). This sucker with distinctive golden or brassy coloration is widespread in Kentucky lakes and streams.

Freshwater drum (*Aplodinotus grunniens*). Commonly called the white perch, the freshwater drum is abundant in Central and Western Kentucky lakes and streams and is an aggressive feeder.

Paddlefish (*Polyodon spathula*). A cylindrical fish with a long, flat snout, it commonly grows to 40 inches in length and is a big river fish that adapts well to lakes. It feeds on plankton. The common name is spoonbill.

Longnose gar (*Lepisosteus osseus*). Found in all major lakes of the state, the longnose gar reaches 50 inches in length and is distinguished by its long, slender bill and toothy mouth.

Some rough fish have economic value and are commercially harvested. Paddlefish eggs and catfish bring in the most dollars to commercial fishermen. However, not all major lakes are open to commercial fishing, and usually commercial fishing is allowed only during the winter months. Commercial fishing tackle includes trotlines, gill nets, hoop nets, slat traps and snag lines. The major lakes open to commercial fishing are Barren River Lake, Herrington Lake, Lake Barkley, Lake Cumberland, and Kentucky Lake.

CATFISH

Barren River Lake ⊶ ⊶ ⊶ ⊶	Lake Barkley ⊶ ⊶ ⊶ ⊶
Buckhorn Lake ⊶ ⊶ ⊶	Lake Cumberland ⊶ ⊶ ⊶
Carr Creek Lake ⊶ ⊶	Lake Malone ⊶ ⊶ ⊶
Cave Run Lake ⊶ ⊶ ⊶	Laurel River Lake ⊶ ⊶ ⊶
Dewey Lake ⊶ ⊶ ⊶	Martins Fork Lake ⊶ ⊶
Fishtrap Lake ⊶ ⊶ ⊶	Nolin River Lake ⊶ ⊶ ⊶
Grayson Lake ⊶ ⊶ ⊶	Paintsville Lake ⊶ ⊶
Greenbo Lake ⊶ ⊶ ⊶	Rough River Lake ⊶ ⊶ ⊶
Green River Lake ⊶ ⊶ ⊶ ⊶	Taylorsville Lake ⊶ ⊶ ⊶ ⊶
Herrington Lake ⊶ ⊶ ⊶	Yatesvillle Lake ⊶ ⊶ ⊶
Kentucky Lake ⊶ ⊶ ⊶ ⊶	

Catfish are abundant in Kentucky's major lakes. During the summer months, large numbers of anglers pursue these "whisker fish," all of which are members of family Ictaluridae. The channel catfish (*Ictalurus punctatus*) is by far the most widely distributed catfish species. Two other important species of catfish caught from Kentucky's major lakes are the flathead catfish (*Pylodictis olivaris*), and the blue catfish (*Ictalurus furcatus*).

Catfish have a smooth, scaleless skin and flexible barbels (whiskers) that enable them to find and taste food in turbid waters. They are popular with anglers because they are easy to catch and are good eating. The downside is their sharp dorsal and pectoral fins, which can inflict painful puncture wounds to the hands of unsuspecting or careless anglers.

Numerous baits are used to catch catfish. The viscera and gills of gizzard shad are a favorite cut bait. Small live shad, shiners, creek chubs, chicken livers, catalpa worms, and crayfish are good catfish bait, too. Catalpa worms (2-inch green caterpillars found on catalpa trees during the summer months) are a favorite bait for use on trotlines or when still-fishing. "Stink baits" appeal to the catfish's strong sense of smell. These strong-smelling concoctions are made from such things as chicken blood and intestines, carp dough, clay, cotton, mustard, and limburger cheese. Often the ingredients are mixed and allowed to turn rancid in a tightly sealed jar. Closely guarded secrets, "stink bait" recipes are sometimes the product of years of experimentation. Sport fishing license holders may use cast nets or seines to catch crayfish and minnows from creeks

This stringer of catfish was taken from Lake Barkley in May 1968. Photograph courtesy of the Kentucky Department of Travel Development.

and lakes for their own use as bait while fishing. Be sure to consult the fishing regulations since there are net and mesh size restrictions. Flathead catfish especially like big creek chubs. Large shiners should be hooked through the back, just in front of the dorsal fin. Creek chubs and gizzard shad are less hardy and should be hooked through the lips. Start the point of the hook below the lower jaw and bring it out through the snout. Crayfish should be hooked through the last joint of the tail so they can crawl on the bottom in a natural manner.

Night is a prime time to catch catfish—on trotlines, limb lines, or with rod and reel. Another popular technique is jug fishing. In jug fishing a length of heavy line and baited hook (on a 1/0 hook) are tied to an empty plastic quart, liter, or pint bottle. Be sure to check fishing regulations before putting out trotlines or limb lines and before jug fishing.

Rock piles, undercut ledges, submerged creek channels, and mudflats are frequented by catfish. Sometimes catfish move off slowly with the bait, and other times they strike hard.

A bottom-bouncing rig is ideal for fishing from a boat in a current, such as in tailwater areas, where snags are a problem. Use a three-way swivel, with the lead weight on the bottom and the hook suspended on a leader to the side so it will trail in the current and not hang up on the bottom.

A slip sinker rig is a good choice for fishing on mud or gravel flats. Tie a No. 2 Eagle Claw hook on an 18-inch leader of 14-pound test monofilament. On the other end of the leader, tie the line to a barrel swivel. On the end of the line from the rod and reel, thread a plastic bead and a 3/4-ounce barrel sinker, then tie the line to the other end of the barrel swivel. The heavy lead weight will take the bait to the bottom, but when the catfish picks up the bait and runs with it, he won't feel any resistance since the line will slip through the weight. Then you've got him. Simply take the slack out of the line and set the hook.

Line breakage is the main reason many big catfish are lost. When line gets old, it becomes brittle. Sunlight and heat are especially harmful to monofilament line. It is best to change your fishing line at least twice during each fishing season. Heavy monofilament line, 17- to 30-pound test, is preferred for catfishing. Some anglers use braided line.

Abrasion from wood or rocks can fray monofilament line very quickly when bottom fishing. If you feel a nick in your line, clip off the weakened section and retie your hook. The palomar knot is an excellent knot for tying on the large hooks (No. 4 to 3/0) used in catfishing. Fingernail clippers worn around your neck on a lanyard are ideal for clipping line.

Channel Catfish

The channel catfish is the most widely distributed catfish in Kentucky. It is found in all the state's rivers and large reservoirs. Hundreds of thousands are stocked in small lakes and farm ponds each year. Frequently, they are raised commercially for food. Coloration is bluish-silver on the back, with a whitish belly, and silvery sides that have small, irregular dark spots. The four pairs of barbels (whiskers) are quite long, and the tail fin is deeply forked. Common names for the channel catfish are "fiddler" and "willow cat."

Adults are commonly 12 to 20 inches long, and on rare occasions 30 inches or more. They are tolerant of turbidity and can live in warm water. Their range extends up the Mississippi Valley to the Plains of Canada, and into the Great Lakes, St. Lawrence River, and drainages of Hudson Bay. The Kentucky state record is 22 pounds, 5 ounces. Wallace Carter of Lawrenceburg caught the fish from an Anderson County farm pond on October 6, 1978. The IGFA all-tackle world record channel catfish weighed 58 pounds and was caught from the Santee-Cooper Reservoir in South Carolina in 1964.

Channel catfish often cruise the bottom looking for food. They frequent shallow flats at night. Bait should be fished right on the bottom. Let the catfish swallow the bait and move off before setting the hook. Rocky areas—gravel, rock piles or riprap—near pond dams and swift water below dams are also frequented by catfish, especially during the spawn.

Flathead Catfish

Flathead catfish, commonly called shovelhead or mudcat, can grow to an enormous size. Kentucky's state record flathead, which weighed 97 pounds and was caught on June 6, 1956, by Esker Carroll from the Green River, eclipses the current all-tackle world record accepted by the International Game Fish Association. The *1996 World Record Game Fishes* lists the IGFA all-tackle world record as weighing 91 pounds, 4 ounces. That flathead was caught from Lake Lewisville in Texas on March 28, 1982. In *Fishes of Kentucky* by William M. Clay there is mention of a 108-pound flathead taken in Kentucky. Coloration is brown to reddish-brown to yellowish above, with dark blotches, and a yellowish to white belly. The fish have wide, flat heads and triangular-shaped tails. The protruding lower jaw has long barbels.

Flatheads commonly reach 36 inches in length and can live for twenty years. They are more common than blue catfish, but less abundant than channels. Young flatheads live in riffles and feed on aquatic insects. Adults are solitary and inhabit deep, sluggish pools, brush piles, and undercut banks, moving at night into the shallows or the head of a pool to feed. They are fish-eaters and do not scavenge like other catfish. The preferred live bait is a wiggling creek chub, shiner minnow, or small sunfish.

Blue Catfish

Common in Kentucky Lake and Lake Barkley, the blue catfish (*Ictalurus furcatus*) is rare or absent in other major lakes in Kentucky. This catfish, which thrives in current, is native to the lower Ohio and Mississippi Rivers and their major river tributaries, including the Tennessee, Cumberland, and Green. The blue catfish is similar in appearance to the channel catfish. The most obvious difference is the channel catfish's rounded anal fin.

Coloration is bluish-gray, with silvery sides and a white belly. It is without spots or other markings. The tail is deeply forked.

Blue catfish can attain enormous size, with 25-pounders being fairly common. The Kentucky state record blue catfish weighed 100 pounds and was caught from the Kentucky Lake tailwaters (Tennessee River) on August 21, 1970, by J.E. Copeland of Benton, Kentucky. The IGFA all-tackle world record blue catfish was caught from the Cooper River in South Carolina on March 14, 1991, and weighed 109 pounds, 4 ounces. Breeding and feeding habits are similar to those of the channel catfish.

Bullheads

Three species of bullheads are found in Kentucky's major lakes. The yellow bullhead (*Ictalurus natalis*) is the most common, since it is found in all the state's river drainages. Bullheads are found most often in headwater tributaries and are not significant to anglers. They rarely exceed 15 inches in length.

CRAPPIE

Barren River Lake ⊷ ⊷ ⊷	Kentucky Lake ⊷ ⊷ ⊷ ⊷
Buckhorn Lake ⊷ ⊷ ⊷ ⊷	Lake Barkley ⊷ ⊷ ⊷ ⊷
Carr Creek Lake ⊷ ⊷	Lake Cumberland ⊷ ⊷
Cave Run Lake ⊷ ⊷	Lake Malone ⊷ ⊷ ⊷
Dale Hollow Lake ⊷ ⊷	Laurel River Lake ⊷
Dewey Lake ⊷ ⊷	Martins Fork Lake ⊷
Fishtrap Lake ⊷ ⊷ ⊷	Nolin River Lake ⊷ ⊷ ⊷
Grayson Lake ⊷ ⊷	Paintsville Lake ⊷
Greenbo Lake ⊷ ⊷	Rough River Lake ⊷ ⊷ ⊷
Green River Lake ⊷ ⊷ ⊷	Taylorsville Lake ⊷ ⊷
Herrington Lake ⊷ ⊷ ⊷	Yatesville Lake ⊷ ⊷ ⊷

Both species of crappie are common in Kentucky, the white crappie (*Promoxis annularis*) and the black crappie (*Promoxis nigromaculatus*). These two members of the sunfish family, Centrarchidae, can be distinguished from one another by coloration and the number of dorsal spines. The white crappie, commonly called newlight, has a silvery olive shading to a darker olive green on its back. It usually has six dorsal spines, in rare cases five. The black crappie, known throughout the South as the spec or calico bass, is also silvery olive, but with dark green to black wormlike markings. The black crappie usually has seven or eight dorsal spines that are equal in length to the anal fins.

Both species are found in all the river drainages of Kentucky, and thus are abundant in the state's major lakes. With varying success, crappie are stocked in many of the state's small lakes and ponds. Native to the Mississippi River and its major tributaries, the white crappie is widely distributed east of Nebraska, from Ontario to the Atlantic coast. The black crappie has a similar geographic range but is the dominant species in the South, from Florida to Texas.

Crappie feed on a variety of organisms, including invertebrates such as crustaceans and insects, but their diet is mostly minnows and other small fish. They are strictly carnivorous.

Crappie fillets, dusted with peppered cornmeal and pan fried in vegetable oil, are a springtime delicacy in Kentucky. They often are prepared with hush puppies, fried potatoes, coleslaw, and fresh asparagus spears.

A white crappie, spinning tackle, and a selection of jigs.

The Kentucky state record crappie (there is no distinction between the two species) is 4 pounds, 6 ounces. Kevin Perry of Mt. Sterling caught the record on June 29, 1997, from a Montgomery County pond. The IGFA all-tackle world record white crappie weighed 5 pounds, 3 ounces and was caught on July 31, 1957, at Enid Dam in Mississippi. The IGFA all-tackle world record black crappie weighed 4 pounds, 8 ounces and was caught on March 1, 1981, from Kerr Lake in Virginia. Crappie seldom grow beyond 15 inches in Kentucky. The majority of the crappie harvested are 8 to 12 inches long. There is a 9-inch minimum size limit in effect at Barren River Lake, Carr Creek Lake, Green River Lake, Nolin River Lake, and Rough River Lake. Three reservoirs have 10-inch minimum size limits—Lake Barkley, Lake Cumberland, and Kentucky Lake.

Crappie enter the shallows to spawn when water temperatures warm to 60 degrees in the spring. Their nests are shallow depressions, arranged in colonies, in 3 to 8 feet of water. Prespawn, they stage on creek channel drop-offs, along stump rows, or atop submerged humps or channel ridges.

Black crappie prefer weeds beds and thrive in clear water. White crappie are more tolerant of turbid waters. When crappie come to the banks, they congregate on brush piles and stump rows. The preferred fishing methods year-round are casting tiny (1/32- to 1/16-ounce) tube jigs or still-fishing live minnows.

HYBRID STRIPED BASS

Barren River Lake ⋈ ⋈ ⋈ ⋈   Herrington Lake ⋈ ⋈ ⋈
Dewey Lake ⋈ ⋈   Rough River Lake ⋈ ⋈ ⋈
Fishtrap Lake ⋈ ⋈ ⋈ ⋈   Taylorsville Lake ⋈ ⋈ ⋈

The hybrid striped bass is Kentucky's newest predator fish. Called the "Sunshine Bass" in Florida, and the "Whiterock" in Georgia, it is an example of interspecific hybridization, the crossing of two species. But the cross must occur in the controlled environment of the hatchery since it does not happen naturally in the wild. Offspring are usually sterile. The original cross is the eggs of the female striped bass (*Morone saxatilus*) mixed with the milt of the male white bass (*Morone chrysops*). The so-called reciprocal cross is the eggs of the female white bass mixed with the milt of the male striped bass. The reciprocal cross is much easier to accomplish since gravid (fertile) striped bass females are often hard to capture in the wild and are difficult to handle without the high risk of stress-related mortality. The striped bass and white bass are true bass, both members of the family Serranidae.

Hybrids do not have a preference for cool water, having about the same temperature and oxygen requirements as white bass. In summer, hybrids can live in the upper levels of the thermocline (a transitional zone where water temperatures drop about 1 degree per foot) and can survive in water into the high 70s.

Identification of the hybrid striped bass appears difficult at first. The best way to learn to differentiate the hybrid from the white bass is to examine specimens side by side. The white bass has a deeper body and arched back It has just one patch of teeth on the back of the tongue. There are faint dark lines on the sides of the white bass, with only one extending to the tail. The hybrid striped bass is more streamlined and has two patches of teeth on the back of the tongue. Several of the dark lines on the sides of hybrid striped bass extend to the tail.

Five major lakes have been stocked with hybrid striped bass—Barren River Lake, Dewey Lake, Fishtrap Lake, Herrington Lake, and Taylorsville Lake. Kentucky's state record hybrid striped bass was caught by Louisville's Mark Wilson on April 27, 1991, from the tailwaters of Barren River Lake. Wilson caught a 20-pound, 8-ouncer, besting the

Hybrid striped bass are agressive feeders that can be caught on spoons, jigs, and topwater lures.

previous state record by 2 pounds, 6 ounces. The IGFA all-tackle world record hybrid striped bass was taken from Leesville Lake in Virginia on May 12, 1989, and weighed 24 pounds, 3 ounces.

Hybrid striped bass can be caught by casting jigs, spinners, and crankbaits in the jumps, or by trolling crankbaits over submerged humps along river channels. When hybrids are suspended, some anglers still-fish with chicken livers. Drifting live shad and trolling crankbaits are also productive fishing methods. These silver streaks are fun to catch on light spinning tackle, but hybrids over 10 pounds are tackle busters. Hybrids can consume fish that are about one-third their body length. For example, a 24-inch hybrid can eat an 8-inch shad.

LARGEMOUTH BASS

Barren River Lake ⊶ ⊶ ⊶ ⊶	Kentucky Lake ⊶ ⊶ ⊶ ⊶
Buckhorn Lake ⊶ ⊶	Lake Barkley ⊶ ⊶ ⊶ ⊶
Carr Creek Lake ⊶ ⊶ ⊶	Lake Cumberland ⊶ ⊶ ⊶
Cave Run Lake ⊶ ⊶	Lake Malone ⊶ ⊶ ⊶
Dale Hollow Lake ⊶ ⊶ ⊶	Laurel River Lake ⊶ ⊶
Dewey Lake ⊶	Martins Fork Lake ⊶ ⊶
Fishtrap Lake ⊶ ⊶ ⊶	Nolin River Lake ⊶ ⊶ ⊶
Grayson Lake ⊶ ⊶	Paintsville Lake ⊶ ⊶
Greenbo Lake ⊶ ⊶	Rough River Lake ⊶ ⊶
Green River Lake ⊶ ⊶ ⊶	Taylorsville Lake ⊶ ⊶ ⊶
Herrington Lake ⊶ ⊶ ⊶	Yatesville Lake ⊶ ⊶ ⊶

The largemouth bass (*Micropterus salmoides*) is Kentucky's most popular native game fish. Common in lakes, rivers, farm ponds, and streams throughout the state, the largemouth is more likely to be found in reservoirs and sluggish waters than high-gradient streams. A member of the sunfish family, Centrarchidae, its geographic range extends from Mexico to Ontario and from the Atlantic coast to the Mississippi Valley.

Coloration deepens in clear water. The largemouth's back and upper sides are olive green, with gold or bronze luster. There are faint, radiating lines on the cheeks, a dark lateral band, and silvery undersides.

The best bass fishing of the year begins in March, when the older female bass move into the shallows and go on feeding sprees before spawning. The largest bass spawn first, but spawning is intermittent. Nest building begins when water temperatures approach 65 degrees, but photoperiod (length of daylight) is an equally important factor in triggering the spawn. In Kentucky's major lakes, the bass spawn begins in April and usually extends into late May.

Spawning occurs when the females' eggs become ripe. The exact day varies between individual fish. One female bass may lay eggs in several nests over a period of weeks. The smaller bass spawn last. Cold snaps may postpone or delay spawning. Only rarely does inclement weather cause the loss of an entire year class of bass. Spawned-out female bass do not begin feeding heavily right after they come off the nest. They usually take a day or two to recover strength. Bass eggs take four to five days to hatch. The male fans the nest to move oxygenated water over the eggs and keep silt from settling on the nest. In a few days, the fry school up over the nest. Males go on feeding sprees after their parental duties are concluded, since while guarding the nest they may go for ten days without eating.

The Kentucky state record largemouth bass weighed 13 pounds, 10 1/4 ounces. It was caught on April 14, 1984, by Dale Wilson of London from Wood Creek Lake. The IGFA all-tackle world record largemouth bass weighed 22 pounds, 4 ounces and was caught on June 2, 1932, from Georgia's Montgomery Lake.

There are many productive fishing lures and techniques for largemouth bass in Kentucky's major lakes. Tournament professional Kevin Van Dam refined the use of jerk baits and encourages anglers to give them a try, especially in the spring. "It's a technique that bass haven't seen at a lot of lakes. . . . With jerk baits you can cover a lot of water and excite fish that aren't necessarily in the mood to bite," said Van Dam, whose spirited approach to fishing shallow-running and suspending crankbaits has helped him win over $300,000 in prize money on the Bassmasters Tournament Trail in his first five seasons.

The Bomber Long A and Smithwick Rattlin' Rogue have been Van Dam's money lures. He fishes the floating models about 75 percent of the time. Suspending lures are used in cold water or after fronts have passed, when bass are sluggish. The lures are fished no deeper than 8 feet.

Jerk baits mimic dying or injured baitfish, moving targets for opportunistic feeders. "Bass are always going to eat the shad that's different in the school, the one that's wounded or doesn't swim like the others." Clear water is the key. "It's a sight-activated presentation. More than with any other lure, you can draw bass from a long way off."

He casts beyond the structure and jerks the rod tip down real hard to get the lure to the working depth. The retrieve is a series of erratic jerks of the rod tip, followed by pauses that make the line go slack. This makes the crankbait dart, float up, and tremble. The slower the retrieve, the longer the pause between jerks. "The lure actually backs up [when you pause]. Any bass that's following can't resist that kind of action. They strike at it out of instinct." Since the bass usually takes the lure when the line is slack, Van Dam said, "you don't know a fish is on until you jerk again and set the hook." Color or size of the jerk bait is not as important as its visibility to the bass. "On sunny days I fish chrome or gold; on cloudy days, chartreuse or pearl." Jerk baits are effective whenever fish relate to shallow structure—logs, rocks, and submerged vegetation.

In the spring, jerk baits can be fished prespawn, and all the way through post-spawn (into June). Position the boat so that casts are parallel to the bank. "Keep the lure over the fish, in the strike zone, for as long as possible. You don't want the lure at the same level or below the fish. . . . The idea is to make the bass come up to take the lure instead of taking the lure down to the bass."

Sunglasses with polarized lenses are a must when fishing jerk baits, as they often allow the angler to see bass as they approach to strike. And since the best fishing is in clear water, casts must be long to prevent spooking fish with the boat.

Van Dam suggested fishing a 5 1/2- or 6-foot graphite rod of medium action, with a fast taper (light tip action). Spinning and casting reels are spooled in line from 6- to 10-pound test, depending on lure size. The lighter the line, the deeper the bait will dive. Hooks on the baits should be kept sharp because many strikes are very light. "They'll slap at it, not even bite it, but you'll catch them."

Another spring and early summer bass lure that is very productive on Kentucky's major lakes is the spinnerbait. Ken Cook, who won the BASS Masters Classic XXI in 1991, proved that the spinnerbait is one of the most versatile lures in bass fishing. A spinnerbait really doesn't look like anything in nature, so why is it effective? "The flashing blade catches the fish's attention, and its vibration bombards the senses. That's why the spinnerbait is a hot lure in stained water. Fish can easily home in on it."

The pulsating skirt makes the lure look like a swimming baitfish. Bass hit the skirt out of hunger or anger. Cook used an unorthodox retrieve to entice strikes from finicky bass. "I like fishing it with what I call a doodling retrieve," Cook said. "I shake the rod tip as I retrieve it slowly. That makes the blade flutter and the skirt fluff and gives it a very erratic action. That's what it took to get these bass to bite." The retrieve made the lure dart left and right like a wounded, frightened baitfish looking for a place to hide.

A popular spinnerbait technique in early spring on Kentucky's major lakes is slow-rolling. The lure is retrieved very slowly, just fast enough to keep the blade moving, as the lure is guided over logs and down channel drop-offs. This presentation works well when bass are holding on the edges of creek channels, prior to moving into shallows.

A summer technique that is hard to beat when bass are deep is Carolina-rigging plastic lizards. This technique became popular when Phenix City, Alabama, angler and lure manufacturer Jack Chancellor won BASS

Fly fishing guide Ron Kruger caught this largemouth bass from Kentucky Lake on a Desperate Diver bass bug he designed.

Masters Classic XV on the Arkansas River. Chancellor didn't fish with lizards, but he popularized the Carolina rig, which is the most widely used technique for fishing with lizards. Carolina-rigging lizards and other plastic baits enables anglers to cover deep water faster and more thoroughly than with crankbaits.

Rigging a plastic bait Carolina-style requires a slip sinker, a red plastic or glass bead, and a small barrel swivel (preferably black). Egg sinkers are sometimes used because they don't get hung up as much as bullet-shaped sinkers. Tie a soft plastic bait to a leader and tie the other end of the leader to the barrel swivel. Thread the line from your fishing rod through the slip sinker and the plastic bead, and then tie it to the other end of the barrel swivel. The bead prevents the heavy sinker from pinching and cutting the line at the knot (where it is attached to the barrel swivel).

The rig is used most often to fish drop-offs. The heavier lead gives the angler a better feel for the bottom contour. The rig is effective because the unweighted lizard floats and drifts just off the bottom, where bass are likely to be suspended. It is an especially effective presentation in submerged vegetation. The lure stays in the strike zone longer, and a bass doesn't have to swim up far to take the bait. Fish the rig as slow as possible for a much more natural presentation than a weighted bait.

A good winter technique is jigging spoons. Professional bass angler Randy Fite has used deep-water tactics to win tournaments and qualify for seven BASS Masters Classics. "Winter is the most difficult time for the average bass angler. They have trouble finding fish because they're schooled up so tightly," said Fite. "But it's a time when you can find the heaviest concentrations of fish you've ever found in your life." Mann-O-Lure and Hopkins Spoon are top brands of jigging spoons. Here are some of his tips on how to find and catch bass during the coldest winter weather.

Bass go deeper in the winter than any other time of the year. The main reason is they follow schools of baitfish (shad) into waters that have the most stable temperatures. Deep water is less affected by extreme temperature changes that occur on the surface. The key to finding winter bass is to use a depth finder to determine the depth at which the shad are holding; schools of shad will show up as one solid mass, layered at a particular depth. Then look for bottom structure at the depth of the shad, since bass tend to feed in relation to structure. Bass will feed when the shad come in contact with the top edge of a steep ledge or the peak of a hump along the channel. Look for bass on the main lake, near the river channel, or near the mouth of major tributaries. On a graph or crystal display bass will show up as larger marks right on the bottom, but at times even big bass may be obscured by swarms of baitfish.

Since bass are shad-oriented during the winter, a chrome finish jigging spoon is a top artificial lure because it imitates a dying shad when jigged vertically. It is critical that the jigging spoon make contact with the bottom structure, but don't hop the bait real high since bass are less active because of the cold water. The lure presentation should be subtle. Bring your rod tip up about 6 inches, then let the lure flutter down while keeping tension on the line by lowering your rod tip at the same rate that the bait falls. Keeping proper tension is critical because if you have slack in your line you will never feel the bass. Strikes will be slight taps and will always come as the lure is falling. If you lower your rod tip too slowly, the lure will stand upright, and lose the fluttering action needed to entice a strike. Fish with a 3/4- to 1-ounce jigging spoon on casting gear, with your reel spooled in 17-pound test line.

In lakes with good forage, adult bass taken during the winter tend to be chunky, high-quality fish, especially the females, which are building egg masses. Bass school by size, so if you catch a 3-pound bass, others are likely to be there. Sometimes big bass feed right in with striped bass or hybrids during the winter.

Al Lindner shows off a largemouth bass.

MUSKELLUNGE

Buckhorn Lake ⋈ ⋈ ⋈	Dale Hollow Lake ⋈ ⋈
Cave Run Lake ⋈ ⋈ ⋈ ⋈	Green River Lake ⋈ ⋈ ⋈ ⋈

The muskellunge (*Esox masquinongy*) is king of Kentucky's major lakes—a voracious predator and big-time brawler on even the heaviest fishing tackle. "Old Briartooth" is a sport fish in a class by himself.

Of the three subspecies, only *E. m. ohioenis*, the Ohio Muskellunge, which is found throughout the Ohio River Valley, is native to Kentucky. In North America, the muskie's range extends from Tennessee and South Carolina, up the Mississippi River valley, and into the Great Lakes and Canada.

The muskie is a member of family Esocidae, which also includes pikes and pickerels. Pollution and siltation almost destroyed native populations. Hatchery propagation and a vigorous stocking program restored the species to much of its historic range in Kentucky. However, reproductive success in Kentucky waters is poor. Since muskie spawn in gravel-bottomed streams, natural reproduction is uncommon in Kentucky's major lakes, and limited to small tributaries. Spawning begins when water temperatures reach 52 degrees. Today, muskie are present in the Green, Licking, and Kentucky River basins, in addition to Tygart's Creek and several other streams that drain into the Ohio River. Cave Run Lake, Buckhorn Lake, and Green River Lake offer the best muskie fishing, with populations supported by annual stockings. Fish over 40 inches long are taken from all three lakes annually.

The elongated, cylindrical fish is beautifully marked. Its body is usually olive to greenish-gray, with golden reflections and darker spots, blotches, or vertical bars. Its mouth is duck-billed, and its powerful jaws are lined with sharp teeth.

Muskies will feed on almost anything, but prefer large shad and suckers, both soft-finned fishes. They dart out and grab their prey from hiding, swallowing it head first. Deadfalls and standing timber are favorite haunts. A muskie may stay in the same general location year after year until it is caught or run off by a larger fish.

Two of the best fishing months in reservoirs are May and September, but many lunkers are taken in the early spring. Crankbaits, jerk baits, buzzbaits, and bucktail spinners are top lures for casting when

Muskie guide David "Crash" Mullins took this 47-incher in late October from Cave Run Lake.

muskies are on shoreline cover. In the summer, muskies go deep. The ticket to success is trolling deep-diving crankbaits parallel to creek channel drop-offs lined with standing timber.

Muskies over 40 inches aren't always the easiest to land. "A big muskie is going to make a run at the boat," said muskie guide David "Crash" Mullins. "It's best to get the trolling motor up. Your line can get wrapped around it and he'll break you off."

Mullins has seen it all, guiding anglers on Cave Run Lake over 150 days a year. "Too many fishermen are undergunned. They're not using stout enough tackle. Their line is too light, or they have old line on their reel." He cringes at the sight of light, woven wire leaders. "If you're going to use a wire leader, use one made from solid wire with a big snap." His monofilament line of choice is Cortland Muskie Mono, 25- to 30-pound. He uses dacron braided line when fishing jerk baits, and a heavy action St. Croix rod.

Kentucky's state record muskie weighed 43 pounds and was caught on March 13, 1978, from Dale Hollow Lake by Porter Hash of Edmonton. The all-tackle world record muskie weighed 67 pounds, 8 ounces and was taken July 24, 1949, by Cal Johnson from the Lake Court Oreilles, near Hayward, Wisconsin.

SAUGER

Kentucky Lake ⚫⚫⚫	Lake Barkley ⚫⚫

The sauger (*Stizostedion canadense*) is a river fish that isn't as widely distributed or abundant in Kentucky as it once was. Since sauger prefer current to slack water, and high-rise dams are a hinderance to migration, sauger do not thrive in the lake environment and have not adjusted as well as other species. In lakes, sauger populations seem to fluctuate wildly.

A member of the family Percidae, the perches and darters, the sauger closely resembles the walleye and is often misidentified by anglers since both fish frequently live in the same waters. Sauger are cool-water fish that begin their spawning run in February when water temperatures are in the upper 40s or low 50s and warm-water species are still inactive. They live and feed near the bottom, fostering the misconceptions that sauger live in deep water and that specialized fishing techniques are needed to catch them. This is not the case at all. Sauger can be caught on spinning tackle casting jigs into water just a few feet deep. They are easy, once you figure out their subtle bite. The tasty fish are best prepared by filleting.

The increased turbidity of rivers, the blocking of spawning routes, and a general lowering of water quality in such important rivers as the upper Cumberland, Tennessee, Kentucky, and Barren have limited the sauger's range. In North America, sauger are found from the Tennessee River in Alabama to New Brunswick, Canada, and west to Oklahoma.

Sauger are regionally popular, and many anglers across the state know very little about these slender, toothy fish that travel in schools. At Kentucky Lake and Lake Barkley, and their tailwaters, there is a 14-inch minimum size limit on sauger. These are the only major lakes in Kentucky which have special regulations for sauger. Otherwise, statewide limits apply—no minimum size limit and a ten-fish daily creel.

The sauger's back is dark to yellowish green, with lighter sides and a silver to whitish belly. The back is crossed with blotch-like saddle bands.

The Kentucky state record is 7 pounds, 7 ounces. Rastie Andrews of Jamestown caught the fish from Lake Cumberland on April 28, 1983. The IGFA all-tackle world record sauger weighed 8 pounds, 12 ounces and was caught from Lake Sakakawea on October 6, 1971.

In late winter and spring, sauger congregate in tailwaters, where they can be caught on 1/8-ounce jigs tipped with minnows.

The saugeye is a cross between a sauger and a walleye which occurs infrequently in nature when the two species interbreed, but can be accomplished easily in a hatchery. Saugeye have been found in the Cumberland River above Lake Cumberland, and are common in the Ohio River. They have been stocked in many reservoirs and streams in Ohio. Gregory Perry of Frenchburg, Kentucky, caught a 24-inch, 3.82-pound saugeye from Bath County's Clear Creek Lake on June 6, 1997, establishing the state record.

SMALLMOUTH BASS

Barren River Lake ⚫⚫
Carr Creek Lake ⚫⚫
Cave Run Lake ⚫
Dale Hollow Lake ⚫⚫⚫⚫
Fishtrap Lake ⚫⚫
Grayson Lake ⚫⚫
Greenbo Lake ⚫⚫

Green River Lake ⚫⚫⚫
Kentucky Lake ⚫⚫⚫
Lake Barkley ⚫
Lake Cumberland ⚫⚫⚫
Laurel River Lake ⚫⚫
Martins Fork Lake ⚫
Paintsville Lake ⚫

Smallmouth bass (*Micropterus dolomieu*) are found throughout central and eastern Kentucky in lakes and rivers, with limited populations in the western third of the state. They are well established in the lower Green River, but are absent in the Purchase Region, where streams flow into the Mississippi. Common names include brown fish, smallie, and bronzeback. They are members of the sunfish family, Centrarchidae. One of Kentucky's top sport fish, smallmouths prefer high-gradient streams (4- to 20-foot drop in elevation per mile) where rock, sand, and gravel are present. They thrive in lakes of moderate to low fertility and feed on insect larvae, minnows, and crayfish.

The drought years in the late 1980s which brought about increases in water clarity throughout the Tennessee River basin have contributed to the growth of an excellent smallmouth bass fishery in Kentucky Lake. The lake yields trophy-size fish to 8 pounds each spring. Dale Hollow Lake and Lake Cumberland are also top smallmouth bass waters.

The smallmouth bass closely resembles the largemouth and spotted bass in body shape, but the smallmouth's tail is wider. The upper body is greenish with a bronze luster and dark vertical bars. The cheek and gill flap have three bronze streaks, radiating from the eye. Its belly is silvery, the eyes reddish. Two other distinguishing characteristics are a small patch of teeth on the tongue and a jaw that does not extend to the eye.

Spawning begins in the spring when water temperatures reach 62 degrees. The fry of smallmouth bass are solid black, distinguishing them from largemouth bass and spotted bass.

For more than forty years the all-tackle world record fish was Kentucky's state record—an 11 pound, 15 ouncer caught by David L. Hayes on July 9, 1955. But in September 1996 the IGFA disqualified

On light tackle there is no fish more fun to catch than smallmouth bass, known for powerful dives and acrobatic leaps.

Hayes' catch. On November 15, 1996, the IGFA certified a 10-pound, 14-ounce smallmouth caught from Dale Hollow Lake on April 24, 1969, by John T. Gorman as the new all-tackle world record.

Smallmouth prefer smaller baits than largemouth bass. Top artificial lures for smallmouth bass are plastic grubs, topwater propeller baits, and shallow-running or suspending crankbaits. Live bait—hellgrammites, lizards, nightcrawlers, crayfish, and minnows—are also highly effective on smallmouth.

Lexington angler Kirk W. Robinson, who avidly fishes Lake Cumberland, fall through spring, usually when water temperature are below 60 degrees, offers these tips:

Fish shale rock banks (45 degree angle) on the lower main lake (below Jamestown Marina), major tributaries, and "short arm" embayments off the main channel. Position the boat in 30 to 40 feet of water.

The live bait of choice is a 3- to 4-inch shiner minnow, hooked from the lower jaw up through the snout. "Fish the shiner like a worm, by casting to the bank and allowing the bait to stairstep down the rock walls," said Robinson. "Patience is a key, it may take five minutes [per cast]."

Robinson uses Stren Magnathin clear line, 6- or 8-pound test, rigged on a 6- to 7-foot rod, and a Shimano Bait Runner 3500 reel. "You fish the reel with the bail closed," said Robinson. "When the fish moves off with the bait, the reel's spool clicks as the fish takes line. That way you know you've got a fish on."

The standard rig is a single BB split shot, positioned 18 inches above a No. 4 Kahle hook. The Kahle style hook allows the shiner to swim in a natural manner. "Be careful not to pinch the split shot too tight on your line," said Robinson. "There's a risk you'll damage the line."

It is critical that the bait stay within a foot or so of the bottom. "When you feel the sinker hit the bottom, reel up a turn. I think there's a much better chance catching the fish that are close to the bottom than those that are suspended off the rock wall."

The other way to fish is to allow the wind to drift the boat down the bank, using the trolling motor to keep the boat perpendicular to the shore. It is possible to have four rods out (in rod holders) when fishing in this manner. When drift fishing, remember that more line (as much as 100 to 200 feet) must be let out for the bait to reach the desired depth.

On windy days, or when the fish are especially deep, Robinson suggested fishing a little heavier weight, a 1/8-ounce bell sinker, which is rigged as a slip sinker above a barrel swivel. The bait trails on the other end of an 18-inch leader, which is tied to the bottom eyelet of the swivel.

Sometimes fish will move as far as 100 feet with the bait in their mouths. Be patient with setting the hook. "It becomes a thinking man's game," said Robinson. "If you set the hook and he's not there, you wonder if you waited too long, or set the hook too soon."

Robinson suggested setting the hook as soon as the fish stops running with the bait. "He's probably turning the minnow around in his mouth and getting ready to swallow it." If a smallmouth hits the bait hard, Robinson suggested setting the hook immediately. "If you don't they'll swallow the bait and be gut hooked."

SPOTTED BASS

Barren River Lake ⚫⚫⚫⚫
Carr Creek Lake ⚫⚫⚫
Cave Run Lake ⚫⚫
Dale Hollow Lake ⚫⚫⚫⚫
Dewey Lake ⚫⚫
Fishtrap Lake ⚫⚫⚫
Grayson Lake ⚫⚫
Green River Lake ⚫⚫
Herrington Lake ⚫⚫⚫

Kentucky Lake ⚫⚫⚫
Lake Barkley ⚫
Lake Cumberland ⚫⚫⚫
Laurel River Lake ⚫⚫⚫
Martins Fork Lake ⚫⚫
Nolin River Lake ⚫⚫⚫⚫
Paintsville Lake ⚫⚫⚫⚫
Rough River Lake ⚫⚫

The spotted bass (*Micropterus punctulatus*) has found a home in Kentucky. On February 27, 1956, Kentucky's General Assembly passed Senate Resolution 70 establishing the spotted bass as Kentucky's official game fish. Soon afterward, the legislation was signed into law by Gov. Albert B. "Happy" Chandler. From that date, the spotted bass became known as the Kentucky bass, a common name that is widely accepted throughout much of the fish's geographic range.

The spotted bass was chosen as the state's official game fish because of its abundance in the Ohio River and tributaries to the south, many of which arise or flow through the Bluegrass State. The preferred habitat is gravel substrate, chunk rock, boulders, or rock walls. In Kentucky's major lakes, spotted bass tend to live in deeper water near dams. They also frequent riprap. The fish eat crayfish, insect larvae, minnows, and salamanders during their aquatic breeding stage.

On January 1, 1988, the minimum size limit on the spotted bass was lifted, enabling anglers to creel spotted bass of any size. The regulation change was made because spotted bass have slow growth rates and most fish never reached the statewide 12-inch minimum size limit. Also, biologists felt that allowing anglers to remove more spotted bass would increase growth rates for largemouth and smallmouth bass.

Spotted bass have physical characteristics and habitat preferences that are similar to those of their cousins, the largemouth and smallmouth bass, but the species is not as widely distributed. Fishery biologists did not recognize that the spotted bass, a member of the sunfish family, Centrarchidae, was a separate species from the largemouth bass until 1927. Adult spotted bass are commonly 8 to 15 inches in length,

Dave Csanda with a spotted bass caught from Kentucky Lake.

weighing 8 ounces to 2 pounds. After reaching 2 3/4 pounds, spotted bass develop a very broad girth which tapers to a sleek, powerful, forked tail. The spotted bass has an olive-green back with irregular markings of darker green. Its sides are paler, with a midlateral band of semiconnected bars. The belly is pearl, with longitudinal rows of dusky (dark green spotted) scales. Its tongue has a small patch of teeth. Somewhat of a regional fish, the spotted bass is found in streams of the Gulf Coast from Texas to the Florida panhandle, and north and west of the Appalachians to eastern Kansas, central Illinois, and southern Pennsylvania. Ichthyologists have taken spotted bass from every major river in Kentucky, except for the Little Sandy.

The state record spotted bass was caught from a farm pond. It is believed that the fish was trapped in the pond by receding flood waters, where it grew to an enormous size. The fish weighed 7 pounds, 10 ounces and was caught by A.E. Sellers of Louisville on June 13, 1970, in Nelson County. The IGFA all-tackle world record spotted bass weighed 8 pounds, 15 ounces and was caught from Lewis Lake in Alabama on March 18, 1978.

Live minnows, nightcrawlers, salamanders, small jigs, and plastic grubs are tops lures for spotted bass, which often can be caught from depths exceeding 30 feet.

STRIPED BASS

Lake Cumberland ⚫◀ ⚫◀ ⚫◀

The striped bass (*Morone saxatilis*) is a nonnative species first stocked in Kentucky waters in 1957. The preferred common name is now striper, since rockfish has fallen out of favor with fishery biologists. The striper's body shape is elongated and less compressed than that of the white bass (*M. chrysops*), with a moderately forked tail. Coloration is dark greenish to blue above, with pale, silvery sides that have seven to eight dusky longitudinal stripes. The base of the tongue has two parallel patches of teeth. Adult stripers can reach 50 pounds in Lake Cumberland, and 20-pounders are common.

Each year 250,000 1 1/2- to 2-inch striped bass fingerlings are stocked in Lake Cumberland, Kentucky's only striped bass lake. Striped bass are also occasionally caught in the winter months from Kentucky Lake, although none are stocked. Those stripers migrated through TVA's system of reservoirs on the Tennessee River. The stocking rate in Lake Cumberland is five fish per acre. It is a put-grow-take fishery, since there is no evidence of natural reproduction in Lake Cumberland, where a trophy fishery developed in the lake in the mid to late 1980s.

The tailwaters below Kentucky Lake and Lake Barkley have experienced exceptional striped bass angling in recent years. Biologists suspect that some natural reproduction may have occurred in the late 1980s in the Ohio River, during a period of high water clarity and increased current. The Ohio River is also stocked annually.

A streamlined, powerful swimmer, the striped bass is an open-water feeder that primarily eats shad. It is a member of the true bass family, Serranidae. During the winter months, striped bass may travel many miles in search of food. A favorite tactic is to herd shad into shallow banks.

Striped bass may be caught by drifting live shad, casting or trolling crankbaits, or casting white deer-hair jigs tipped with pork rind strips or plastic curlytails. Other productive fishing techniques are vertical jigging slab spoons and casting topwater lures. The Cordell Redfin, retrieved so that it wobbles across the surface like a wounded shad, is a good choice for surface action.

Tim Tarter of Nancy, Kentucky, who pioneered drifting live shad on planer boards in Lake Cumberland, stands with a 29-pounder taken in early March.

During the summer months, striped bass seek out water that is about 68 degrees, and may go down to depths in excess of 50 feet in Lake Cumberland.

Kentucky's state record striped bass, which weighed 58 pounds, 4 ounces, was caught December 11, 1985, from Lake Cumberland by Roger Foster of Somerset. The IGFA all-tackle world record landlocked striped bass was caught in California in 1992. It weighed 67 pounds, 8 ounces.

Prized as a terrific game fish, the striper is excellent tasting if prepared properly. Be sure to remove the band of dark flesh from fillets.

SUNFISH SPECIES

Barren River Lake ⊷ ⊷ ⊷	Kentucky Lake ⊷ ⊷ ⊷ ⊷
Buckhorn Lake ⊷ ⊷	Lake Barkley ⊷ ⊷ ⊷ ⊷
Carr Creek Lake ⊷ ⊷	Lake Cumberland ⊷ ⊷ ⊷
Cave Run Lake ⊷ ⊷ ⊷	Lake Malone ⊷ ⊷ ⊷
Dale Hollow Lake ⊷ ⊷ ⊷	Laurel River Lake ⊷ ⊷ ⊷
Dewey Lake ⊷ ⊷ ⊷	Martins Fork Lake ⊷
Grayson Lake ⊷ ⊷ ⊷	Nolin River Lake ⊷ ⊷
Greenbo Lake ⊷	Rough River Lake ⊷ ⊷ ⊷
Green River Lake ⊷ ⊷	Taylorsville Lake ⊷ ⊷ ⊷
Herrington Lake ⊷ ⊷ ⊷	Yatesville Lake ⊷ ⊷ ⊷ ⊷

Kentucky's major lakes support several species of sunfish. Some are found in large numbers, others are scarce. All are native species, but some have been stocked to establish populations or bolster existing ones. The sunfish that anglers are most likely to encounter in Kentucky's major lakes are bluegill, green, longear, and redear.

Bluegill

The bluegill (*Lepomis macrochirus*) is the most popular panfish in Kentucky, but it does not get the respect it deserves. Anglers and biologists alike tend to consider the bluegill as more of a forage fish than a game fish species. This is because bluegill are the main food of largemouth bass and catfish in ponds and small lakes. Largemouth, spotted, and smallmouth bass feed on bluegill in our major lakes, but to a much lesser extent, since shad is a more preferred food.

What the bluegill lacks in size and glamour, it makes up for in fighting ability and food value. An abundant native species and one of our best-tasting fish, bluegill are easy to catch and their white flesh is sweet and firm.

A member of family Centrarchidae, the bluegill is found in all stream drainages of the state, and hence, all the major lakes. It is Kentucky's most widely distributed sunfish. In North America, the bluegill's range extends from northeastern Mexico to Florida, and north to the Great Lakes.

Adult bluegills are saucer-shaped, beautiful fish. Their coloration is

Bluegill are the most common sunfish species in our major lakes. The average bluegill caught is about 7 inches.

variable, but generally they are olive green with emerald, copper, and bluish reflections on their sides, with dark backs. Their lower sides and belly are whitish to yellow. Breeding males may have bright red breasts.

The current Kentucky state record bluegill weighed 4 pounds, 3 ounces. It was caught on August 5, 1980, by Phil M. Conyers of Madisonville. Conyers was bass fishing with spinning tackle and a 6-inch plastic worm in a strip mine lake in Hopkins County when the monster bluegill struck. The IGFA all-tackle world record bluegill weighed just 9 ounces more than Conyer's state record catch. It weighed 4 pounds, 12 ounces and was caught on April 9, 1950, from Alabama's Ketona Lake. The average adult bluegill in Kentucky's manmade impoundments is a 7-incher.

Bluegills and other sunfish species feed mostly on aquatic and terrestrial insects, insect larvae, scuds, mollusks, and algae. They often raid the nests of other fish—including black bass—to prey on fish eggs and small fry. Some of the best sunfish angling of the year occurs during mayfly hatches in late spring and early summer, when bluegills come to the surface to take the emerging insects.

Bluegill move around a great deal except during the spawn, when they become fiercely territorial. Spawning begins in May and continues into June, when water temperatures reach into the 70s. Their nests are circular and are clustered in colonies in shoreline shallows.

Green Sunfish

The green sunfish (*Lepomis cyanellus*) is an abundant species found in all of Kentucky's major lakes. Adults are commonly 7 inches, rarely larger. Coloration is pale green above with darker greenish reflections, paler on the sides, and whitish below. The side of its head has emerald-green mottlings. The green sunfish has a rather large mouth (compared to other sunfish species) and rounded pectoral fins, and the opercular flap has a dark spot, bordered with white. The fish often hybridizes with other sunfish species, with the resulting offspring showing intermediate characteristics.

The geographic range of the green sunfish extends from New Mexico and Colorado eastward to southern Ontario and New York. Tolerant of turbidity, the green sunfish thrives in streams and tends to become over-crowded in small ponds.

The Kentucky state record green sunfish weighed 1 pound, 2 ounces. It was caught on July 31, 1982, by John Meriwether of Henderson from a farm pond in Ballard County.

Longear Sunfish

The longear sunfish (*Lepomis megalotis*) is common in all of Kentucky's major lakes, and abundant in the clear lakes of Eastern Kentucky. Our most colorful sunfish, and arguably Kentucky's most beautiful sport fish, the longear is a bright-colored little fish, hence the common name "sun granny." Its body is olive-green above, and yellowish to red on the belly. It has a long, black opercular flap, bordered in white. The side of its head is bright emerald-blue, with bars of orange radiating backward from the snout across the cheek.

The Kentucky state record longear sunfish weighed 7.2 ounces and was caught by Richard Masters of Crestwood in a Taylor County farm pond on May 12, 1989. Generally, adults are 4 to 7 inches long, too small to interest anglers. The longear sunfish prefers clear, shallow embayments. Its geographic range extends from Minnesota eastward, to South Carolina.

The longear sunfish is common in rocky lakes. Photograph by John Wyatt.

Redear Sunfish (Shellcracker)

The redear sunfish (*Lepomis microlophus*), commonly called the shellcracker, has limited distribution in Kentucky's major lakes. Of the state's twenty-two major reservoirs, Kentucky Lake's population is the best. The redear's geographic range begins in Mexico and northern Florida and extends north to western Kentucky and North Carolina. The shellcracker, similar in appearance to the pumpkinseed (*Lepomis gibbosus*), thrives in clear lakes and ponds, especially those with aquatic vegetation.

An adult redear can reach 10 inches. Its back is a deep olive green, and the upper sides are brassy with a purplish tinge. Its lower sides are silvery with a yellowish tinge. The opercular flap is red or orange on the lower edge. The Kentucky state record shellcracker weighed 3 pounds, 1 ounce and was caught on May 24, 1982, from a Shelby County farm pond by Betty Traux of Finchville.

When fishing for bluegills and other sunfish, keep the tackle simple. All that is needed is a pole or ultralight spinning tackle, live bait, and a bobber. A cane pole works great, but I prefer fishing with a 10- or 12-foot fiberglass pole. These poles are very sensitive, so even the slightest nibble can be detected. The telescoping poles are easily stored and are light enough for even small children to handle.

On light tackle even small fish put up a big fight. The lightest monofilament line, 4- to 6-pound test, is okay for panfish, but remember that light line kinks and twists easily. I prefer to use 10- or 12-pound test monofilament on poles. A little heavier line makes it possible to straighten out light wire hooks rather than break the line when snagged on cover. Ultralight spinning tackle has some obvious advantages over a pole because the bait can be cast to likely fish-holding structures such as downed treetops, stumps, weed beds, standing timber, or flats adjacent to submerged creek channels.

Live bait catches more fish than artificial lures, especially in cool water. Red worms, bits of nightcrawler, crickets, and wax worms are great bluegill bait. Some of the best live baits are free for the taking. A compost pile—made from grass clippings, vegetable kitchen waste, leaves, small sticks and weeds—will attract earthworms to shady areas of your yard. Not only will a compost pile keep you in red worms, but it will create rich, organic soil for your garden or flower bed.

August is the time to start collecting bagworms, a great bluegill bait. Bagworms are found mostly on evergreens and seem to prefer Eastern red cedar, which is abundant throughout Kentucky. The 3/4-inch caterpillars are just the right size to thread on a No. 10 bream hook. Use a small pair of scissors to cut open the bags and get at the fish bait.

If fishing with a bobber, make sure just enough weight is used to stabilize the float so that it rides upright in the water. A pea-sized lead split shot is usually enough weight. Attach the lead to the fishing line about 6 inches above the hook. Bobbers can be attached directly to the line or rigged so that they slip on the line to a depth determined by a bobber stop. A piece of rubber band tied to your fishing line with an overhand knot makes a good bobber stop. Simply position the piece of rubber band at the depth you want to fish.

Reading a fishing bobber is an art of observation. Obviously, if the bobber goes all the way under the water, the fish has taken the bait. But most strikes are less obvious. A slight rise in the bobber signals that the fish had sucked in the bait from above. If the bobber starts to the right, it means a fish has inhaled the bait from the left side.

Combine artificials with live bait for more success. Tip a 1/32-ounce bluegill jig with a wax worm and you will get more strikes. Wet flies and tiny jigs can be fished on ultralight spinning tackle by the use of a clear casting float, which has eyelets on both ends. A fly or tiny spinner is tied to an 18-inch leader, which is knotted to one end of the float. The line from the reel and rod is tied to the eyelet on the other end of the float. The rig is easily cast because of the weight of the float. The best retrieve uses an erratic stop-and-go action.

Artificial bugs and flies fished on a flyrod are ideal for catching bluegills during the spring and early summer.

TROUT

Dale Hollow Lake ⚬⚬⚬	Laurel River Lake ⚬⚬⚬⚬
Greenbo Lake ⚬⚬⚬⚬	Paintsville Lake ⚬⚬⚬

There are three species of trout established in Kentucky's major lakes and/or their tailwaters. All three are nonnative species, introduced to take advantage of cool-water habitats.

Rainbow Trout

The rainbow trout (*Oncorhynchus mykiss*) was introduced into selected cool-water streams, lakes, and tailwaters. While Greenbo Lake, Laurel River Lake, and Paintsville Lake are the only major lakes in Kentucky which receive rainbows, thirteen tailwaters profiled in this book are stocked annually. The rainbow thrives in tailwaters because of daily discharges of cool, oxygenated waters, which seldom reach 70 degrees even in the hottest summer weather. The Lake Cumberland tailwaters, which extends for more than 70 miles to the Tennessee line, southeast of Tompkinsville, is Kentucky's top rainbow trout river. Laurel River Lake is the state's top rainbow trout lake. Since there is no natural reproduction, these reservoir trout are "put-grow-take" fisheries.

A member of family Salmonidae, the salmons and trouts, the rainbow is a high-quality sport fish also prized as table fare. The rainbow is native to the west coast, from Baja, California, to Alaska. Sea-run rainbows are called steelhead.

Coloration is spectacular, especially in the fall. The rainbow's back is light green, and the silvery sides have a distinct pinkish red band. Its belly is white, and black spots are sprinkled about the fish's back, sides, head, and tail.

In Kentucky, the stocking size is 8 to 10 inches, but adults may grow to 10 pounds, living on a diet of aquatic insects and forage fish. The Kentucky state record is 14 pounds, 6 ounces. Jim Mattingly of Somerset caught the fish from the Lake Cumberland tailwaters on September 10, 1972. The IGFA all-tackle world record rainbow trout weighed 42 pounds, 2 ounces and was caught at Bell Island, Alaska, on June 22, 1970.

Anglers must possess a trout permit (in addition to a fishing license) to fish for trout in Kentucky. Trout permits cost $5 for both residents and nonresidents. When still-fishing, rainbow trout can be caught on live, organic, and prepared baits, such as nightcrawlers, kernel corn, cheese, and Berkley Power Baits. Fishing over lights at night is very popular with houseboaters. In tailwater, rainbows can be caught on crankbaits and spinners fished on ultralight spinning tackle. Fly fisher-men use nymphs, dry flies, and streamers to coax rainbows into striking.

Brown Trout

The brown trout (*Salmo trutta*) is a stocky, beautiful fish with a squarish tail and brown body. On its sides, back, and dorsal fin it has dark spots and red spots, both surrounded by white halos.

Brown trout have a preferred temperature range of 50 to 65 de-grees. They have been stocked in the tailwaters of two Kentucky reser-voirs—Lake Cumberland and Herrington Lake. In addition, 30,000 brown trout were stocked in Laurel River Lake in 1995 to supplement the rainbow trout stockings.

The Kentucky state record is 18 pounds, 8 ounces. Randy Gibson of

Brown trout are stocked in the tailwaters of Herrington Lake and Lake Cumberland.

Bakerton caught the brown from the Lake Cumberland tailwaters on June 11, 1988. The IGFA all-tackle world record brown trout weighed 40 pounds, 4 ounces and was caught at Herber Springs, Arkansas, on May 9, 1992.

Lake Trout

The lake trout (*Salvelinus namaycush*) is a deep-water species found throughout Canada, Alaska, and the Great Lakes states. "Lakers" have white mouths and numerous white spots on a bluish-gray back, dorsal fin, and tail, which is very forked.

Only one major lake in Kentucky, Dale Hollow Lake, has been stocked with lake trout, which require very cold water, 40 to 55 degrees. Lake trout were first stocked in 1975. Annual stockings in Dale Hollow Lake vary from 10,000 to 60,000 fish per year. The stocking size is 5 to 6 inches. Lake trout up to 20 inches (a four-year-old fish) are caught.

The Kentucky state record lake trout weighed 5 pounds, 5 ounces and was caught by John E. McDonogh of Jeffersontown from the Cumberland River on April 4, 1983. The IGFA all-tackle world record lake trout weighed 66 pounds, 8 ounces and was caught from Great Bear Lake in Canada, on July 19, 1991.

A drift boat is an ideal way to float the Lake Cumberland tailwaters.

WALLEYE

Carr Creek Lake ⊶ ⊶ ⊶   Laurel River Lake ⊶ ⊶ ⊶
Dale Hollow Lake ⊶ ⊶ ⊶ ⊶   Martins Fork Lake ⊶ ⊶ ⊶
Green River Lake ⊶ ⊶   Nolin River Lake ⊶ ⊶ ⊶ ⊶
Lake Cumberland ⊶ ⊶ ⊶   Paintsville Lake ⊶ ⊶ ⊶

The walleye (*Stizostedion vitreum*) is native to Kentucky, but the southern strain of fish that inhabited the state's rivers has all but disappeared. A northern strain of walleye more suitable to lake environments was stocked as fry in Kentucky waters beginning in the late 1960s. In 1973, when the Minor Clark Fish Hatchery opened, department personnel began collecting broodstock in-state and producing walleye fingerlings (1 1/4-inchers) for stocking. A member of the perch family, Percidae, the walleye's common name is pickerel.

The walleye is fairly distinctive in appearance. It has large, glassy

A weight-forward spinner (like the Hot n' Tot Pygmy) baited with a live nightcrawler is a good choice when walleye are shallow or suspended along flooded timber.

eyes and a prominent dark blotch on the first dorsal fin. The ghostly stare of the walleye is a result of light reflected back through the pupil. Coloration is dark green on the back. The yellowish sides have faint markings, and the belly is milk white. The sauger, which closely resembles the walleye, is darker, with distinctive saddlelike markings across its back and sides.

The walleye's geographic range extends from the Tennessee River basin northward, on both sides of the Appalachians, to Quebec and the southern Hudson Bay region, and on to northwestern Canada. Walleye are common in the Missouri and upper Mississippi Rivers. The fish was first identified in Kentucky by Rafinesque in 1820. A specimen taken from the Ohio River was named *Perca salmonea*.

Adults are commonly up to 24 inches long, rarely more than 30 inches. Kentucky's state record walleye weighed 21 pounds, 8 ounces and was caught by Abe Black of Shaker Heights, Ohio. The fish was taken from the Lake Cumberland headwaters on October 1, 1958. The IGFA all-tackle world record was caught on August 2, 1960, from Tennessee's Old Hickory Lake. It tipped the scales at 25 pounds.

Walleye runs into river headwaters and tailwater areas below dams start in the late winter (under normal water conditions) in February, when water temperatures reach 45 to 46 degrees. Walleye spawning temperatures range from about 52 to 55 degrees. They spawn on rocky shores of lakes and riprap along dams, where their eggs hatch in the cracks and crevices, safe from predators. Females are very fertile, producing as many as 20,000 to 50,000 eggs per pound of body weight. Kentucky waters that have walleye runs include the Nolin River, Cumberland River, the Big South Fork of the Cumberland River, and the Laurel River between Laurel River Dam and the river's mouth. To a much lesser degree there are walleye runs in the Cumberland River below Wolf Creek Dam, in the headwaters of Laurel River Lake, and in the headwaters of Paintsville Lake.

Kentucky anglers are just learning to fish for walleye using traditional tackle and techniques. The Lindy Rig, perfected over twenty-five years ago, is a popular live bait rig for walleye. It is made with a 1/8- to 1/2-ounce walking slip sinker and a barrel swivel for a stop. A floating plastic jig, baited with a minnow, nightcrawler, or leech, is attached to one end of a 30-inch leader, with the other end tied to the barrel swivel. The suggested hook size is No. 4 or No. 6. The rig is drifted or trolled across a flat. The best way to fish the rig is to occasionally raise and lower the rod tip. The slack line between the slip sinker and bait allows the walleye time to suck in the bait. The least resistance can cause a short hit. A deep-diving crankbait or a spinner rig, baited with a nightcrawler, will also catch walleye when trolled across long, sloping points or flats.

Night fishermen catch walleye on jigging spoons by fishing on the dark side of the boat—away from the light of gas lanterns or floating beams directed down into the water. A 1/4- or 1/2-ounce Hopkins spoon is a good choice. Walleye often suspend in the shadows below the swirls of shad which are drawn to the light. Let the jigging spoon free fall, then slowly jig it. Walleye will hit the spoon on the fall.

Walleye are also caught on weight-forward spinners (such as the Erie Dearie) baited with nightcrawlers. This tactic is most effective in the spring when lake levels are high and walleye locate at the edges of flooded timber along the shoreline.

Rick Markesbery (right) unhooks a big walleye caught from Paintsville Lake by Dan Wilson.

WHITE BASS

Cave Run Lake ⚬⚬⚬
Dewey Lake ⚬
Fishtrap Lake ⚬⚬
Grayson Lake ⚬⚬
Green River Lake ⚬⚬⚬⚬
Herrington Lake ⚬⚬⚬
Kentucky Lake ⚬⚬

Lake Barkley ⚬⚬⚬⚬
Lake Cumberland ⚬⚬⚬
Laurel River Lake ⚬⚬⚬
Nolin River Lake ⚬⚬⚬⚬
Rough River Lake ⚬⚬
Taylorsville Lake ⚬⚬⚬

The white bass (*Morone chrysops*) is a true bass, a member of family Serranidae. It is found in streams and rivers throughout the state; therefore, it is present in many of Kentucky's major lakes. The deep-bodied silvery fish has a small head and terminal mouth. There are two separate dorsal (back) fins; the first has nine spines. The belly is milk white. The back is bluish-sliver with metallic reflections. Its sides have dusky, broken stripes. Adults are 10 to 14 inches long, rarely 18 inches.

For most of the year it is an open-water (pelagic) species in lakes, but in the spring the spawning urge makes schools of white bass congregate in lake headwater tributaries, or in rivers below dams which halt their migrations. Spawning begins as soon as water temperatures approach 50 to 55 degrees. They may make spawning runs accompanied by striped bass or hybrid striped bass where populations intermingle.

There are good to excellent white bass fisheries in Lake Barkley, Cave Run Lake, Fishtrap Lake, Green River Lake, Herrington Lake, Kentucky Lake, Nolin River Lake, Rough River Lake, and Taylorsville Lake. White bass are also found in abundance in the Ohio River and lower Green River, in Daviess and McLean Counties, south and west of Owensboro.

The white bass is a powerful swimmer that is great fun to catch on light spinning tackle. The best fishing is in the spring when white bass congregate below dams and make spawning runs to headwater tributaries of lakes. Their primary food is minnows, shiners, and shad (threadfin and gizzard). During the summer, white bass school up and chase swarms of shad on the surface. Plunker and fly combinations, white curlytail jigs, Roostertail spinners, and slab spoons are cast into "jumps." White bass are also caught trolling crankbaits, with streamer flies, spinners,

White bass are abundant in Kentucky's major lakes and offer anglers excellent fishing opportunities in the spring and summer.

spoons, or small jigs trailing on a leader. At night, white bass are caught over lights by still-fishing with minnows.

White bass are surprisingly good table fare if prepared properly. The skin and the strip of dark meat should be removed from fillets before cooking. Bread the fillets in lightly peppered corn meal and fry them in vegetable oil in an iron skillet.

Two 5-pound white bass, one caught from Kentucky Lake in 1943 and the other taken from Herrington Lake in 1957, are tied for the state record. The IGFA all-tackle world record weighed 6 pounds, 13 ounces and was caught from Lake Orange in Virginia on July 31, 1989.

THE LAKES

If a little madness be a necessary requisite to obtain the ultimate in the pleasure of angling—then, O Lord, give me insanity!

—John Alden Knight (1936)

INTRODUCTION

Kentucky has a mix of lake types and sport fish guaranteed to test the skill of any angler. The lake types range from flatland reservoirs dominated by warm-water species to deep, clear mountain lakes, where cool-water species thrive. Kentucky's major lakes are manmade impoundments built for flood control, water supply, and navigation, with fishing and outdoor recreation as secondary considerations. All but two of Kentucky's major lakes are storage impoundments, built in headwater tributaries. Only Kentucky Lake and Lake Barkley are main stem reservoirs, which are characterized by high exchange rates of water. It takes just eighteen to nineteen days (depending on lake level) for water that has entered these reservoirs to flow through the dam. This continual exchange of water is the major reason why their nutrient levels and fish production are higher.

The trophic state, or relative fertility, of Kentucky's major lake were assessed using the Carlson Trophic State Index (TSI) for chlorophyll *a*. This method allows lakes to be ranked numerically, according to increased eutrophy, and provides for a distinction, according to TSI value, between oligotrophic, mesotrophic, and eutrophic lakes. The trophic state index listed for each lake is from the Kentucky Division of Water's 1994 Report to Congress on Water Quality.

The lakes profiled in this book aren't just the largest lakes (some are quite small). Each, however, has a unique distinction that I believe makes it worthy of inclusion from an angling standpoint. Lakes in eastern Kentucky are generally smaller and less fertile than lakes in western and central Kentucky, where rivers have bigger, wider floodplains. Due to eastern Kentucky's mountainous topography, it takes a much higher dam to back up as much water as is held back in flatlands. Mountain lakes have less embayment habitat too, which has an effect on some fish species. For example, there may be limited spawning areas for largemouth bass.

The twenty-two lakes profiled in this chapter, in alphabetical order, are: Barren River Lake, Buckhorn Lake, Carr Creek Lake, Cave Run Lake, Dale Hollow Lake, Dewey Lake, Fishtrap Lake, Grayson Lake, Green River Lake, Greenbo Lake, Herrington Lake, Kentucky Lake, Lake Barkley, Lake Cumberland, Lake Malone, Laurel River Lake, Martins Fork Lake, Nolin River Lake, Paintsville Lake, Rough River Lake, Taylorsville Lake, and Yatesville Lake. Each lake profile includes location, size, trophic state index, lake manager's office, managing fishery biologist, lake level/fishing report line, marinas, boat launching ramps, and local tourism information.

The fishing information on each lake starts with an overview. This includes a wide variety of information such as fishery management programs of the past, current outstanding fisheries, environmental problems, significant lake bed features or structure (such as standing timber or weed beds) that have an impact on fishing, and idle speed restrictions.

The fish species at each lake are listed in descending order of importance to anglers and their relative quality, as assessed by the managing fishery biologist. The amount of detail provided for a particular species is proportional to its significance to anglers at that lake, or its overall quality in Kentucky. Every attempt was made to give the most up-to-date information on the fishery's status. The fisheries are rated as being

The modern bass boat revolutionized fishing on large reservoirs. Photograph courtesy of Ranger Boats.

poor, fair, good or excellent by the managing fishery biologist. This helps anglers evaluate fishing opportunities and compare them with other lakes. Tailwater fishing opportunities will also be discussed. This will include a species list and detailed information on significant fisheries.

U.S. Army Corps of Engineers Lake Maps

The U.S. Army Corps of Engineers operates eighteen lakes in Kentucky. Their color brochures of these projects show lake outlines, the locations of boat launching ramps, day-use areas, campgrounds, and local access roads. The brochures can be obtained free from Corps district offices and the resource manager's office at each lake. Topographic maps (scale 1/24,000) that show preimpoundment lake bed features and depth contours are available for twelve of the reservoirs, and navigation charts are available for one reservoir.

Listed below are the U.S. Army Corps of Engineer district offices, the lakes for which topographic maps and navigation charts are available, and the cost of the maps

U.S. Army Corps of Engineers, Louisville District, Box 59, Louisville, KY 40201-0059. For map orders telephone (502) 582-5739 or (502) 582-5010. Maps are available for Barren River Lake, Buckhorn Lake, Carr Creek Lake, Cave Run Lake, Green River Lake, Nolin River Lake, Rough River Lake, and Taylorsville Lake.

The maps cost 75 cents per lake, plus $1 for shipping and handling on orders over $3. Payment may be made by check or money order. The black and white maps are composed of multiple sheets, each measuring 14 1/2 by 21 inches.

U.S. Army Corps of Engineers, Nashville District, Box 1070, Nashville, TN 37202. For map orders telephone (615) 736-7864. Maps are available for Dale Hollow Lake, $5.35; Lake Barkley, $4.00 (11 by 17 inches) or $8.00 (24 by 32 inches); Lake Cumberland, $12.00; and Laurel River Lake, $6.50. Shipping and handling is $3.00 for orders under $30.00. The black and white maps are composed of multiple sheets, each measuring 14 1/2 by 21 inches. The Lake Barkley navigation chart is in color. Payment may be made by check or money order.

U.S. Army Corps of Engineers, Huntington District, 502 8th Street, Huntington, WV 25701-2070. For map orders telephone (304) 529-5293. A limited quantity of maps are available only for Yatesville Lake. The black and white maps are composed of multiple sheets, each measuring 14 1/2 by 21 inches. The cost is $5.25, plus $3.00 postage and handling. Payment may be made by check or money order.

Tailwaters

Some of the best fishing opportunities in Kentucky are the tailwaters of our major lakes. Tailwaters, however small, are particularly attractive to game fish when discharge rates are the highest. Some fish are swept through dams during periods of heavy discharge, others are drawn to tailwaters because of the swift current. In the winter the water discharged is usually warmer than the water in the river downstream, while during the hot summer months, it is often cooler.

Numerous species can be found in tailwaters. Catfish, largemouth bass, crappie, smallmouth bass, and muskie are among the species attracted to tailwaters year-round because shad and other food fishes congregate there. White bass, sauger, striped bass, striped bass hybrids, and walleye stack up in tailwaters in the spring because dams halt their seasonal migrations in search of suitable spawning areas. Rainbow and, to a lesser degree, brown trout are seasonally stocked in some tailwaters so they can take advantage of cool waters discharged from the lake's lower depths.

Anglers fish the tailwaters below the dam at Green River Lake.

Most tailwaters have developed facilities for anglers—parking areas, chemical toilets, picnic tables, and walkways with railings in dangerous areas above the current. Anglers are reminded to obey all safety regulations posted in tailwater areas. Never tie a boat up to the dam, stay out of restricted areas marked by buoys, and be aware that heavy discharges create dangerous currents and boils. Anglers wading in tailwater areas should pay particular attention to water levels. If you are fishing near the dam and you hear an alarm sound, head for the safety of the shore immediately. Rapidly rising water levels can overwhelm a wading angler and dislodge boats from their mooring.

BARREN RIVER LAKE

Bluegill ⚬⚬⚬
Catfish ⚬⚬⚬⚬
Crappie ⚬⚬⚬
Hybrid Striped Bass ⚬⚬⚬⚬

Largemouth Bass ⚬⚬⚬⚬
Smallmouth Bass ⚬⚬
Spotted Bass ⚬⚬⚬⚬
Tailwaters ⚬⚬⚬

Location Barren River Lake is about 103 miles south of Louisville in Barren, Monroe, and Allen Counties. The main access highways are Interstate 65 and U.S. 31E. The dam is on Ky. 252, southwest of Glasgow. The lake was impounded from the Barren River, a tributary to the Green River. The gates were closed on the dam in March 1964, but the lake did not reach seasonal pool until 1965.

Size The 10,000-acre lake at summer pool, elevation 552, has 140 miles of shoreline, is 33 miles long, and is about 70 feet deep above the dam. There is a substantial winter drawdown, 27 feet to elevation 525, which reduces the surface acreage to 4,340. At winter pool the upper half of the lake is very shallow. The drawdown goes all the way to the preimpoundment elevations of the old river channel, and miles of mudflats are exposed.

Trophic State Index (TSI) Barren River Lake has a TSI of 50, which ranks it as a mesotrophic lake (moderate fertility). The Beaver Creek embayment, 1,565 acres, has a TSI of 57, ranking it as eutrophic (high fertility).

Lake Manager's Office U.S. Army Corps of Engineers, Resource Manager's Office, Barren River Lake, 11088 Finney Road, Glasgow, KY 42141-9642, telephone (502) 646-2055.

Managing Fishery Biologist Kentucky Department of Fish and Wildlife Resources, Southwestern Fishery District, B.D. Laflin, District Biologist, 4800 Nashville Road, Bowling Green, KY 42101, telephone (502) 842-3677

Lake Level/Fishing Report Line The U.S. Army Corps of Engineers lake information line is (502) 646-2122.

Marinas There are four marinas. *Walnut Creek Marina*, open April 15

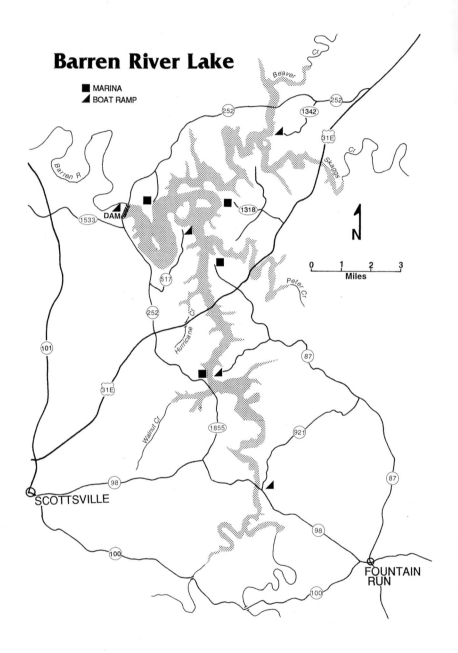

Barren River Lake

■ MARINA
▲ BOAT RAMP

Beaver Cr

252
1342
31E
252
Skaggs Cr
Barren R
1533
DAM
1318
517
Peter Cr
252
101
Hurricane Cr
31E
87
1855
921
Walnut Cr
98
87
SCOTTSVILLE
100
98
FOUNTAIN RUN
100

0 1 2 3
Miles

N

to October 15, is about 6 miles south of the dam, on Ky. 1855. The address and telephone number are 1994 Walnut Creek Road, Scottsville, KY 42164, (502) 622-5858. *Barren River Lake State Resort Park Dock*, open March 1 to November 30 (but could be open later or earlier depending on lake level), is 10 miles southwest of Glasgow, on U.S. 31E. The address and telephone number are 1850 State Park Road, Lucas, KY 42156, (502) 646-2357. *Sawyer's Landing Marina*, open February 15 to November 30 (call to make arrangements for use at other times), is 2 miles northeast of the dam, off Ky. 252. The address and telephone number are 1261 Peninsula Road, Glasgow, KY 42141, (502) 646-2223. There is a $2 fee to launch at the adjacent Peninsula boat ramp, $25 for an annual pass, with discounts available to senior citizens. *The Narrows Marina*, open April 15 to October 15, is about 11 miles southwest of Glasgow, off U.S. 31E. The address and telephone number are South Lucas Road, Lucas, KY 42156, (502) 646-5253. There is a $2 fee to launch at the adjacent Narrows boat ramp, $25 for an annual pass, with discounts available to senior citizens.

Boat Launching Ramps   There are four boat launching ramps on the lake in addition to the ramps at the marinas. *Austin* boat ramp is off Ky. 87, about 5 miles southwest of Barren River Lake State Resort Park. *Brown's Ford* boat ramp is off Ky. 98, at the lake headwaters. *Bailey's Point* boat ramp is off Ky. 517, about 6 miles southeast of the dam. There is a $2 fee to launch, $25 for an annual pass, with discounts available to senior citizens. *Beaver Creek* boat ramp is the closest ramp to Glasgow, off U.S. 31E. There is a $2 fee to launch, $25 for an annual pass, with discounts available to senior citizens.

Local Tourism Information   Glasgow/Barren County Chamber of Commerce, 118 E. Public Square, Glasgow, KY 42141, telephone (502) 651-3161.

Fishing   Barren River Lake is a flatland, warm-water reservoir with high-quality populations of largemouth bass, hybrid striped bass, catfish, and crappie. The upper lake is predominated by shallow flats, with numerous stump beds and scattered pockets of standing timber. The lower lake has a more varied shoreline, which includes boulders, shale bluffs, and four islands in a horseshoe bend around Bailey's Point. Shad is the primary forage for game fish. Both gizzard and threadfin shad are present in the lake. In 1965 and 1966 a total of 2,672 adult threadfin shad were stocked in the lake. There have been numerous die-offs of shad through the years, the most recent during the winter of 1995-96. Preimpoundment surveys of the Barren River found 85 species of fish, dominated numerically by rock bass, black bass (mainly spotted bass), and catfish. Walleye, muskellunge, and rock bass were found in preimpoundment surveys, but are not present in the lake today.

Largemouth Bass   The largemouth bass fishery is rated excellent, and the outlook is for a large population of 10- to 15-inch fish. In recent years, the largemouth bass has replaced the crappie as the most sought-after game fish species at Barren River Lake. About 80 percent of the black bass in the lake are largemouth. "Largemouth bass up to 22 inches are caught by anglers," said fishery biologist B.D. Laflin. "It takes three-plus years for a largemouth bass to reach harvestable size [15 inches]."

Barren River Lake arguably has Kentucky's third best largemouth bass fishery behind Kentucky Lake and Lake Barkley. It is a popular lake for tournaments, too. "We have lots of 3- to 5-pounders, but we rarely see big bass [8- to 10-pounders]." The Beaver Creek arm of the reservoir is a top bass producer. It is eutrophic because of treated sewage effluent from Glasgow. "There's a higher productivity level, but there haven't been any major fish kills or algae blooms."

Laflin said fishing pressure has remained pretty steady in the 1990s. A 1992 creel survey found that the average largemouth bass harvested was a 13.8-incher weighing 1.33 pounds. The creel survey conducted during 1996 was the first since a 15-inch minimum size limit was established for largemouth and smallmouth bass on March 1, 1993. "A really nice fishery has developed since 1993," said Laflin. "Quality has increased and the numbers are stable."

Various baits can be used, depending on the season. The spinnerbait is a top spring lure, when the bass move up onto the brushy flats in the upper lake as the water warms. During the summer, fish Carolina-rigged plastic baits on main lake flats and deep-diving crankbaits in chartreuse or crayfish patterns across deep points. In the winter, when the lake is low, fish jig and pork rind combinations along river channel drop-offs.

Hybrid Striped Bass   The hybrid striped bass fishery is rated excellent, and the outlook is for numerous fish over 18 inches and a strong year class of sublegal fish coming on which will provide good fall fishing. Barren River Lake, one of only five lakes in Kentucky stocked with hybrid striped bass, may offer the best opportunity for a trophy fish over 10 pounds. During the summer of 1994, hybrids up to 26 inches were gill netted in the lake during routine sampling.

Hybrids were first released in the reservoir in 1979. The initial stocking was about 226,000. Hybrid fry, hatched in mid-May, are raised on a plankton diet at the Minor E. Clark Fish Hatchery near Morehead. Typically, hybrids are stocked when they reach 1 1/2 to 2 inches in length in June. The annual stocking rate has varied from about 10 to 20 fish per acre. About 300,000 hybrids were stocked in 1996. "We increased the number to compensate for the fish lost when the lake is drawn down to winter pool," said Ted Crowell, assistant director of the fisheries division.

Laflin said the fishery receives only moderate pressure. Some of the best fishing of the year occurs in the spring, when high water covers parking lots and grassy areas around shoreline campgrounds. That is when hybrids move into the shallows to feed on crayfish, shad, and minnows. Concentrations of hybrids are found around the islands off the old river channel, just above the dam to Bailey's Point. In the fall, hybrids are caught by trolling and casting jigs and spoons, still-fishing on the bottom with live crayfish, and drifting live shad.

For white bass, striped bass, and hybrids there is a twenty-fish daily creel, singly or combined, but no more than five may be 15 inches or longer.

Catfish The outlook for catfish is excellent, with many 1- to 4-pound channel catfish available to anglers. Barren River Lake may be one of Kentucky's best kept catfishing secrets. "There's some real good fish, big numbers and very little fishing pressure," said Laflin. "The catfish are healthy and have a fast growth rate." The fishery is rated excellent. "I don't know that one area of the lake is better than the other for catfish," said Laflin. "Wherever you fish, you need to find dingy water."

Barren River Lake supports both channel and flathead catfish. Laflin said trotlines, jugs, and limb lines (in the spring) are used to catch catfish from the lake. A few are caught by anglers trolling crankbaits on main lake flats. Catfish populations are renewed by natural reproduction; there is no supplemental stocking. "The average channel cat being caught from Barren is about an 18- to 22-incher," said Laflin. "There's not as many flatheads, but generally they're much larger." Flatheads up to 50 pounds have been taken from Barren River Lake.

In the spring, the upper lake offers the best fishing, especially the areas where riprap covers the banks adjacent to highway bridge abutments. "Prespawn [April and early May] there are some good catches made by bank fishermen," said Barren County conservation officer Donald Depp. "After the spawn catfish hang around for a few weeks to feed on the riprap." On summer nights, fishing over lights from the bank is popular around bridges, Depp said. Some catches are accidental. "A lot of catfish are caught by hybrid anglers when they're fishing on the bottom with nightcrawlers or crayfish."

In Barren County, Depp recommends catfishing near the Ky. 252 bridge over Beaver Creek and the U.S. 31E bridge over Peter's Creek. In Allen County, two good fishing spots are Walnut Creek boat ramp, off Ky. 1855, and Brown's Ford boat ramp off Ky. 98, at the lake headwaters. "At most of these places there's plenty of parking spaces [for bank fishermen]." Another good catfishing area is the riprap near the state park. "Very early in the spring [February through March] when it's still cold there's good fishing in the upper lake," said Depp. "The lake level is down to the old river channel. We have a lot of guys that build fires and fish from the banks, with good success."

Crappie The crappie fishery is rated good. The outlook is for numerous 9- to 10-inch white crappie and a strong year class of 6- to 8-inch black crappie which should reach legal size in the fall. "Overall, the population is doing fine," said Laflin. "Black crappie still dominate the population."

Fishing pressure is moderate to heavy, seasonally. Trap netting in the fall of 1994 showed that the majority of the black crappie population were either 10-inch fish or 2- to 3-inchers. The average weight of a seven-year-old, 10-inch black crappie was 0.59 pounds. White crappie were 3-and 4-inchers and 10- to 12-inchers. The average weight of a five-year-old, 12-inch white crappie was 0.96 pounds. Few intermediate crappie were sampled, attesting to the subpar reproduction in recent years. "There were low numbers of crappie spawned in 1990 and 1992," said Laflin. Crappie growth in Barren River Lake is considered good. The best crappie fishing is in the tributaries—Beaver, Skaggs, and Peter Creeks in the lower lake, and Walnut Creek at midlake.

There is a 9-inch minimum size limit.

Spotted Bass The spotted bass fishery is rated excellent, and the outlook is for numerous 12- to 15-inch fish. It is no surprise that Barren River Lake has an excellent spotted bass fishery since spotted bass was the most abundant black bass in the preimpoundment surveys. "There are some really huge spotted bass," said Laflin. The rocky bluffs on the lower lake hold spotted bass, which can be caught on tube jigs, plastic grubs, and live minnows. The average Kentucky bass harvested in 1992 was a 12.4-incher weighing 0.82 pounds. Samples taken by electrofishing in April and May of 1992 found spotted bass up to 16 inches long. The spotted bass fishery represents about 15 percent of the lake's black bass.

Smallmouth Bass   The smallmouth bass fishery is rated fair to good, and the outlook is for slightly improving fishing in rocky areas of the lower lake. The smallmouth is a bonus fish in Barren River Lake. "The best fishing occurs when the fish come up shallow on the rocks in the cool-weather months," said Laflin. Fish shale bluffs and gradually sloping gravel points. That same time of year, also try points and sweeping bends in the channel. Cast jigs, crankbaits, and live minnows on shallow flats adjacent to the old river channel.

"Creel survey data from 1992 show the highest harvest is in March [233] and April [296]," said Gerry Buynak, bass biologist for the Kentucky Department of Fish and Wildlife Resources. Smallmouth made up about 5 percent of all black bass harvested that year—a total of 1,175.

When the lake water is stratified, the smallmouth bass population is concentrated in the lower lake, from Barren River Lake State Resort Park to the dam. "During the cooler months smallmouth tend to scatter out all over the lake," said Buynak.

The average smallmouth bass being harvested is a 15.2-incher that weighs about 1.65 pounds, but fish weighing 3 to 4 pounds are being caught. There is a 15-inch minimum size limit, with a combined daily creel of six on largemouth and smallmouth bass in Barren River Lake.

White Bass   The white bass fishery is rated fair, and the outlook is for an improving population of smaller fish. In recent years, Barren River Lake's white bass fishery has been suppressed somewhat. "Numbers are not real good," said Laflin. "[The population] is not at the level we expect." Laflin said this is due to poor reproduction. "There's a spring [spawning] run but there aren't many fish."

While most fish stay close to the lake during their spawning run, Laflin said that in a good year white bass can go as far as 60 miles upriver, all the way to Tompkinsville, near the headwaters of the Barren River. "[In recent years] the spring weather has not been conducive to white bass runs," said Laflin. "We've had low rainfall in March." When water levels are right, white bass go about 10 miles up Skaggs Creek. There are also minor runs in White Oak Creek, Long Creek, and Beaver Creek.

Vary your strategy by the season. Small white or yellow Roostertail spinners are a good early spring lure. Summer jump action is sporadic. "There are not a lot of jumps and they are small," said Laflin. "Jumps usually occur around Grass and Goose Islands, off the beach at the state park, the narrows [near the mouth of Skagg's Creek], and off Bailey's Point." Slab spoons, shallow-running crankbaits, jigs and the Little

George spinner are the best lures when white bass are jumping. Live minnows are the best bait for night fishing over lanterns.

White bass receive only moderate fishing pressure. The last decent spawn was in 1994, the year class that has now reached harvestable size. The average adult white bass taken is an 11- to 12-incher.

White bass are native to the Barren River, but in the spring of 1965 360 adult white bass were released in the lake to bolster native populations. There have been no other stockings of white bass since the lake was impounded.

Bluegill The bluegill fishery is rated good, and the outlook is for numerous 6- to 7-inch fish. A number of factors have combined to create an improved outlook for larger bluegill. "Because of the high shad kill the past two winters there's been more predation on bluegill by bass," said Laflin. "There's been quite a few larger bluegill than normal [7- and 8-inchers] caught in the summer of 1996." Also, high water during May and June in 1995 and 1996 has improved spawning conditions for bluegill, and may mean more bluegills in the future.

"Bluegill are spread out all over the lake," said Laflin. During the late spring, fish shallow flats around willow trees. In the summer, drift fish deep along rocks bluffs in the lower lake. Fish crickets, red worms, and wax worms on ultralight spinning tackle.

Tailwater Fishing Opportunities

How good is fishing in the Barren River Lake tailwaters? It looks too shallow to produce much, but Louisville's Mark Wilson might tell you otherwise. On April 27, 1991, Wilson caught a 20-pound, 8-ounce hybrid striped bass, besting the previous state record by 2 pounds, 6 ounces. "It took me 35 minutes to get it in," Wilson said. "It's the first hybrid I ever caught. My arms got so tired." Wilson caught his record fish on a 1/8-ounce brown Stanley jig, tipped with a live crayfish.

The heavy discharge from the 27-foot drawdown is responsible for hybrids escaping into the tailwaters. On January, 5, 1994, Laflin and his crew sampled 184 hybrids while electrofishing the tailwaters. The hybrids ranged in size from 5 to 27 inches long, and thirty-eight fish were over 20 inches long. Most of the hybrids average 2 to 3 pounds, but when sampling the tailwaters by electrofishing one spring, Laflin and his crew shocked up a 30-inch hybrid. "The tailwaters supports a good fishery for hybrids that lasts into the early summer," said Laflin. "The hybrids are just hanging around. At times there are some real big ones in there, some are 8 to 9 pounds." Hybrids are drawn to the tailwaters during periods of high discharge in the spring, and during the fall, when the lake's level is drawn down, Laflin suspects that hybrids go through the dam to the river below.

The hybrids are usually caught by anglers still-fishing at night with live bait—crayfish and nightcrawlers. Most of the fish are caught in the bucket, or concrete spill basin. "The hybrids [suspend] around the big pillars that break up the flow," Laflin said. When the fishing is hot, there's likely to be a big crowd of fishermen, Laflin said, adding, "sometimes the hybrids don't start biting until two or three o'clock in the morning."

During periods of moderate to heavy discharge, an eddy is created off the main channel in a small slough (an old river channel) that is just downstream, well within walking distance of the dam. "That's where most of the crappie fishing is done," Laflin said.

Other fish are also available in the tailwaters. White bass come up into tailwaters in fair numbers during the spring. April through November, 18,600 rainbow trout are stocked. About six miles of the tailwaters is considered trout habitat.

There is a boat launching ramp below the dam for access to the tailwaters.

Barren River Lake Dam.

BUCKHORN LAKE

Bluegill ⊶ ⊶	Largemouth Bass ⊶ ⊶
Catfish ⊶ ⊶ ⊶	Muskellunge ⊶ ⊶ ⊶
Crappie ⊶ ⊶ ⊶ ⊶	Tailwaters ⊶ ⊶ ⊶

Location   Buckhorn Lake is in Perry and Leslie Counties, about 28 miles west of Hazard. Completed in 1961, the lake was built by the Louisville District of the U.S. Army Corps of Engineers on the middle fork of the Kentucky River. The dam is 43.3 miles above the middle fork's confluence with the north fork in Beattyville, and the drainage area above the dam is 408 square miles. The main access highways are Ky. 28, Ky. 1833, and Ky. 257.

Size   Buckhorn Lake is 21 miles long at summer pool (elevation 782) and has 1,230 surface acres, with 65 miles of shoreline. At winter pool, elevation 757, the lake is drawn down to 550 surface acres. Averaging about 25 feet deep, Buckhorn Lake is 60 feet deep above the dam.

Trophic State Index (TSI)   Buckhorn Lake's TSI of 38 ranks it as an oligotrophic lake (low fertility).

Lake Manager's Office   U.S. Army Corps of Engineers, Resource Manager's Office, Buckhorn Lake, 1325 Buckhorn Dam Road, Buckhorn, KY 41721, telephone (606) 398-7251.

Managing Fishery Biologist   Kentucky Department of Fish and Wildlife Resources, Eastern Fishery District, Steve Reeser, District Biologist, 2744 Lake Road, Prestonsburg, KY 41653, telephone (606) 886-9575.

Lake Level/Fishing Report Line   The U.S. Army Corps of Engineers lake information line is (606) 398-7157.

Marinas   There is one marina. *The Buckhorn Lake State Resort Park Marina*, open April 1 to October 31, is on Ky. 1833, where the road ends in the water. The address and telephone number are 4414 Gays Creek Road, Buckhorn, KY 41721, (606) 398-7510.

Boat Launching Ramps   There are five boat launching ramps on the

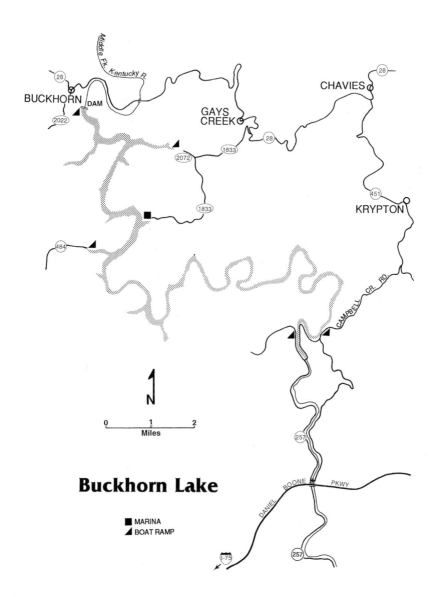

Buckhorn Lake

■ MARINA
◢ BOAT RAMP

lake in addition to the ramp at the marina. There is no fee to launch a boat at any of these five ramps as of spring 1997, but user fees are being considered for the future. The 25-foot drawdown to winter pool makes launching difficult at some ramps because of mud. At winter pool, the best ramp to launch from is at the Buckhorn Lake State Resort Park marina. Drift and debris collects on the main lake when the water comes up in the spring. When high water recedes, the drift left behind is piled on the shore and burned. Floating debris is corralled with log booms and tied off to the shore. *Confluence* boat ramp is off Ky. 257 in the upper lake, about 11 miles southwest of Krypton, Kentucky. *Dam* boat ramp is off Ky. 28, about 1 mile east of Buckhorn. *Gays Creek* boat ramp is off Ky. 1833, 5 miles north of Buckhorn Lake State Resort Park. *Leatherwood* boat ramp is on the west side of the lake where Ky. 484 ends in the lake. *The Trace Branch* boat ramp is off Campbell Creek Road, 8 miles southwest of Krypton.

Local Tourism Information   Perry County Tourism Commission, 601 Main Street, Suite 3, Hazard, KY 41701, telephone (606) 439-2659.

Fishing   Buckhorn Lake is a highland reservoir with a surprising amount of shallow water. Usually mountain lakes are exceedingly deep and crystal clear. Fish cover includes scattered weed beds, pockets of standing timber, submerged road beds, and drift piles near the dam. The lake has a growing reputation for producing big muskies, with perhaps the best chance in the state of boating a fish over 40 inches. While muskie density is lower than at Cave Run Lake or Green River Lake, Buckhorn Lake has good potential for a high-quality muskie fishing experience. The fact that the lake is difficult to reach and facilities are limited in the immediate area may be a contributing factor to lower fishing pressure on muskies than at other lakes.

Buckhorn also has populations of white bass, spotted bass, longear sunfish, warmouth, carp, freshwater drum, largemouth bass, bluegill, crappie, and catfish. The main forage fish is gizzard shad. An attempt was made to establish threadfin shad, but the population succumbed to winter kill. The lake was last stocked with threadfins in 1992.

Muskellunge   The muskie fishery is rated good, and the outlook is for numerous 30-inch fish in the lower third of the lake, from Leatherwood Creek to the dam. Local angler Chris Haley believes Buckhorn Lake offers the best chance to catch a 40-inch muskie anywhere in the state. "I've had better days here than at Cave Run Lake," said Haley, who grew up in Hazard. "There's not as much fishing pressure on muskies."

Over several seasons in the 1990s, Haley took more than 20 muskies over 40 inches long from Buckhorn Lake. Fall is his favorite time to fish for muskies at the reservoir. "The muskies are at the mouths of creeks on wood cover in 10 to 20 feet of water in the summer, but in late August they start to move up on shallow flats adjacent to creek channels," said Haley. "They tend to school up in weed beds." In September, before the winter drawdown, Haley catches a lot of muskies in the afternoons. "Buckhorn cools off fast in the fall. A good rain will bring the fish up shallow." Otter Creek and Meetinghouse Branch are two of the best creeks for muskie.

Swim Whiz crankbaits, Suick jerk baits, and Grim Reaper (500 or 900 series) bucktail spinners are top lures on the lake. In the spring Haley prefers to fish white- or silver-colored lures, in the summer, chartreuse and black, and in the fall, yellow or orange. He fishes orange lures at the heads of creeks and silver lures on the main lake. "In the fall I think they're trying to fatten up by eating carp and suckers. Maybe that's why orange is so effective." When he fishes a bucktail, it is usually white and chartreuse or orange and black.

Two factors may be at work to keep muskies densities at Buckhorn Lake lower than the state's other two muskie lakes. The first factor is the severe winter drawdown (25 feet), which allows some fish to escape through the dam into the tailwaters, where high catch rates are reported in the late fall. Second, almost all of the muskies caught from Buckhorn Lake are kept by anglers. There is a very low release rate at Buckhorn, whereas at Cave Run Lake and Green River Lake the muskie release rate approaches 50 percent, according to creel data.

In 1993 an estimated 282 muskies were caught, including 171 over 30-inches in length. According to creel survey data, the average keeper was a 35.4-incher. Ninety three of the 171 keepers were over 38 inches in length. May was the best fishing month for keeper muskie, followed by June, September, and October.

According to stocking records, 17,343 muskie were released in Buckhorn Lake from 1980 through 1993, with average lengths ranging from 9 inches to 13.5 inches. Buckhorn Lake is one of only three impoundments and fourteen streams in Kentucky which are stocked with muskies annually. Muskies are stocked in Buckhorn Lake because the fish were native to the middle fork of the Kentucky River. The stocked muskies attain legal size (30 inches) in their third growing season.

When summer comes, Haley starts trolling. "The best time to fish is the first three hours of the morning, when the lake is shrouded in heavy fog." The average depth and bottom structure make the lake ideally suited to trolling. "It's a flat bottomed, relatively shallow lake," said Haley. "Typically, you're trolling over 15 to 30 feet of water, with the muskies suspended at 10 to 12 feet." The lower eight miles of the lake offers the best trolling water, including Leatherwood, Otter, and Turkey Creeks.

Haley suggested trying several lures when trolling. "You never know, from day to day, what they want." Crankbaits like the Swim Whiz, Believer, and Bill Norman have a wide wobble. "The jointed Believer puts out a clicking noise because the wobbling action makes the rear set of treble hooks hit the tail." Lipped crankbaits with tighter action are good too. "It depends on what type of mood the fish are in," said Haley. In clear water, fish black and silver (the shad pattern) or brown with a yellow belly (the sucker pattern). Firetiger and chartreuse are top colors in stained water, Haley said.

In hot weather muskies follow bait fish out from the banks to deeper water as the day progresses. Since the muskie's eyes are on the top of its head, it wants to come up to take a bait, Haley said. "Something that runs under a muskie can spook him." The exception is in the spring. "A muskie will tear up a bait that's churning up the bottom in the shallows, thinking it's a spawning sucker or carp." He said in the summer muskies tend to suspend off three types of cover—false points that come out from rock cliff lines, areas where old roadbeds enter the lake, and deep drop-offs. "A combination of all three is best," said Haley.

Surprisingly, Buckhorn has that kind of variety of cover. There are islands and weed beds, small pockets of standing timber, old roadbeds, rocky points, even huge pockets of floating driftwood near the dam. Drift piles are tough places to fish, but there are muskies suspended under all that debris. In the upper lake there are miles of shallow flats near submerged channels, ideal places to catch big fish when they begin moving up shallow. "Later in the fall, the best fishing is in the afternoons, when carp, suckers, and other forage move up onto shallow flats where the water is being warmed by the sun," said Haley. "You can catch some really big muskies on big jerk baits in one or two feet of water."

Haley fishes bucktails (in-line spinners) fast. "I crank them just under the surface so that the blades put out a big wake." A change in tactics is needed on muskies that follow up a lure repeatedly on a fast retrieve. "Leave the fish alone for ten or fifteen minutes so he can cool down, then go back with a [floating] shallow-running crankbait," said Haley. "Twitch the lure on the surface. Make it pop. He'll come up and eat it."

Crappie The crappie fishery is rated excellent, and the outlook is for excellent numbers and size distribution. Fishing pressure is low. The best time of the year to fish is February to April, during winter drawdown period when crappie are confined to the river channel in the upper end of the lake. At winter pool there is very little water above Leatherwood Creek. With the lake reduced to roughly half it size at seasonal pool, crappie congregate on stumps and other wood structure in water less than 10 feet deep. "There's a noticeable current, and schools of crappie can sometimes be found in the eddies, on the inside turns of the winding river channel," said Dan Wilson, the former eastern district fishery biologist. Some fishermen are afraid to take their boats up the river because they worry about running aground or damaging their outboard motor's propeller, Wilson said. Although crappie may appear vulnerable at low water, Wilson said many anglers overlook the opportunity. Crappie become much harder to find in numbers once the lake reaches season pool. The water usually begins rising in late March or early April.

"The exploitation rate [percent of the lake's fish caught each season] is 23 percent," said Wilson. "That's a lot lower than at most lakes [where it approaches 50 percent]."

The size of the crappie being caught is surprising too. The average harvested fish is a 7- to 11-inch white crappie, but population samples have yielded fish up to 14 inches. Both white and black crappie are present. "The crappie are pretty decent size, the growth rate is average, and there's several year classes in the population," noted Wilson. No minimum size limit is in effect, and the statewide daily creel limit applies—thirty crappie per day.

Wilson said mark and recapture studies, which use tagged fish to help estimate harvest, have shown that the most crappie are taken in April, May, and July, based on tag returns. "Crappie fishing can be good throughout the winter, but it depends on flow and water turbidity [how muddy the water becomes]." The best fishing is when the lake is low and clear.

Largemouth Bass The largemouth bass fishery is rated fair, and the outlook is for low numbers but catch rates similar to Fishtrap Lake and other mountain reservoirs. Most bass are 12 to 16 inches long, and fishing pressure is moderate.

"Density is low due to extreme environmental conditions," said eastern district fishery biologist Steve Reeser. "But there's some quality-size fish in the lake." Murky, high water in the spring and a severe drawdown in the fall have a major effect on spawning success and the survival of young-of-the-year bass. "During the summer when the lake [thermally] stratifies there isn't suitable oxygen below 15 feet," said Reeser.

In the spring, the best bass fishing is from Leatherwood Creek on down the lake to Gay's Creek, generally in the mid to lower section of the lake.

Night fishing is very popular during the summer months, when anglers cast plastic baits and crankbaits to wood cover on flats.

Reeser said bass growth rates have remained stable during the 1990s. Largemouth bass reach 10.7 inches at age two and 14.1 inches at age four. "The largest bass we sampled this spring while electrofishing was a 16-incher," said Reeser. The 15-inch minimum size limit, established on January, 1, 1991, is responsible for increased numbers of 11- to 15-inch fish. Buckhorn Lake has no smallmouth bass and very few spotted bass.

Catfish   The outlook for catfish is good, with stable populations of both channels and flatheads. Flatheads up to 50 pounds have been caught from the lake. During the summer, fish for flatheads at night on channel flats in the upper lake with large creek chub, shiner, or sucker minnows. Channel catfish can be caught in the lower lake off rocky banks by fishing nightcrawlers.

Bluegill   The bluegill fishery is rated fair, and the outlook is for adequate numbers but small size. In Buckhorn Lake it takes a bluegill four years to reach 6 inches in length, so most are only 5 to 6 inches long. Some of the best fishing is around the huge drift piles near the dam. Fish with light tackle and live bait—worms, crickets, wax worms, or meal worms.

Tailwater Fishing Opportunities

The Buckhorn Lake tailwaters supports cool-water fisheries and boasts one of the highest catch rates for muskie of any tailwaters in Kentucky. In summer, the middle fork of the Kentucky River below Buckhorn Dam is a pool and riffle stream. In an August 1993 sampling, biologists shocked up several 35- to 40-inch muskies within five miles below the dam.

Other species are also present. Sauger, spotted bass, and rainbow are taken by anglers. The sauger are descendants from the fish stocked in the Kentucky River during the early 1980s. Walleye have been stocked in the tailwaters periodically since the late 1980s. "These are excess fish from the hatchery," said Reeser. "About 20,000 fry [1 1/2-inchers] are stocked annually." The stocked rainbow trout are also popular with anglers. Last year trout were released monthly, April through November, for a total of 6,100 fish.

There is no boat launching ramp in the tailwaters, so anglers are limited to fishing from the bank, a canoe, or a cartop boat.

Buckhorn Lake Dam.

CARR CREEK LAKE

Bluegill ➤◄ ➤◄	Smallmouth Bass ➤◄ ➤◄
Catfish ➤◄ ➤◄	Spotted Bass ➤◄ ➤◄ ➤◄
Crappie ➤◄ ➤◄	Walleye ➤◄ ➤◄ ➤◄
Largemouth Bass ➤◄ ➤◄ ➤◄	Tailwaters ➤◄ ➤◄ ➤◄

Location   For more than twenty years it was known as Carr Fork Lake, but in January 1997, Congress officially changed the name of the project to Carr Creek Lake. By whatever name, the lake is in Knott County, about 16 miles east of Hazard, on Ky. 15. The dam is 8.8 miles above the mouth of Carr Fork, a tributary to the North Fork of the Kentucky River. The drainage area above the dam is 58 square miles.

Size   The 710-acre lake is 8.2 miles long at elevation 1,027. The scenic mountain lake was completed in December 1975 and has a maximum depth of about 65 feet, with an average depth of about 40 feet. In the summer the lake can become very clear, despite annual fertilization.

The small reservoir has a seasonal drawdown of 10 feet. There are three small dams in headwater tributaries (Defeated Creek, Shingle Creek, and Little Carr Fork Branch) to prevent sediment from being deposited in the lake.

Trophic State Index (TSI)   Carr Creek Lake has a TSI of 53, which ranks it as a eutrophic lake (high fertility).

Lake Manager's Office   U.S. Army Corps of Engineers, Carr Creek Lake, Resource Manager's Office, HCR 32, Box 520, Sassafras, KY 41759, telephone (606) 642-3308.

Managing Fishery Biologist   Kentucky Department of Fish and Wildlife Resources, Eastern Fishery District, Steve Reeser, District Biologist, 2744 Lake Road, Prestonsburg, KY 41653, telephone (606) 886-9575.

Lake Level/Fishing Report Line   The U.S. Army Corps of Engineers lake information line is (606) 642-3307.

Marinas   There is one marina. *Red Fox Marina*, open year-round, is about 4 miles east of Vicco, off Ky. 15. The out-of-state owner's address

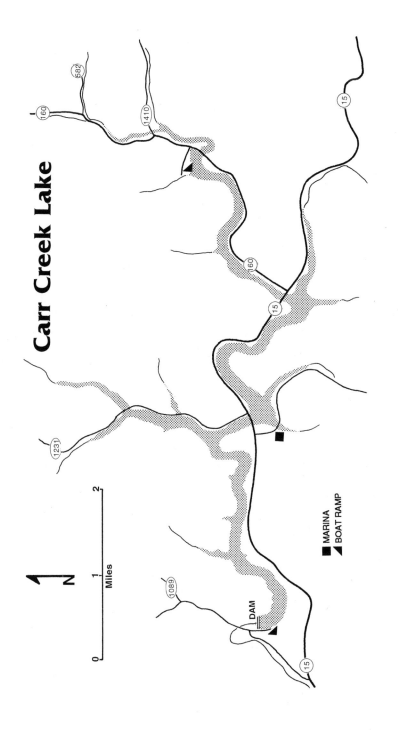

Carr Creek Lake

MARINA
BOAT RAMP

N
Miles
0 1 2

Carr Creek Lake • 75

and local telephone number are Box 263, Hurricane, WV 25526, (606) 642-3239.

Boat Launching Ramps   There are two boat launching ramps on the lake in addition to the ramp at the marina. There is a $2 fee to launch at all boat ramps, $25 for an annual pass, with discounts available to senior citizens. *Dam* boat launching ramp is on the south side of the lake, off Ky. 1089. *Littcarr* boat launching ramp is at the head of the lake, off Ky. 160.

Local Tourism Information   Knott County Tourism Commission, Box 508, Hindman, KY 41822, telephone (606) 785-5881.

Fishing   Carr Creek Lake, a highland reservoir, supports populations of largemouth, smallmouth, and spotted bass, redear sunfish, crappie, bluegill, walleye, and channel catfish. Bullheads and longear sunfish are also present.

Extensive creel survey work on the lake has provided biologists with data necessary for intensive management. Fish attractors (pine trees and stake beds) have been placed in the lake at several locations, some marked by buoys. The lake has three coves that have standing timber, and there are small scattered beds of aquatic vegetation. Both gizzard and thread-fin shad were present at one time, but the threadfin shad have all but disappeared and no supplemental stockings have been made since 1992. Carr Creek Lake has been fertilized since 1981.

Largemouth Bass   The largemouth bass fishery is rated good, and the outlook is for a stable population. Recent improvements in the fishery are due to improved water quality, several strong year classes spawned in the early 1990s, and the change to a 15-inch minimum size limit, said district fishery biologist Steve Reeser.

In the late 1980s, the bass fishery was in poor shape, so a supplemental stocking program was initiated. For five years, until 1997, about 7,500 11- to 13-inch bass were stocked annually to boost the population. The stocked fish were marked by clipping a portion of their fins. "The stocked fish really didn't contribute to the fishery," said Reeser. "Less than 3 percent of the stocked fished survived to spawn." Reeser said the lake's largemouth bass fishery recovered on its own. Fishing pressure continues to be heavy, and has increased steadily since 1992, especially tournament fishing.

Fish for largemouth bass around standing timber, weed beds, rocky banks and cliffs, and the riprap near the dam. Jig and pork rind combinations and plastic worms (black and grape) are popular lures in the summer, when the best fishing is at night. In spring and fall, fish a No. 7 Model A Bomber in the firetiger pattern. There are usually some bass jumps in the fall, but the best fall fishing is during murky water conditions in November, when good fish are caught by casting crayfish-colored crankbaits across rocky points. Schooling bass are caught off submerged humps in the winter by anglers jigging spoons.

Carr Creek Lake produces 5-pounders on a regular basis, but the average largemouth bass being caught is a 12- to 14-inch fish. Creel clerk Ronnie Mosley said numbers of bass over 15 inches declined in 1996. About 60 percent of the black bass in Carr Fork are largemouth.

Walleye   The walleye fishery is rated good, and the outlook is for numerous 15- to 18-inch fish. Walleye continue to improve in size and distribution, and catch rates have climbed in recent years. "This past year [1996] was the best so far," said Mosley. "There's some real good fish in the lake."

Spring and summer are especially good. In the spring, when walleye are shallow, the most productive technique is casting live nightcrawlers to the banks. Some of the best fishing, however, occurs in the summer, when walleye relate to structure—points and drop-offs. "A lot of walleye are being caught at night over lights on jigging spoons and live shad," said Mosley. "And some are being caught by anglers trolling Erie Dearie [weight-forward] spinners baited with nightcrawlers." Mosley said walleye are being caught all over the lake. The section of the lake from the mouth of Irishman Creek embayment to the dam seems to hold the most walleye.

Growth is excellent. Walleye reach 15.5 inches in two years," said Reeser. "Carr Creek Lake now has a faster walleye growth rate than Paintsville Lake." Creel survey data show that the average walleye being caught is a 16- to 20-inch fish, and 10-pounders are caught from the lake frequently in the spring.

During the summer, Carr Creek Lake stratifies thermally at about 17 feet, resulting in the loss of dissolved oxygen in deeper water. "You'll find that the walleye suspend right at that stratification depth," said Mosley.

The first year walleye were stocked was 1984, when 35,000 1.3-inch fish were released. Between 1985 and 1992, about 273,000 walleye fingerlings and 3.5 million fry were stocked. The stocking rate is now about 60,000 fry a year.

Spotted Bass   The spotted bass fishery is rated good, and the outlook is for numerous 8- to 10-inch fish. Growth is good and the fishery is underutilized. According to 1993 creel survey data, fifty-five spotted bass were caught and thirteen were creeled. The average size harvested was 10.5 inches. "I've seen some spotted bass up to 13 inches," said Mosley. Spotted bass, which make up about 30 percent of the black bass population, are caught off rocky points on jigs and live minnows.

Crappie   The crappie fishery is rated fair to good, and the outlook is for a stable population, after a decline in quality in 1996. Fishing pressure is heavy. Reeser said it is hoped that the 9-inch minimum size limit, which became effective in 1994, will halt further declines in quality by limiting harvest.

Fish around deadfalls and fish attractors. Decent numbers of big crappie are still being caught from the lake each spring. Mosley said he sees crappie in the 10- to 13-inch size range, 13- to 14-inch range, and a few truly big fish. "Last spring [in 1996] I checked a fisherman with a 17-inch crappie that weighed about 3 pounds."

Smallmouth Bass   The smallmouth bass fishery is fair, and the outlook is for a stable to improving population. It is a small, self-sustaining population. Smallmouth are native to the Kentucky River drainage. Limited supplemental stockings were made in the past but have been discontinued. "It's a remnant population," said district fishery biologist Steve Reeser. About 10 percent of the black bass in the lake are smallmouth. "We see more smallmouth in the lower half of the lake and the Littcarr [embayment]," Reeser said. "Fish are taken off the riprap on the dam."

According to 1993 creel survey data, 377 smallmouth bass were caught, and 19 were harvested. The average size creeled was a 17.7-incher. A 15-inch minimum size limit on smallmouth and largemouth bass was initiated on January 1, 1991. Smallmouth up to 6 pounds have been taken.

Popular smallmouth lures are brown, green, and motor oil-colored jigs and crayfish-colored crankbaits.

Bluegill   The bluegill fishery is rated fair, and the outlook is for numerous small fish. Most bluegill are about 6 inches long, with a few over 7 inches. They are caught around docks and off rock walls on crickets, wax worms, and meal worms.

Catfish   The catfish fishery is rated fair, and the outlook is for low numbers of 1- to 3-pound channel catfish. The lake also supports yellow bullheads and white catfish (*Ictalurus catus*), an uncommon species associated with pay lakes and commercial fisheries that is native to the Atlantic coastal states. "We're not sure how white catfish got in the lake," said Reeser. "Whether it was an illegal stocking or they were mixed in with the channel catfish that have been stocked in the lake periodically over the years."

The best catfish angling of the year at Carr Creek Lake occurs in May and June, when catfish congregate on riprap banks to spawn. Fish with nightcrawlers or prepared dough baits.

Tailwater Fishing Opportunities

Year-round discharges of cool, oxygenated water makes for good trout fishing in the small tailwater area. Rainbow trout are stocked monthly, April through November, for a total of 12,600 fish a year. There is about a mile of cool-water habitat, with few holdover trout.

"At times some real nice walleye are in the tailwaters," said Mosley. "Increased flow draws them in close to the dam." Reeser said it is likely that the walleye escaped from the lake.

Carr Creek Lake Dam.

CAVE RUN LAKE

Bluegill ◄ ◄ ◄
Catfish ◄ ◄ ◄
Crappie ◄ ◄
Largemouth ◄ ◄
Muskellunge ◄ ◄ ◄ ◄

Smallmouth Bass ◄
Spotted Bass ◄ ◄
White Bass ◄ ◄ ◄
Tailwaters ◄ ◄ ◄ ◄

Location   Cave Run Lake is in Menifee, Morgan, Bath, and Rowan Counties, about 15 miles southwest of Morehead. The major access highways are Interstate 64, U.S. 60, Ky. 801, and Ky. 1274. The project was completed in 1974 at a cost of $83 million. The dam is 173.6 miles upstream of the mouth of the Licking River, which empties into the Ohio River at Covington.

Size   At summer pool (elevation 730), Cave Run Lake is 8,270 acres and 48.1 miles long. The 6-foot winter drawdown to elevation 724 creates a lake with 7,390 surface acres of water. The scenic reservoir is in Daniel Boone National Forest, set against a backdrop of wooded hills. Many of the lakes' embayments are filled with standing timber. There are 166 miles of shoreline at summer pool.

Trophic State Index (TSI)   Cave Run Lake has a TSI of 45, which ranks it as a mesotrophic lake (moderate fertility).

Lake Manager's Office   U.S. Army Corps of Engineers, Cave Run Lake, Resource Manager's Office, 150 Highway Ky. 826, Moorehead, KY 40351, telephone (606) 784-9709.

Managing Fishery Biologist   Kentucky Department of Fish and Wildlife Resources, Northeastern Fishery District, Lewis Kornman, District Biologist, Minor Clark Fish Hatchery, 120 Fish Hatchery Road, Morehead, KY 40351, telephone (606) 784-6872.

Lake Level/Fishing Report Line   The U.S. Army Corps of Engineers lake information line is (606) 783-7001.

Marinas   There are two marinas. *Scott Creek Marina*, open year-round (boat rentals April 1 to November 15 only), is 5 miles south of Farmers, on Ky. 801. The address and telephone number are Box 174, Morehead, KY 40351, (606) 784-9666. *Longbow Marina*, open year-round (boat rent-

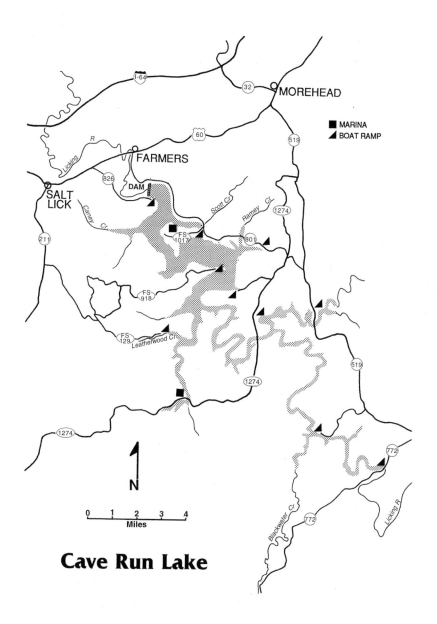

MOREHEAD

■ MARINA
▲ BOAT RAMP

FARMERS

SALT LICK

Cave Run Lake

N

0 1 2 3 4
Miles

als April 1 to November 15 only), is 7 miles east of Frenchburg, on Ky. 1274. The address and telephone number are HCR 71, Box 1220, Frenchburg, KY 40322, (606) 768-2929.

Boat Launching Ramps   There are nine boat launching ramps on the lake in addition to the ramps at the marinas. There is no fee to launch at any of the boat ramps on Cave Run Lake. *Bangor* boat ramp is off Ky. 1274, on the Menifee/Morgan County line. *Blackwater* boat ramp is off Ky. 976, near the mouth of Blackwater Creek. *Claylick* boat ramp is off Ky. 1274, 10 miles up the lake from the dam. *Leatherwood* boat ramp is off Forest Service Road 129, on the west shore of the lake. *Poppin Rock* boat ramp is off Ky. 519, on the North Fork of the Licking River. *Twenty Six* boat ramp is off Ky. 772, at the extreme upper end of the lake on the Licking River. *Twin Knobs* boat ramp is off Ky. 801, about six miles southeast of the dam. *Warix Run* boat ramp is off Ky. 801, about 12 miles southeast of the dam. *Zilpo* boat ramp is off Forest Service Road 918, on the west shore of the lake.

Local Tourism Information   Morehead Tourist Commission, 150 East First Street, Morehead, KY 40351, telephone (606) 784-6221 or toll free (800) 654-1944.

Fishing   Even before the Licking River was impounded, local anglers were harvesting muskies with regularity from Kentucky's fifth largest river, which drains an area of 3,670 square miles to the east of Kentucky's Bluegrass Region. Given the muskie-producing ability of the river system, it is not surprising that a reservoir created from these waters would become Kentucky's top fishing hole for "Old Briartooth," yielding 50-inch fish on occasion. Formation of the lake, and the opening of the Minor E. Clark Hatchery, set the stage for the emergence of a high-quality muskie fishery, now recognized as one of the region's best, with catch rates surpassing some of the best muskie waters in the Great Lakes states.

It is not a typical mountain lake, as fertility levels increase in the upper reaches of the reservoir and decrease near the dam. The lake can be very clear in the summer but is prone to muddy up after heavy rains above the lake.

The lake's other sport fish species include largemouth bass, smallmouth bass, spotted bass, white bass, crappie, bluegill, and catfish. A 4-acre cove rotenone study in 1995 in the lower lake yielded a total standing crop of 150 pounds of fish per acre, 52 pounds of which were gizzard shad.

Muskellunge   The muskie fishery is rated good to excellent, and the outlook is for many 30- to 45-inch fish. The population is maintained by annual stockings and a very small amount of natural reproduction.

Generally, anglers fish the upper lake and tributary flats in the spring, troll the main lake and mouths of major tributaries in the summer, and cast timbered coves in the fall. The best time to fish on Cave Run Lake, especially during the fall, is a drizzly, overcast day, what anglers refer to as "muskie weather."

The fishing year begins in late February or early March, depending on the severity of the winter. In the spring, fish shallow coves because muskies tend to relate more to bottom contour than structure in cold water. The Warix Run embayment is a good example of an area muskies prefer in the spring where there are shallow flats but immediate access to deep water. There is no visible structure. What you have there are two ditches that hold fish. Old roadbeds and channel breaks in just a few feet of water are capable of holding muskies in the spring, too. A muskie can be right up next to the bank in water that you would think is way too shallow.

Muskies seem to prefer smaller lures early in the year. A steady retrieve is always best, even in cool water. Beginning muskie fishermen make the mistake of retrieving their lures too slowly, or worse yet, stopping the retrieve if a muskie is seen following the bait. If anything, speed up the retrieve or rip the lure through the water with a sweep of the rod if a fish follows your lure to the boat. Sometimes that will trigger a strike. That is why a figure eight of the lure at the boat often evokes a response. The muskie thinks the lure (forage fish) is trying to escape.

The upper lake is best in the spring because water temperatures are higher. There can be as much as 10 degrees difference between water temperatures in the North Fork of the Licking River and the main lake. Fish the northeast-facing coves and banks because the prevailing southwest winds blow in surface layers of warmer water. Beaver Creek is a good place to fish in late April and early May because a lot of active fish seem to move out onto points and into the standing timber on the edge of flats.

In summer, troll the old river channel, especially around Zilpo Flats and timbered channels in Beaver Creek and other major embayments. Fish deep-diving crankbaits such as the Bomber, Hellbender, and Swim Whizz.

Don't overlook weed beds year-round. David "Crash" Mullins of

Olive Hill, who guides exclusively for muskies about 150 days a year, fishes weed beds a lot, especially in the fall before the drawdown. One of the best weed beds on the lake is in Scott Creek, up past the moored sailboats. The weed bed is barely visible below the surface and is sandwiched between the creek channel and shoreline flooded timber.

The best fishing in the fall usually begins in September, when the shad move to the backs of bays as the water begins to cool down. Mullins believes the prime fall fishing occurs when water temperatures are above 53 degrees. "Below 50 degrees, things start slowing down. You have to fish deeper and slower." Muskies eventually move out from the coves to deeper water, beginning in November. "You get more bites earlier [in the fall], but the bigger fish come in late October and November."

Mullins fishes bucktails a lot in the fall. In October 1995 he caught a 47-incher on a black bucktail with chartreuse blades. "Colored blades have become something of a trend in recent years," said Mullins, who prefers to fish the Grim Reaper model 650 bucktail, a 6-inch in-line spinnerbait which has double Colorado blades. "Any fluorescent colors are okay. I also like red and orange."

In the fall Mullins also fishes balsa wood twitch baits. "You want a lure with a wide wobble. I like to twitch it on the surface, then bring it in with a steady retrieve." Color preferences for twitch baits are red, chartreuse, or black back, with silver sides. "Firetiger is also a good choice."

Most strikes happen in the first or last 5 feet of the retrieve, Mullins said. "You wouldn't believe how many hits I get at the boat. I always figure eight my lure at the boat." He personally caught over forty muskies in 1995.

"I think we're getting better quality fish in Cave Run Lake since the department began stocking the 13- to 15-inch fish [instead of smaller fingerlings]," said Mullins. "A muskie can reach 35 inches in just three years. No other place I know of is producing fish that good in such a short time."

Largemouth Bass   The largemouth bass fishery is rated fair to good, and the outlook is for numerous fish under 13 inches and increased numbers of fish over 16 inches. The slot limit, now in its second year, is fine tuning Cave Run Lake's largemouth bass fishery. During the past decade, bass numbers have increased due to the 15-inch minimum size limit. "When the size limit was changed from 12 to 15 inches in 1985 we had about 1.2 pounds of bass per acre of water. By 1993 it had grown to 14 pounds per acre," said Kentucky's bass biologist Gerry Buynak, quoting numbers from a size limit evaluation. But he also noticed some declines in growth rates, decreased survival for smaller bass, and a decline in the condition of bass in the fall. There were no big increases in the number of keepers, bass over 15 inches, or the number of keepers creeled. "The bulk of the bass were just under the size limit," said Buynak.

This stockpiling is the reason the Kentucky Fish and Wildlife Commission voted to change to a slot limit, which became effective March 1, 1996. Under the slot limit, largemouth bass that measure 13 to 16 inches cannot be kept. "It's a temporary change, maybe for two years, to try to offset some of those negative factors," said Buynak. "Then we'll go back to a 15-inch minimum size limit."

Ted Crowell, assistant director of fisheries, believes the slot limit will work at Cave Run Lake because the average fisherman has no problem with keeping fish to eat. Creeling fish has always been a part of the department's bass management philosophy, Crowell said. Is the return to a 12-inch minimum size limit a viable management option? No way, Crowell said. That would nullify a decade of progress made at the lake.

Different lures are appropriate during different seasons. Spinnerbaits are a top lure in the spring, when bass are in the shallow, wooded coves. Flippin' jigs are also productive around shoreline deadfalls. During the summer, when the lake tends to get very clear, most bass fishing is done at night. Texas-rigged plastic worms and deep-diving crankbaits are favorite lures. In the fall, topwater lures like the Pop-R and crankbaits like the Shad Rap and Bomber Long A are fished in scattered jumps and across main lake points as the water begins to cool down. Bass hotspots on the lake include the south bank of Caney Creek, where shallow, timbered flats are adjacent to the creek channel; the mouth of Warix Run, where submerged roadbeds converge; and the beach off Zilpo Recreation Area, where roadbeds and rock piles often hold big fish early in the year.

White Bass The white bass fishery is rated good, and the outlook is for a good population, with many fish in the 12- to 15-inch range and some fish up to 17 inches. The best fishing continues to be during midlake jumps in June, July, and late September.

Slowly and quietly over the past five years a white bass fishery has developed in Cave Run Lake. Until recently, few anglers knew the fishery existed, said district fishery biologist Lew Kornman. The white bass fishery may have started from a few holdover fish in the Licking River, since white bass, striped bass hybrids, and striped bass have never been stocked in Cave Run Lake by the Kentucky Department of Fish and Wildlife Resources. Or it may be that white bass were illegally stocked. No one knows for certain. "For years it was rare to see a white bass," said Kornman. Most of the white bass being caught are running 12 to 15 inches long. "It's as good a quality as I've seen."

White bass attract attention during the summer and early fall when they start jumping in the lower lake, chasing schools of small shad. "We first noticed white bass jumps in the Zilpo Flats areas," said Kornman. "We've also heard of jumps at the mouth of Caney Creek and near the marina in Scott Creek." Trolling small spinners, streamer flies or curlytail grubs on an 18-inch leader behind a deep-running crankbait is the ticket to catching white bass during the summer months.

Kornman made several suggestions for finding hungry bass. When the lake is high, white bass can be caught from the bank in Scott Creek at the Ky. 801 bridge. "There's a channel, and fish sometimes move through this area when there's current." During periods of high discharge, Kornman said, white bass are caught in the Cave Run tailwaters, although there's no noticeable spring run below the dam. Kornman also suggested anglers try the area between Claylick and Warix Run. "There's an old roadbed near the channel." He has also observed big white bass up to 18 inches long in the Licking River arm of the upper lake in the fall.

Bluegill   Often overlooked by anglers, the bluegill fishery is rated good, and the outlook is for numerous 6- to 7-inch fish.

Catfish   The outlook for catfish is good numbers of 1- to 3-pound channel catfish and some large flatheads. The fishery is rated good. Catfish are overlooked by anglers at Cave Run Lake.

Smallmouth Bass   The smallmouth bass fishery is rated fair to poor, and the outlook is for low numbers of fish under 13 inches and even fewer fish over 16 inches.

Smallmouth populations are concentrated in the lower end of lake, where banks are littered with chunk rock. "The farther up the lake you go, the fewer smallmouth you'll find," said Lew Kornman, the northeastern district fishery biologist. "The greatest number of smallmouth are on the rocky cliffs along Ky. 801, from the dam to Scott Creek." Kornman said he has sampled smallmouth from the riprap on the face of the dam and the deep, rocky banks near Twin Knobs.

"We also see smallmouth on some banks from Warix Run to the Claylick boat ramp, and we've even taken a few up the lake at the confluence of Beaver Creek and the Licking River. . . . You've got to know where to fish," said Kornman. "You can't catch smallmouth just anywhere [on this lake]."

Creel survey data from 1994 show that the average smallmouth bass harvested was 16.8 inches long, and that smallmouth bass represented 17.7 percent of all black bass harvested. Catches of smallmouth bass up to 6 pounds (about 21 inches long) have been reported. "Smallmouth catches are incidental," said Kornman. "There's not much fishing pressure."

Native to the Licking River, smallmouth bass occur less frequently in the upper reaches of the drainage where Cave Run Lake was impounded, so the lake received supplemental stockings. "The main years fish were stocked was 1987 through 1989," said Kornman. Age and growth data show that it takes seven years for a smallmouth to reach 17.2 inches in Cave Run Lake. That means fish stocked in the late 1980s are now reaching trophy size. There is a slot limit on smallmouth bass. All smallmouth (and largemouth) bass between 13 and 16 inches must be released. Smallmouth bass numbers are not expected to increase in the long run.

Spotted Bass　The spotted bass fishery is rated fair, and the outlook is for increasing numbers of 8- to 10-inch fish. In 1984 Cave Run Lake became the first reservoir in Kentucky to remove the size limit on spotted bass. Four years later, on January 1, 1988, the regulation was broadened to include all Kentucky lakes and streams. "To my knowledge we're the first state to enact such a regulation on a statewide basis," said Pete Pfeiffer, director of fisheries.

Removing the minimum size limit on spotted bass has been well received all over the state, not just at Cave Run Lake. "Its acceptance by the angling public has been the greatest," said Crowell. "Increased pressure on spotted bass has reduced competition between all the bass species and has helped to buffer the effects of more restrictive size limits [on largemouth and smallmouth bass]."

The best fishing is in the lower two-thirds of the lake. Fish small jigs, live minnows, and deep-diving crankbaits off the rock bluffs along Ky. 801.

Crappie　The crappie fishery is rated fair, and the outlook is for good fishing in the upper lake for 8- to 10-inch fish. Crappie populations in Cave Run Lake are very cyclic. "At certain times crappie fishing can be good, relatively speaking, but there's not good fishing every year," said Lew Kornman. "It seems like every third year it's a bust." Fishing pressure is heavy seasonally.

According to creel survey data, crappie anglers made 5,680 trips in 1994, or 23 percent of all fishing trips on Cave Run Lake. "Crappie is the third most sought-after species behind muskie and largemouth bass." Kornman estimated that white crappie make up about 90 percent of the population, and black crappie the remaining 10 percent.

Crappie in Cave Run Lake have a fairly slow growth rate. "Late in their fourth year they become harvestable size [about 9 to 10 inches]." In 1994, 81,013 crappie were caught. Of those caught, 38,889 were harvested. The average white crappie kept by anglers was a 10-incher. The average black crappie kept was an 11.5-incher. Kornman said the size of white crappie being harvested has shown steady improvement in the last decade: 7.2 inches in 1986; 9.2 inches in 1989; and 9.6 in 1993.

Live minnows and chartreuse 1/16-ounce tube jigs and Roadrunner jigs are top producing lures. In the spring, crappie typically locate in 5 to 20 feet of water on stumps, brush, and deadfalls in coves and on channel banks near deep water. Some of the top areas of the lake for crappie fishing include Beaver Creek; Licking River, upstream to the Ky. 1274 bridge; and the old roadbeds between Claylick and Warix Run boat launching ramps. "There's lots of standing timber in the lake, but a lot of the trees don't have limbs," said Kornman. "Brushy, leafy, new-fallen trees make much better crappie cover." Kornman also suggested fishing around road culverts and fish attractors, which are marked by buoys.

Tailwater Fishing Opportunities

The Cave Run Lake tailwaters supports high-quality fisheries. "There's a real diversity of fish, and quite a few species of mussels [which indicate high water quality]," said Kornman. "It's a unique river." It seems that when the discharge rate is high, the fish move up into the tailwaters, Kornman said. "Then they drop back downstream into deeper pools when the discharge rate subsides." There is a boat launching ramp in the tailwaters.

The number one fish in the tailwaters is the muskie. "In the 33 miles below the dam there's about 400 acres of muskie-pool habitat," Kornman said. "The best water is in the upper 20 miles." For years, adult muskie have been electrofished from the tailwaters by biologists and taken to the nearby Minor Clark Hatchery, where they are stripped of their eggs and milt. Then the fish are taken back to the tailwaters. Likewise, large broodfish taken from other streams have been released

Fishing guide James Baker shows a 13-inch crappie caught from Cave Run Lake.

in the tailwaters, Kornman said. The eggs from the river fish are of better quality.

Other species also can be found. There are some smallmouth in the Licking River, but most are farther downstream. Sauger, crappie, and white bass are taken from the tailwaters in the spring. Seventy-five hundred rainbow trout are stocked in the tailwaters each year between October and the following June.

Cave Run Lake Dam.

DALE HOLLOW LAKE

Bluegill ⚬⚬⚬	Smallmouth Bass ⚬⚬⚬⚬
Crappie ⚬⚬	Spotted Bass ⚬⚬⚬⚬
Largemouth Bass ⚬⚬⚬	Trout ⚬⚬⚬
Muskellunge ⚬⚬	Walleye ⚬⚬⚬⚬
Redear Sunfish ⚬⚬⚬⚬	Tailwaters ⚬⚬⚬

Location Dale Hollow Lake is Kentucky's oldest major reservoir. Construction began in 1942 but was halted until the end of World War II. One of the first impoundments built by the U.S. Army Corps of Engineers under the Flood Control Act of 1938, the cost of the project was $52.3 million. About 130 miles south of Lexington, the lake straddles the Kentucky-Tennessee border. The waters lap Kentucky's Cumberland and Clinton Counties and four counties in Tennessee—Clay, Overton, Pickett and Fentress. Take Ky. 61 from Burkesville, or Ky. 553 or Ky. 738 from Albany, for access to the Kentucky potion of the lake. Sulphur Creek, Illwill Creek, Fanny's Creek, and Wolf River are the major Kentucky embayments of the lake. Most of the 61-mile-long lake is in Tennessee.

Size Impounded from the Obey River, Dale Hollow Lake is 27,700 acres at summer pool (elevation 651). The winter drawdown reduces the lake to 21,880 acres at elevation 631. At summer pool, about 4,819 surface acres (17.4 percent) of Dale Hollow Lake is in Kentucky—2,049 acres in Cumberland County and 2,770 acres in Clinton County. The lake is 160 feet deep just above the dam.

Trophic State Index (TSI) Dale Hollow Lake has a TSI of 33, which ranks it as an oligotrophic lake (low fertility).

Lake Manager's Office U.S. Army Corps of Engineers, Dale Hollow Lake, Resource Manager's Office, 5050 Dam Road, Celina, TN 38551, telephone (615) 243-3136.

Managing Fishery Biologist Kentucky Department of Fish and Wildlife Resources, Southeastern Fishery District, Doug Stephens, District Biologist, 2073 N. Highway 25 West, Williamsburg, KY 40769, telephone (606) 549-1332. Tennessee Wildlife Resources Agency, Anders

Dale Hollow Lake

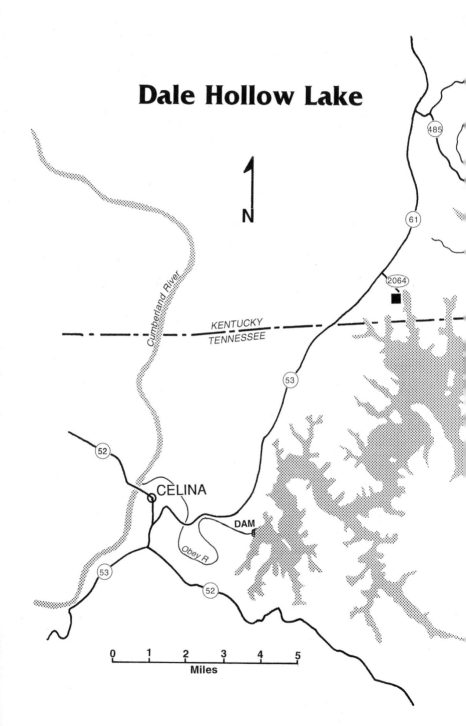

485

61

2064

N

Cumberland River

KENTUCKY
TENNESSEE

53

52

CELINA

DAM

Obey R

53

52

| 0 | 1 | 2 | 3 | 4 | 5 |
Miles

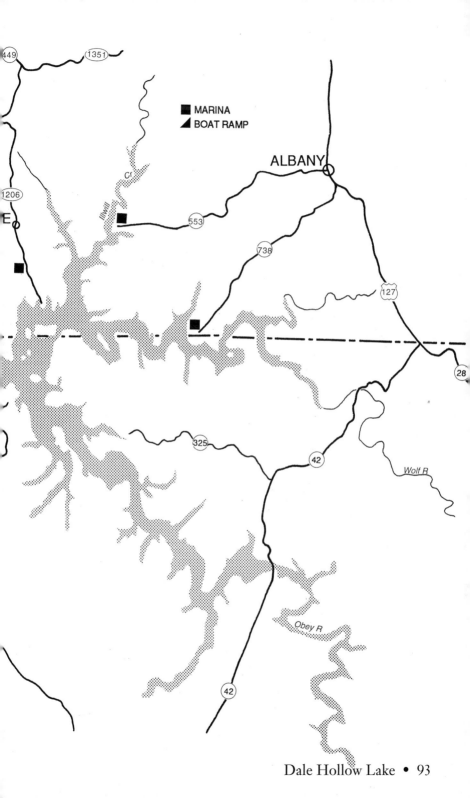

MARINA
BOAT RAMP

ALBANY

Dale Hollow Lake • 93

Myhr, Regional Reservoir Biologist, 216 E. Penfield Street, Crossville, TN 38555, telephone (615) 484-9571.

Lake Level/Fishing Report Line   The U.S. Army Corps of Engineers lake information line is (800) 938-4665. Another option is (800) 261-LAKE. Follow the recorded instructions to receive reports on the automated information line.

Marinas   There are five marinas on the Kentucky portion of the lake. *Hendrick's Creek Resort*, open seasonally (March 1 through November 30), is 15 miles south of Burkesville, off Ky. 61. The address and telephone number are 945 Hendrick's Creek Road, Burkesville, KY 42717, (502) 433-7172. *Sulphur Creek Marina*, open seasonally (April 1 through October 31), is 5 miles south of Kettle, off Ky. 485. The address and telephone number are 3498 Sulphur Creek Road, Burkesville, KY 42717, (502) 433-7272. *Wisdom Fishing Camp*, open seasonally (March 1 through November 30), is 8 miles southeast of Albany, off Ky. 553. The address and telephone number are Route 2, Box 220, Albany, KY 42602, (606) 387-5821. *Wolf River Resort*, open seasonally (April 1 through October 31), is 12 miles southeast of Albany, off Ky. 738. The address and telephone number are Route 2, Box 751, Albany, KY 42602, (606) 387-5841. *Dale Hollow Lake State Resort Park Marina*, open year-round, is 12 miles south of Burkesville, off Ky. 1206. The address and telephone number are 6371 State Park Road, Bow, KY 42717, (502) 433-7490.

Boat Launching Ramps   The only boat launching ramps on the Kentucky portion of the lake are the ramps at the marinas. There is no fee to launch a boat at any of these five ramps as of the spring of 1997, but user fees are being considered for the future.

Local Tourism Information   Albany/Clinton County Chamber of Commerce, Albany, KY 42602, telephone (606) 387-8724.

Fishing   A reservoir of outstanding beauty, Dale Hollow Lake has everything an angler could wish for—high-quality fish populations, cool, clear, highly oxygenated waters, and impressive scenery. The rolling hills that surround the lake are rich in timber resources. Beech, oak, maple, and evergreen trees grow right to the water's edge in secluded coves. Rugged cliffs tower over windswept points. When you fish at Dale Hollow Lake during the winter months you share the water with migrating bald eagles.

The lake is famous for its remarkable smallmouth bass fishery, which has yielded three IGFA all-tackle world records. For more than forty years the top fish was Kentucky's state record—an 11-pound, 15-ouncer caught by David L. Hayes on July 9, 1955. But in September 1996 the IGFA, who took over record-keeping responsibilities for freshwater fish from *Field and Stream* magazine in 1978, disqualified Hayes's catch. According to an affidavit filed by fishing guide John Barlow more than forty years ago and only recently discovered by freelance outdoor writer Eldon Davis, Hayes's smallmouth bass had been stuffed with lead weights and outboard motor parts. As soon as Hayes' record was disqualified, the all-tackle world record was awarded to Paul Beal of Noblesville, Indiana., who caught a 10-pound, 8-ouncer from Hendricks Creek in 1986. "That was the heaviest smallmouth we had on record," said Stephany Wilken, world record secretary for the IGFA. On November 15, 1996, however, Beal's record was surpassed when the IGFA received documentation on a 10-pound, 14-ounce smallmouth caught in the lake on April 24, 1969, by John T. Gorman. "The Freshwater Fishing Hall of Fame approached us," said Wilken. "They provided us with substantial information about the fish." The bass was 26 1/4 inches long and had a 21 1/2-inch girth. Dale Hollow Lake also produced Kentucky's state record muskie, a 43-pounder caught March 13, 1978, by Porter Hash.

Other game fish species include walleye, spotted bass, largemouth bass, trout (rainbow and lake), bluegill, redears, and crappie. Forage includes alewives, threadfin, and gizzard shad. Fishery biologists from both Kentucky and Tennessee state agencies jointly manage the fisheries. A reciprocal license agreement exists between the two states, which means either state's fishing license will be honored in both Kentucky waters and Tennessee waters.

Smallmouth Bass   The smallmouth bass fishery is rated excellent, and the outlook is for numerous fish over 3 pounds. The status of the fishery today is much improved from the late 1980s, when catch rates and the size of the fish being harvested were in decline. To remedy the situation, Tennessee adopted very restrictive regulations in 1992, raising the minimum size limit on smallmouth bass at the lake to 18 inches and lowering the daily creel limit to two fish.

Wayne Pollock, who was chief of fisheries for the Tennessee Wildlife Resources Agency at the time, said the regulation change was necessary to revitalize the fishery. He said the change was widely supported by fishermen despite its severe restrictions on harvest. After closely monitoring the effect of the regulation change for the past four years, biologists began to see much improved numbers of big fish. Prior to 1992 there was no minimum size limit and a ten-fish daily creel in the Tennessee waters of the lake.

Kentucky adopted the restrictive smallmouth limits on March 1, 1994. Previously, there had been a 12-inch minimum size limit and a six-fish daily creel in the Kentucky portion of the lake. "We basically adopted Tennessee's regulation for smallmouth," said Ted Crowell, assistant director of fisheries for the Kentucky Department of Fish and Wildlife Resources. "But not their limits on other black bass species."

The two states have philosophical differences of opinion about largemouth bass regulations but are working together to adopt consistent regulations. "This was a case where we could get ahead of the game. There were signs our smallmouth fishery could go bad," said Pollock. "It's difficult to maintain a trophy fishery. [Fishing pressure] was having an impact."

The cold weather months are the best time to fish for smallmouth bass at Dale Hollow Lake. "It can get good if water conditions are stable and they aren't pulling [dropping the level of the lake]," said Billy Westmorland, a fishing book author and host of a popular syndicated TV fishing show, who frequently conducts seminars at sport shows on smallmouth bass fishing.

The action starts to really heat up in early spring. "Most of the bigger fish are in 20 to 25 feet of water. Fish the channels, banks, and points, and up the bigger creeks."

Numerous baits can lure a smallmouth. The Silver Buddy crankbait, grubs, and tube jigs are all good late winter and early spring lures. The Silver Buddy, a vibrating, blade-type bait that imitates the action of a shad, is one of Westmorland's favorites. "It's the easiest lure to use because you fish it on the bottom. Just cast it out and keep the line tight as it sinks." The technique is to jerk the bait off the bottom, then watch the line as the lure flutters back down. "The strike always comes when the lure is falling," Westmorland said. "When you're fishing a 1/2-ounce or 3/4-ounce lure you can get in some deep water in a hurry. That's the way it was designed to be fished."

Westmorland, who always uses spinning gear when fishing for smallmouth bass, catches a lot of fish on 4-inch tube jigs and 3- and 4-inch straight tail plastic grubs. One of his favorites is the Berkley Power Grub. "If you stay with a 4-inch grub you'll catch fewer fish, but you'll catch bigger ones." As for color, something dark is always good, Westmorland explained. "Black, smoke, and pumpkin and pepper are good choices."

Billy Westmorland, author of *Them Ol' Brown Fish*, pioneered smallmouth bass fishing on Dale Hollow Lake. Photograph courtesy of Billy Westmorland.

During the winter fewer smallmouth bass are in the backs of the coves. "It's too early for that," Westmorland said, "but it could happen as early as February if we get a lot of rain and the lake jumps up." Smallmouth come up shallow when the lake begins to fill up with warmer water. Bass are drawn to the murky shallows, where creeks empty into the lake, to feed on crayfish emerging from the mud. March is always a good time to catch a big smallmouth, Westmorland said. "You can reach them with deep-diving crankbaits that time of year."

The smallmouth bass is the most abundant species of black bass in Dale Hollow Lake as reflected by harvest. According to creel data collected in 1993, there were twice as many smallmouth taken by anglers than largemouth bass. "The 70,000 smallmouth caught had an average weight of 3.2 pounds. The 36,000 largemouth averaged 2.5 pounds, and the 14,000 spotted bass had an average weight of 1.6 pounds," said Pollock. In Dale Hollow Lake it takes a smallmouth bass about five years to reach 18 inches and a weight of about 3 pounds.

"We have a good database for trend analysis," said Pollock. "We've had a creel survey at the lake for the last fourteen years." Pollock said the outlook for smallmouth bass looks good in the future. "There was a good smallmouth spawn in 1993. There's plenty of smaller fish coming on."

Largemouth Bass The largemouth bass fishery is rated good, and the outlook is for numerous 12- to 16-inch fish. Largemouth bass quality and quantity are holding steady despite rising fishing pressure.

Largemouth bass creel and size limits are different on the Kentucky and Tennessee portions of Dale Hollow Lake. Tennessee has a ten-fish daily creel with no minimum size limit, and Kentucky has a six-fish daily creel with a 12-inch minimum size limit.

The largemouth bass is found throughout Dale Hollow Lake, but population densities are dependent on habitat. "Dale Hollow is a deep and rocky, clear lake," said Doug Stephens, a Kentucky district fishery biologist. "It's more suited to smallmouth bass." But, Stephens said, high populations of largemouth bass are in some embayments. The weed beds scattered around the lake are especially attractive to largemouth bass. "We were surprised by the numbers [sampled] in the shallow headwaters of Wolf River," he said. "We saw some decent fish."

Danny Scott, assistant chief of the fisheries division for the Tennessee Wildlife Resources Agency, said the average largemouth bass being creeled in the Tennessee portion of the lake is a 2.4-pounder. "According to the most recent creel data [1993], anglers harvested 13,868 largemouth and caught and released another 31,000." About 57 percent of the fishermen on Dale Hollow Lake are bass anglers, Scott said. "Fishing pressure is continuing to escalate. We're considering more restrictive limits."

Muskellunge The muskie fishery is rated fair to good, and the outlook is for a small number of high-quality 30- to 45-inch fish. Muskies are overlooked by many anglers who fish Dale Hollow Lake. Reed Tatum, a fishery biologist with the Tennessee Wildlife Resources Agency, said muskie were native to the Obey River but disappeared after the turn of the century because of water quality degradation and habitat destruction associated with coal mining and timber harvesting. "The muskie in the lake now are descendants of fish from Chautauqua Lake [in western New York]." Stockings were made in the late 1950s, but no muskies have been placed in Dale Hollow Lake since then. The population is sustained by natural reproduction, Tatum said.

Over the years, muskie numbers have fluctuated. "There was lots of fishing pressure on muskies in the early 1980s, and a lot of fish were caught and removed from the lake," said Willard Parnell of Edmonton, Kentucky, who has fished the lake since it opened. "In the last few years muskies have made a pretty decent comeback."

Parnell said he has taken some memorable muskies from the lake in the past, including a 49 1/2-inch 30-pounder. "I've had the most success in the afternoons." He's caught muskie from a variety of cover in the lake—deep, smooth-bottomed coves, shoreline deadfalls, and beds of rooted aquatic vegetation in the shallows. He said 15 to 20 feet is a good depth to troll, since sometimes muskies suspend out in open water at staggered depths. "Mainly I'm trolling, but I've caught a few fish casting." Most of the muskie he catches are released. "[In this population] if you keep what you catch it cuts down fast on the number of fish out there."

Some of the crankbaits Parnell has used with success in Dale Hollow Lake include Bomber, Hellbender, Bill Norman, and Swim Whiz. "Recently, I've been fishing smaller lines and lures."

Parnell does not believe muskies are spread out all over Dale Hollow Lake. "Like a lot of lakes up north, there's isn't any fish in about 80 percent of the water." He said Irons Creek, Sulphur Creek, and Hendrick's Creek hold muskies. In the spring he fishes weed beds in 8 to 12 feet of water.

Dale Hollow Lake continues to show potential for yielding big fish because of its size and the relatively low fishing pressure. Anglers should note that the daily creel limit is one muskie, with a 30-inch minimum size limit.

Walleye   The walleye fishery is rated good to excellent, and the outlook is for numerous 14- to 18-inch fish. Walleye are probably the most popular with anglers at Dale Hollow Lake, behind the three black bass species—largemouth, smallmouth and spotted bass. "According to creel survey data from 1993, 17,400 walleye were caught and harvested," said Danny Scott, assistant chief of fisheries division for the Tennessee Wildlife Resource Agency. "The average walleye weighs 2.73 pounds." Each year walleye up to 10 pounds are taken from the lake. Scott said about 23 percent of the anglers on the lake are fishing for walleye, including many nonresidents from the Great Lakes states. "At certain times of the year there's more out-of-state anglers on the water than residents." In both the Kentucky and Tennessee portions of the reservoir there is a ten-fish daily creel on walleye, with a 16-inch minimum size limit.

Scott characterizes the lake's walleye as a seasonal fishery, with the peak of fishing pressure during the early spring. "The main walleye spawning run is on the West Fork of the Obey River," Scott said. "Walleye are spawning in the lake, too." They are native to the Cumberland River and its tributaries, which include the Obey River.

Predation on walleye eggs and fry by alewives, a nonnative forage fish, limits natural reproduction. "We stock the lake every other year," Scott said. "The stocking rate is 10 [2- to 3-inch fingerlings] for every acre of water." The walleye come from Tennessee's Eagle Bend Hatchery, in Clinton.

Billy Westmorland, who spent a great deal of time fishing for walleye during the summer and fall of 1996, said he found the most fish on drop-offs and points. "Pretty much the same kind of places you'll find bass, where a fish can swim for five seconds and be in deep water." Westmorland found that the walleye got deeper as the fall progressed, and he caught fish as deep as 40 feet in November. "They move out as the lake level drops." During the fall, Westmorland believes, walleye are more structure orientated. "I think the contour of the bottom and the closeness of the break is more important than the substrate of the bottom," said Westmorland. "Walleye will hang on stumps, but an area doesn't have to have stumps to hold walleye."

He fishes points and flats around islands and sweeping turns of the old river channel. "If you go over a wad of walleye on a point and mark them on the graph, they move, but if you mark individual fish over a flat it doesn't seem to affect them as much."

Billy Westmorland displays a walleye caught on a spinner rig baited with a live nightcrawler.

During the summer, water temperature is more important. "[In summer] walleye follow the thermocline," Westmorland said. "The thermocline [bands of thermally stratified water] drops through the summer, and the walleye follow it down because they prefer cooler water. . . . Usually walleye are right on top of the thermocline. They're easy to catch there." When the lake water "turns over" in the fall, the thermocline disappears as temperatures become consistent throughout the water column. During the fall and winter months, the best walleye fishing on Dale Hollow Lake is in the midsection of the reservoir, just across the state line in Tennessee. "Walleye are scattered all over the lake in the spring, but this time of year, the Kentucky portion of the lake is too shallow, due to the drawdown," said Westmorland.

Westmorland fishes spinner rigs all summer and fall on Dale Hollow Lake and offered the following recommendations: If windy, fish 2 1/2- to 3-ounce bottom bouncers. "If it's calm, a 2-ounce bottom bouncer is ideal." Colors and blade sizes vary at the whim of the walleye. "One day they hit one color better than others." Bead and blade colors that seem to work best are red, green and yellow, red and yellow, yellow, and chartreuse. Number 3 blades seem to catch more fish than any other size, but larger blades (No. 4 or No. 5) work better on days when walleye are more aggressive. Trolling speed is critical. "Sometimes they want the end of the weight dragging the bottom, or just thumping it every now and then."

Spotted Bass   The spotted bass fishery is rated excellent, and the outlook is for numerous 12- to 14-inch fish. "The average spotted bass harvested is about a 14-incher," said Anders Myhr, regional reservoir biologist for the Tennessee Wildlife Resources Agency. "But the lake produces lots of 2- to 3-pounders."

"It's a reservoir-wide fishery," said Myhr. "Spotted bass are actively fished for in the spring into June." Early in the year, fish the backs of embayments, where the water warms up faster. "Later [in the spring] a popular tactic is to float a worm along the main lake channel bluffs."

In a recent creel survey, 4,100 spotted bass were harvested, with an average weight of 1.58 pounds. "That's a 13- to 14-inch spotted bass," Scott said. "That's a good fish. We would like to see more spotted bass creeled."

Crappie   The crappie fishery is rated fair, and the outlook is for 7- to 8-inch black crappie and 8- to 9-inch white crappie. Water conditions are much more conducive to black crappie, whose preferred habitat is rooted aquatic vegetation. "Creel surveys tell us the black crappie harvest fluctuates from about 2,000 to 10,000 fish a year," said Myhr. "[By comparison] it's a small fishery, but the black crappie being caught are some good ones, pound plus fish [10- to 12-inchers]."

Myhr said the difficulty in maintaining good year classes of crappie has led to supplemental stockings. "In the fall of 1995 we put 295,000 4-inch black [nose] crappie in Dale Hollow Lake," said Myhr. "They are genetically marked fish that have a black stripe down their face [nose] to their chin." The distinct markings make the fish easily identifiable from native fish and help biologists assess natural reproduction and determine crappie catch rates.

The white crappie population is smaller and confined mainly to the Wolf River embayment, Myhr said. "The average white crappie harvested is a 8- to 9-incher."

There is no minimum size limit on crappie, but Myhr said he hopes to establish a 10-inch limit in the future.

Bluegill The bluegill fishery is rated good, and the outlook is for a stable population. Some of the best fishing is in the summer, when bluegill are caught by drift fishing live bait, crickets, or bits of nightcrawler along main lake channel bluffs and points. The average bluegill being harvested is a 6- to 8-incher, but bluegill up to 10 inches are taken.

Redear Sunfish (Shellcrackers) The redear sunfish fishery is rated excellent, and the outlook is for numerous 8- to 10-inch fish. It is believed that shellcrackers were illegally or accidentally introduced into Dale Hollow Lake, but the population is flourishing. Catches of fish up to 2 pounds are being made by anglers who can locate schools around rooted aquatic vegetation. The invasion of an exotic species, an Asiatic clam in the 1960s in the Tennessee River basin, is believed to be responsible for the expansion of shellcracker populations, since the sunfish feed heavily on mollusks. Fish red worms or wax worms on light spinning tackle near the bottom around submerged weed beds.

Trout The trout fishery is rated good to excellent, and the outlook is for numerous 12- to 14-inch rainbow trout and 12- to 18-inch lake trout. Both species are sustained by stockings. "Every once in a while we find some wild fish, but the natural reproduction is not significant enough to support the populations," said John Mayer, a trout biologist with the Tennessee Wildlife Resources Agency. "Trout populations are doing well, and trout fishing is very popular, especially during the summer."

The lake trout (*Salvelinus namaycush*), a deep-water species found throughout Canada, Alaska, and the Great Lakes states, was first introduced into Dale Hollow Lake in 1975. "Lake trout are stocked just about every year," said Mayer. "The numbers vary from 10,000 to 60,000 a year." The stocking size is 5 to 6 inches. Mayer said lake trout up to 20 inches (four-year-old fish) are being caught. "During the early fall there's lots of fishermen at the dam, trolling [spoons and crankbaits on] downriggers."

Rainbow trout (*Oncorhynchus mykiss*) have been stocked in Dale Hollow Lake since the 1960s. "We stock about 90,000 fish a year," said Mayer. "The stocking size is 9 inches." Rainbows up to 7 pounds are taken. Still-fishing at night over lights with nightcrawlers, power baits, kernel corn, and cheese is the most popular way to catch rainbow trout during the summer months.

Size and creel limits on trout at Dale Hollow Lake are seasonal in both the Kentucky and Tennessee portions of the reservoir. The fish are stocked in the fall. The restrictive size limit during the winter months allows the trout an opportunity to disperse from the stocking site and grow some before they are caught. November 1 through March 31 there is a 22-inch minimum size limit and a two-fish daily creel. April 1 through October 31 there is no minimum size limit and a seven-fish daily creel (however, no more than two may be lake trout).

Trout populations are sustained by alewives, threadfin and gizzard shad. "It was a hard winter 1995-96 and there was a significant kill of shad," said Mayer. "So we stocked some threadfins in early March [1996]."

Tailwater Fishing Opportunities

The Dale Hollow Lake tailwaters, about 6 miles of trout water on the Obey River, is stocked annually with 100,000 rainbow and 5,000 brown trout. Walleye, sauger, and striped bass are also taken from the Dale Hollow tailwaters. "There's lots of bait fishermen," said Mayer. "You can find some good fish if you get away from the ramps."

DEWEY LAKE

Bluegill ◄◄◄	Largemouth Bass ◄
Catfish ◄◄◄	Spotted Bass ◄◄
Crappie ◄◄	White Bass ◄
Hybrid Striped Bass ◄◄	Tailwaters ◄

Location   Dewey Lake is about 120 miles east of Lexington in Floyd County. The dam is about 4 miles northeast of Prestonsburg, off Ky. 3. Impounded from the John's Creek, a tributary to the Levisa Fork of the Big Sandy River, Dewey Lake opened in the spring of 1951. The cost of the project was $7.8 million. The main access highways are U.S. 23/460, Ky. 302 (formerly Ky. 3), and Ky. 194.

Size   The lake has 1,100 acres at summer pool (elevation 650), and 900 acres at winter pool (elevation 645). It has 52 miles of shoreline, is 50 feet deep just above the dam, and is 18.5 miles long.

Trophic State Index (TSI)   Dewey Lake has a TSI of 50, which ranks it as a mesotrophic lake (moderate fertility).

Lake Manager's Office   U.S. Army Corps of Engineers, Dewey Lake, Resource Manager's Office, HC 70, Box 540, Van Lear, KY 41265, telephone (606) 886-6709.

Managing Fishery Biologist   Kentucky Department of Fish and Wildlife Resources, Eastern Fishery District, Steve Reeser, District Biologist, 2744 Lake Road, Prestonsburg, KY 41653, telephone (606) 886-9575.

Lake Level/Fishing Report Line   The U.S. Army Corps of Engineers lake information line is (606) 886-6398.

Marinas   There is one marina. The *Jenny Wiley State Resort Park Marina*, open year-round, is 5 miles northeast of Prestonsburg, off Ky. 302. The address and telephone number are 39 Jenny Wiley Road, Prestonsburg, KY 41653, (606) 886-2711.

Boat Launching Ramps   There are two boat launching ramps on the lake in addition to the ramp at the marina. There is no fee to launch a boat at any ramp on the lake. *Terry* boat launching ramp is in Jenny

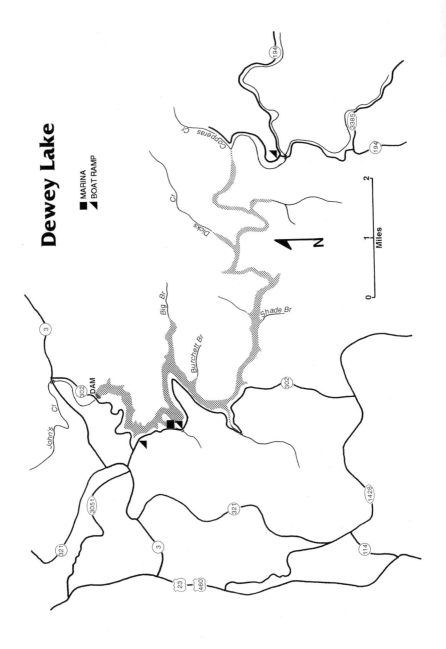

Dewey Lake

■ MARINA
◤ BOAT RAMP

Wiley State Resort Park, off Ky. 302. *German* boat launching ramp is 22 miles east of the dam at the head of the lake, off Ky. 194.

Local Tourism Information   Prestonsburg Tourism Commission, 1 Hal Rogers Drive, Prestonsburg, KY 41653, telephone (606) 886-1341 or toll free (800) 844-4704.

Fishing   Over the years, siltation from surface mining in the John's Creek drainage and associated water quality problems have had a severe impact on the lake, limiting spawning areas and affecting fish growth and reproduction. Early spring rains tend to muddy up the lake. The aquatic vegetation that thrived in the shallow headwaters of the lake during the drought years of the 1980s has all but disappeared.

For ten years, beginning in 1975, the tiger muskie, a sterile cross between the male northern pike (*Esox lucius*) and female silver muskellunge (*Esox masquinongy ohioensis*), was stocked in the lake. The stockings were discontinued in 1985 because project goals were never met. There was poor growth and survival of adult fish, and angler success was low.

Today, Dewey Lake supports populations of hybrid striped bass, spotted and largemouth bass, bluegill, white bass, crappie, and channel catfish. The main forage fish is the gizzard shad.

Catfish   The channel catfish fishery is rated good, and the outlook is for a stable population of 1- to 3-pound fish. Dewey Lake has been known for years as one of the top catfish lakes in Eastern Kentucky. There are good numbers of fish and significant fishing pressure. "A lot of people realize it's good fishing," said eastern district fishery biologist Steve Reeser. "It's no secret."

The lake supports populations of both channel and flathead catfish, with channel catfish being the dominant species. "The average channel taken is an 11- to 20-inch fish," Reeser said. "Occasionally, surplus fish from the hatchery are placed in the lake, but this is a reproducing population." A 20-inch channel weighs about 3 1/2 pounds. Reeser occasionally receives a report of a big flathead being caught. "I've heard of some 40- to 50-pounders being taken."

Catfish are caught year-round, but a majority of the fishing occurs at night in the upper half of the lake during the summer on the shallow flats off the river channel. A boat is needed to reach the best fishing areas. An overlooked time to fish might be during the early spring, when catfish are concentrated in the lower lake before the water level rises to summer pool.

Trotlines and jug fishing are legal, under state regulations.

Bluegill   The bluegill fishery is rated good, and the outlook is for numerous 6- to 8-inch fish. Fish in the shallows of the upper lake for fast action during the spawn. The best technique is to fish live bait—red worms, crickets, or wax worms—on a fly rod or cane pole. Drop the baited hook (with a small float attached as a strike indicator) along the edge of shoreline cover.

Hybrid Striped Bass   The hybrid striped bass fishery is rated fair, and the outlook is for low numbers of fish up to 20 inches. "There are some indications that the fishery may not be well established," said Reeser. The stocking program began in 1993. "The white bass population was so low," said fishery biologist Benjy Kinman. "We didn't think it would ever come back because of siltation in the headwaters."

Kinman said there's a good chance the hybrid striped bass will replace the white bass as the lake's open-water predator, feeding primarily on shad and other minnows. "With hybrids you're not relying on spawning success," said Kinman. "You're bypassing that life cycle. The population is maintained by annual stocking." Hybrid stockings in other small mountain reservoirs have met with success, Kinman said. Since hybrids are highly migratory, high discharge rates through dams can cause fish to be lost downstream. Kinman does not think that will be a problem at Dewey because the seasonal drawdown is minimal.

On March 1, 1995, the daily creel limit for white bass and striped bass hybrids was changed to five, with a 15-inch minimum size limit. "[The change] was intended to simplify the regulations, not protect the white bass," said Kinman. "It will prevent anglers from taking undersize hybrids, which are misidentified as white bass."

Kinman said Dewey received its first stocking of hybrids in the fall of 1993. "They were not the normal size we stock. They were held at the hatchery longer than usual," said Kinman. The fingerlings averaged 5.2 inches and were stocked at the rate of twenty-one fish per acre. Kinman said the hybrid stocking was postponed from the normal early summer so as not to interfere with a crappie growth study that was winding down. In 1994 Dewey received its second stocking of hybrids, which were fry. "The second year our stocking goal is usually ten fish per acre," said Kinman. Hybrids in excess of 19 inches have been taken since the fall of 1995.

Crappie   The crappie fishery is rated fair, and the outlook is for 6- to 8-inch fish. "Very slow growth has resulted in a stunted population," said Reeser. Both white and black crappie are present, with black crappie predominating the catch in the upper lake. White crappie up to 11 inches are taken, but there are very few big fish. Fish cover on the edge of the old river channel with live minnows and 1/32-ounce tube jigs. In the lower lake fish wood cover, deadfalls, and stumps.

Largemouth Bass   The largemouth bass fishery is rated poor, and the outlook is for low numbers of keeper fish. "Anglers have commented that the fishing has improved in recent years," said Reeser. "But environmental conditions, muddy water, and siltation continue to inhibit reproduction, and growth is slow." Fish the upper lake in the spring and the lower lake the rest of the year. There is a 15-inch minimum size limit.

Spotted Bass   The spotted bass fishery is fair, and the outlook is for very few fish over 12 inches. There are decent numbers, but most fish are 6 to 10 inches in length. Fish rock structures in the lower lake with live minnows and 1/8-ounce jigs.

White Bass   The white bass fishery is rated poor, and the outlook is for a further decline in numbers. In recent years, white bass have dropped considerably. "There's a real small [spring] run now," said Reeser. "In the past [the run] was pretty good." White bass populations have been severely impacted by siltation in the headwaters. With the change to a 15-inch minimum size for white bass and hybrid striped bass on March 1, 1995 (a move to protect the small hybrids), the chance of catching a keeper white bass is slim.

Tailwater Fishing Opportunities

Stocked monthly (except July and August), the tailwaters receive 6,550 rainbow trout each year.

FISHTRAP LAKE

Catfish ⚬⚬⚬	Smallmouth Bass ⚬⚬
Crappie ⚬⚬⚬	Spotted Bass ⚬⚬⚬
Hybrid Striped Bass ⚬⚬⚬⚬	White Bass ⚬⚬
Largemouth Bass ⚬⚬⚬	Tailwaters ⚬⚬⚬

Location   Fishtrap Lake is about 147 miles southeast of Lexington in Pike County. The dam is about 15 miles southeast of Pikeville, off Ky. 1789. It was impounded from the Levisa Fork, a tributary to the Big Sandy River. Construction on the 195-foot-high and 1,100-foot-long dam began in 1962.

Size   The 16.5-mile reservoir opened in 1968. Its summer pool elevation is 757 feet, and there is a 32-foot drawdown to winter pool (elevation 725). The 1,131-acre lake has 40 miles of shoreline and is 84 feet deep just above the dam.

Trophic State Index (TSI)   Fishtrap Lake has a TSI of 42, which ranks it as a mesotrophic lake (moderate fertility).

Lake Manager's Office   U.S. Army Corps of Engineers, Fishtrap Lake, 2204 Fishtrap Road, Shelbiana, KY 41562, telephone (606) 437-7496.

Managing Fishery Biologist   Kentucky Department of Fish and Wildlife Resources, Eastern Fishery District, Steve Reeser, District Biologist, 2744 Lake Road, Prestonsburg, KY 41653, telephone (606) 886-9575.

Lake Level/Fishing Report Line   The U.S. Army Corps of Engineers lake information line is (606) 437-9426.

Marinas   There is one marina on the lake. *Mastin Fishtrap Marina*, open year-round, is 15 miles southeast of Pikeville, off Ky. 1789. The address and telephone number are Box 61, Virgie, KY 41572, (606) 432-6894.

Boat Launching Ramps   There are two boat launching ramps on the lake in addition to the ramp at the marina. However, launching is not possible at boat ramps at winter pool because of low water. Beginning in 1997, there will be a $2 fee to launch at the boat ramps, $25 for an annual pass, with discounts available to senior citizens. *Lick Creek* boat

Fishtrap Lake

■ MARINA
◤ BOAT RAMP

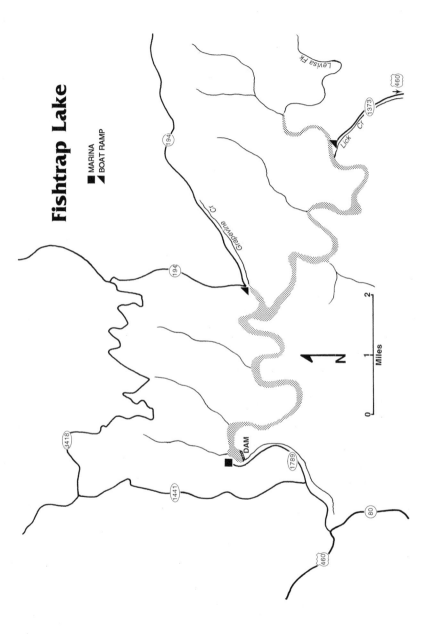

ramp is in the upper lake, off U.S. 460. *Grapevine Creek* boat ramp is mid-lake, off Ky. 194.

Local Tourism Information   Pikeville/Pike County Tourism Commission, 101 Huffman Avenue, Pikeville, KY 41501, telephone (606) 432-5063 or toll free (800) 844-7453.

Fishing   Fishtrap Lake is a steep-sided, highland reservoir with surprising potential. "It's a sleeper lake," said Steve Reeser, eastern district fishery biologist. "It doesn't have the numbers, but has quality fish." In the past the lake was plagued by siltation and water quality problems associated with surface mining, but water quality seems have made some improvements in the last several years. The lake has no flooded timber or rooted aquatic vegetation but does have lots of deadfalls, stump beds, and rocky substrate.

On November 26, 1996, a potentially catastrophic situation was averted. Thousands of gallons of black water from a coal washing operation came into the lake but was diluted by timely rains with no immediate effect on fish populations. "We were very fortunate. We got 2 inches of rain and took on 32 feet of water, raising the lake to summer pool," said Rodney Holbrook, resource manager for the U.S. Army Corps of Engineers. The black water spill occurred when a leak developed in a sediment pond at the Buchanan Number 1 Mine near Oakwood, Virginia. No major fish kill was observed.

The lake's top two species are hybrid striped bass and crappie, but it also sustains populations of largemouth bass, bluegill, white bass, and channel catfish. Occasionally a smallmouth bass is caught. The severe drawdown to winter pool (32 feet) that makes boat launching difficult for anglers may have some benefits to the fishery. "Predators don't have to work as hard [to catch prey]," said Reeser.

Hybrid Striped Bass   The hybrid striped bass fishery is rated good to excellent, and the outlook is for numerous keepers, with some fish weighing up to 8 pounds.

Fishtrap Lake offers a good opportunity for trophy fish because of good growth and relatively light fishing pressure. "Hybrids aren't being targeted, most catches are incidental," said Reeser. A 1995 creel survey showed that the average hybrid harvested was a 15.7-incher that weighed 2.1 pounds. "From the fish we've seen in recent samples, I really expected a greater harvest. "But the harvest has been more than 1 pound per acre, which was our goal, and compares favorably with other hybrid fisheries [in the state]."

Hybrids were first introduced into the lake in 1990 after declines in the white bass population became evident. The stocking rate is about 20 fish per surface acre of water, or 25,000 a year. The fry are stocked in June. Growth is good, said Reeser. "Hybrids reach 15 inches at 2 1/2 years." They have adapted well to Fishtrap Lake and are expected to be the lake's main fishery in the future. Most fish are confined to the lower half of the lake, with the best fishing after the fall drawdown. There is a fair spawning run in the headwaters in April and scattered jump action on the main lake in May and June. During the summer, when the lake thermally stratifies, hybrids go deep (15 to 20 feet) and usually locate just above the thermocline.

Gizzard shad is the main forage fish, but hybrids in the lake also feed on crayfish. Crayfish were found in the stomachs of some fish during age and growth studies in the fall of 1994. Brown, 1/4-ounce jigs tipped with a live crayfish are a top lure when hybrids suspend on rocky points and submerged humps.

Here are some seasonal tips. To catch hybrids in the spring, fish the headwaters with small jigs and spinners. Move with the fish to the lower lake in late spring. In summer and fall, concentrate on probing the deep water with electronics to locate schools of shad and hybrids suspended nearby. At night during the late spring and summer, jigging spoons and still-fishing live minnows (shad or shiners) will catch hybrids over lights. During the day, troll or cast crankbaits and jigs. During the heat of summer, try trolling small spoons or white streamers on leaders behind Bombers and other deep-diving crankbaits.

There is a 15-inch minimum size limit, with a daily creel of five fish.

Crappie The crappie fishery is rated good, and the outlook is for a stable population, with increased numbers of quality-sized fish. Trap netting in the fall of 1995 revealed good numbers of 9- to 11-inch fish, and the 1996 season was the best in years. A size limit may be considered in the future, depending on how much fishing pressure is affecting the fishery. The bigger crappie are caught fishing live minnows on deep structure along submerged channels.

Largemouth Bass The largemouth bass fishery is rated good, and the outlook is for increased numbers of keepers and an even size distribution in the population. "There are good numbers of fish in the population from 6 to 20 inches," said Reeser. "The relative weights are good too." The lake has always offered good potential for catching lunkers up to 7 pounds, but lack of spawning habitat limits the population.

Fishing pressure is very seasonal, offering anglers a good chance to have the lake to themselves in the fall, winter, and early spring. Some of the best fishing of the year is during the early fall, when the lake first stabilizes after the fall drawdown and bass are concentrated in the lower 3 miles.

Bass exhibit very good growth. "There's lots of shad and [the drawdown] crowds up the bass and increases predation [on the shad]," said Reeser. A largemouth bass reaches 12 inches at two years of age. A 1989 creel survey showed that 987 largemouth bass were harvested, and the average size was 12.8 inches. At that time a 12-inch minimum size limit was in effect on largemouth and smallmouth bass. A 15-inch minimum size limit on largemouth and smallmouth bass was initiated on January 1, 1991. "The most recent creel survey in 1995 showed a lower catch rate, but the average fish harvested weighed 2.25 pounds and was 16.3 inches long," said Reeser.

At times, Fishtrap Lake bass fishing can be feast or famine. When the conditions are right, anglers can really catch the bass wadded up in shallow water. This sometimes occurs in late March or early April before the lake comes up to summer pool.

Smallmouth Bass   The smallmouth bass fishery is rated fair, and the outlook is for a small but stable population. A 1989 creel survey showed that only twenty-five smallmouth bass were harvested, and the average fish creeled was 15.7 inches long. Then a 15-inch minimum size limit on largemouth and smallmouth bass was initiated on January 1, 1991. Four years later, during the 1995 creel survey, an increase in size was noted. The average fish harvested was 16.3 inches and weighed 2.13 pounds. "In the last couple of years we've noticed more quality fish," Reeser said. "Anglers are doing particularly well upriver, in Levisa Fork."

Spotted Bass   The spotted bass fishery is rated good, and the outlook is for a stable population of 8- to 12-inch fish. In 1989 the average spotted bass creeled was 11.8 inches long. It is estimated that spotted bass make up about 20 percent of all black bass in Fishtrap Lake. "The population is doing well and is concentrated on the rocky banks of the lower lake," said Reeser.

White Bass   The fishery is rated fair to good, and the outlook is for a stable but small population. There is still a spawning run in April, but population growth is limited by poor spawning habitat. Reeser said gill netting in the fall of 1994 showed that white bass ranged in size from 10 to 17 inches, with most fish being 10 to 12 inches.

Catfish   The catfish fishery is rated good, and the outlook is for numerous 1- to 3-pound channel catfish. "The lake also has some nice flatheads, weighing 10 to 30 pounds," said Reeser. "There's a few jug fishermen who take flatheads at night."

In 1995, according to creel survey data, 3,018 channel catfish were harvested, about 1.8 pounds per acre of water. "Catfish anglers have the second highest success rate (43.2 percent) at the lake," said Reeser. "Only crappie anglers had more success (56.9 percent)."

Tailwater Fishing Opportunities

The tailwaters produce good fishing for several species. Stocked monthly (except July, August, and September) with rainbow trout, the tailwaters receive 14,250 fish a year. "There are some holdover trout," said Reeser. Hybrid striped bass escape from the lake during periods of high discharge and create some excellent fishing in the spring. "We heard of an 8 1/2-pound hybrid being caught in the river below Pikeville," said Reeser. Other species include white bass, sauger, and walleye, which are stocked in the Russell Fork of the Big Sandy River, just a few miles downstream of the dam.

GRAYSON LAKE

Bluegill ⋈ ⋈ ⋈	Smallmouth Bass ⋈ ⋈
Catfish ⋈ ⋈ ⋈	Spotted Bass ⋈ ⋈
Crappie ⋈ ⋈	White Bass ⋈ ⋈
Largemouth Bass ⋈ ⋈	Tailwaters ⋈

Location   Grayson Lake is in Carter and Elliott Counties. The main access highways are Ky. 7, Ky. 182, and Ky. 504. The dam is about 7 miles south of Grayson, off Ky. 7. Construction began in 1964, and the lake opened in April 1969.

Grayson Lake is beautiful in the fall. Above Bruin Creek boat ramp there are big boulders in the water and towering rock cliffs along the shore. There is standing timber in the side hollows on the west bank of the lake, and scattered beds of aquatic vegetation provide numerous fishing opportunities.

Size   Impounded from the Little Sandy River, Grayson Lake is relatively narrow. The 19.7-miles lake has 74.2 miles of shoreline, and its maximum depth is 60 feet, near the dam. At summer pool (elevation 645) the lake has 1,510 surface acres. The winter pool elevation is 637, which reduces the surface acreage to 1,160.

Trophic State Index (TSI)   Grayson Lake has a TSI of 48, which ranks it as a mesotrophic lake (moderate fertility).

Lake Manager's Office   U.S. Army Corps of Engineers, Grayson Lake, Resource Manager's Office, Route 2, Box 258, Grayson, KY 41143, telephone (606) 474-5107 or (606) 474-5815.

Managing Fishery Biologist   Kentucky Department of Fish and Wildlife Resources, Northeastern Fishery District, Lewis Kornman, District Biologist, Minor Clark Fish Hatchery, 120 Fish Hatchery Road, Morehead, KY 40351, telephone (606) 784-6872.

Lake Level/Fishing Report Line   The U.S. Army Corps of Engineers lake information line is (606) 474-7476.

Marinas   There is one marina. *Grayson Lake Marina*, open year-round (boat rentals April 1 to October 31), is 7 miles south of Grayson, off Ky. 7. The address and telephone number are Grayson Lake Marina, Route

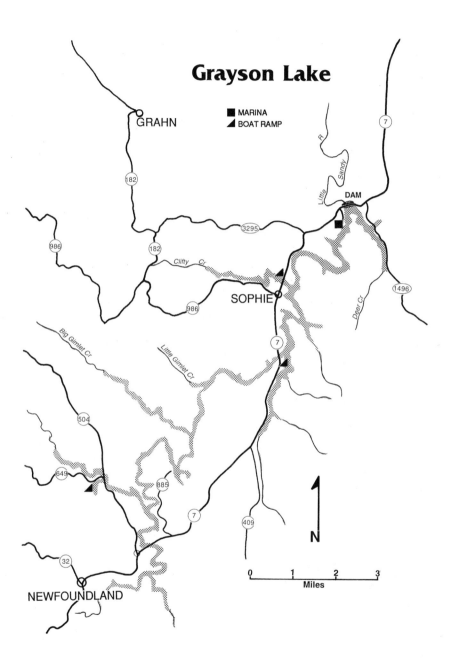

Grayson Lake

■ MARINA
▲ BOAT RAMP

GRAHN

182

986

182

3295

Clifty Cr

986

SOPHIE

Little Sandy R

DAM

1496

Deer Cr

7

7

Big Gimlet Cr

Little Gimlet Cr

504

649

885

7

409

32

NEWFOUNDLAND

0   1   2   3
Miles

N

Grayson Lake • 117

2, Box 256, Grayson, KY 41143, (606) 474-4513. There is a $2 fee to launch at the damsite boat ramp (adjacent to the marina), $25 for an annual pass, with discounts available to senior citizens.

Boat Launching Ramps   There are three boat launching ramps on the lake in addition to the ramp at the marina. There is no fee to launch a boat at any of these three ramps. *Clifty Creek* boat ramp is 2 miles west of the dam, off Ky. 7. *Bruin Creek* boat ramp is 4 miles west of the dam, off Ky. 7. *Caney Creek* boat ramp is 11 miles west of the dam, off Ky. 504.

Local Tourism Information   Grayson Area Chamber of Commerce, Box 612, Grayson, KY 41143, telephone (606) 474-4401.

Fishing   Grayson Lake is a reservoir of varied character. Above Bruin Creek, the lakeshore changes from rolling, green hills to a scenic rock canyon, with numerous waterfalls cascading off 50- to 150-foot limestone bluffs. Fish populations include largemouth, smallmouth, and spotted bass, bluegill, catfish, crappie, and white bass. To bolster the forage base of gizzard shad, threadfin shad were stocked for several years, beginning in 1987, but the fish succumbed to winter kill. A fertilization program began in the early 1990s.

During the summer months pleasure boat traffic is extremely heavy. A 1 1/2-mile stretch of the lake near the old beach is called "The Bongoes" by locals because 2-foot waves bounce back and forth, slapping off the rock walls during heavy boat traffic. Consequently, most summer fishing is done at night.

Largemouth Bass   The largemouth bass fishery is rated fair to good, and the outlook is for numerous sublegal fish. Keeper-size fish are relatively low in number, but there are lots of 12- to 14-inch fish. The largemouth is the dominant species, representing about 81 percent of all black bass in the lake. Grayson Lake was the first major lake in Kentucky (1982) to have a 15-inch minimum size limit on bass.

Local bass angler Kevin Mullins said the mid to upper lake offers the best fishing. "[In the spring] bass move up fast to spawn," said Mullins. "Deer Creek, Greenbrier Creek, and Bruin Creek are top spawning embayments. They get pretty heavily fished." He suggested fishing black jig and pork rind combinations and crayfish-colored or pearl and chartreuse-colored ShadRap crankbaits around flooded timber and submerged brush in the shallows in spring. "At night I'd fish a purple Bagley DB3 crankbait."

Postspawn, dragging Carolina-rigged lizards over submerged humps and drop-offs is a good strategy in the late afternoons, Mullins said. "There are a lot of submerged roadbeds in Clifty, Bruin, and Greenbrier Creeks that bass use as highways." Texas-rigged 6-inch black grape plastic worms, fished with a 3/8- or 1/4-ounce bullet sinker, are popular after dark during the summer months off steep points and bluffs.

The best bass fishing of the year may be in the fall. "Some of my best days have come in October and November," said Mullins. Fish topwater lures, Rapalas, Rattlin' Rogues, or chugger-type poppers in the upper lake prior the fall drawdown.

Smallmouth Bass   The smallmouth bass fishery is rated fair to good, and the outlook is for improving numbers of high-quality fish. A growing population can be found mid-lake between Clifty Creek and Bruin Creek.

Mullins said smallmouth are caught on spinnerbaits more than any other lure. Some of the best fishing is at night on the point across from the dam and the riprap on the face of the dam. "Smallmouth are really coming on," said Mullins." [The fishing] seems to be getting better because we're seeing more smallmouth caught during our Thursday and Saturday night tournaments." Mullins recommends fishing with black spinnerbaits during the dark of the moon, purple and black when the moon is bright, and white and chartreuse during the day in the spring (when water temperatures approach 60 degrees).

Smallmouth were stocked in the lake for six years beginning in 1980 and ending in 1989, with the goal of establishing a self-sustaining population. They now make up about 3 percent of the black bass in the lake. There are good numbers of 10- to 13-inch fish.

Spotted Bass   The spotted bass fishery is rated fair, and the outlook is for a declining population. Spotted bass make up about 16 percent of the black bass in the lake. Only a few spotted bass longer than 11 inches are caught by anglers; most fish are under 10 inches. Fish the rock bluffs in the "Bongoes" and the cliff lines between Big and Little Gimlet Creeks.

White Bass   The white bass fishery is rated fair, and the outlook is for scattered concentrations of fish. There aren't many white bass, but a few are huge—some up to 18 inches long. In the spring there is a small white bass run in the headwaters. During the early summer, troll the old beach (no longer used) at the state park, where white bass suspend off the sandy, gradually sloping bottom; during the late summer and early fall, be on the lookout for jumps on the main lake.

Catfish   The catfish fishery is rated good, and the outlook is for numerous 1- to 2-pound channel catfish and 1- to 3-pound flatheads. There's a stable population of channel catfish. This fishery is somewhat overlooked. Most are in the 12- to 19-inch size range. During the summer some big flathead catfish are caught by jug fishing with live bluegills.

Crappie The crappie fishery is rated fair, and the outlook is for an unpredictable population that is plagued by slow growth. There are few fish over 10 inches, and the best fishing of the year occurs in the upper lake in the spring. Fish woody structure in shallow coves off the lake's main channel.

Considering the numbers the lake produced in the past, crappie populations have made a turnaround. "Populations are better now, not great, but much improved," said district fishery biologist Lew Kornman. "The average crappie is about a 7- to 8-incher, and crappie numbers are vastly reduced." On March 1, 1995, a thirty-fish daily creel limit with no minimum size limit went into effect. Prior to that there had been no daily creel limit, which biologists hoped would help fight the overpopulation problem.

Kornman said several factors may be influencing improved crappie size—more predation of young crappie since the establishment of a 15-inch minimum-size limit on bass, overall lower density of crappie in the lake in recent years, and a fertilization project aimed at boosting young bass survival that also increased the number of small shad available as forage for crappie.

"The idea [of the fertilization] is to affect the shad population at the right time," said Ted Crowell, assistant fisheries director. "By starting earlier in the spring you're promoting the growth of plankton when the shad spawn needs it most." The trick is to stop the fertilization at the beginning of the summer so the shad won't outgrow the predators—small bass and crappie.

Bluegill The bluegill fishery is rated good, and the outlook is for numerous 6- to 7-inch fish. "The bluegill fishery is overlooked by many anglers," said Kornman. Large numbers of small bass in the lake help to keep bluegill numbers down, promoting good growth.

Tailwater Fishing Opportunities

Suitable for fishing from a canoe, the bank, or wading, the tailwaters are quite small. The dam's tailrace is lined with riprap. A total of 7,500 rainbow trout are stocked in the tailwaters annually. Stockings are made monthly, except July, August, and September. Cool-water habitat extends for about a half mile downstream. It is doubtful that there are many, if any, holdover trout.

Grayson Lake Dam on Ky. 7 in Carter County impounds a 1,510-acre reservoir at summer pool (elevation 645).

GREENBO LAKE

Bluegill ⋙	Largemouth Bass ⋙ ⋙
Catfish ⋙ ⋙ ⋙	Rainbow Trout ⋙ ⋙ ⋙ ⋙
Crappie ⋙ ⋙	Smallmouth Bass ⋙ ⋙

Location   Greenbo Lake is about 107 miles east of Lexington in Greenup County, 8 miles south of Greenup, off Ky. 1. The major access highways are Interstate 64 and U.S. 23. Impounded in 1955, the lake was built at a cost of $235,000. The Greenbo Lake Association raised $110,000, and the Kentucky Department of Fish and Wildlife Resources chipped in $125,000, which paid for the design of the lake and construction of the concrete and earthen dam. Greenbo Lake is clear most of the year, which makes it very difficult to fish.

Size   The 181-acre impoundment, surrounded by woodlands, is steep sided and has a maximum depth of 60 feet. There is little or no pool fluctuation. The lake is not fed by any streams of substantial size, so the major influx of water comes from runoff after heavy rainstorms.

Trophic State Index (TSI)   Greenbo Lake has a TSI of 48, which ranks it as a mesotrophic lake (moderate fertility).

Lake Manager's Office   Greenbo Lake State Resort Park, HC 60, Box 562, Greenup, KY 41144, telephone (606) 473-7324.

Managing Fishery Biologist   Kentucky Department of Fish and Wildlife Resources, Northeastern Fishery District, Al Surmont, District Assistant Biologist, Minor Clark Fish Hatchery, 120 Fish Hatchery Road Morehead, KY 40351, telephone (606) 784-6872.

Lake Level/Fishing Report Line   There is no lake information line.

Marinas   There is one marina. *Greenbo Lake State Resort Park Marina*, open seasonally (March 1 to October 31), is 8 miles south of Greenup, off Ky. 1. The address and telephone number are HC 60, Box 562, Greenup, KY 41144, (606) 473-7324.

Boat Launching Ramps   There is one boat launching ramp on the lake. It is adjacent to the marina. There is no fee to launch.

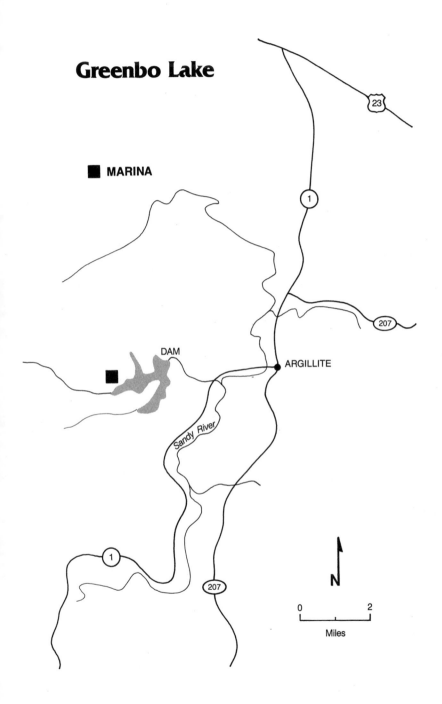

Greenbo Lake

MARINA

DAM

ARGILLITE

Sandy River

N

0   2

Miles

Local Tourism Information   Ashland Area Convention and Visitors Bureau, 728 Greenup Avenue, Ashland, KY 41105, telephone (606) 329-1007 or toll free (800) 377-6249.

Fishing   Greenbo Lake is not a major impoundment compared to the other reservoirs profiled in this book, but it has a unique status which earned the lake a special place in Kentucky angling lore. Greenbo Lake is the only body of water in Kentucky to produce two state record largemouth bass.

What makes the story truly intriguing is that both fish were caught by the same man. Delbert Grizzle, of Flatwoods, caught the bass within eleven months of each other, on September 21, 1965, and August 3, 1966. Grizzle's formula for success was pretty simple. He fished at night and cast an unweighted, 6-inch plastic worm (wine, black, blue, and purple were favorite colors) to the bank and worked it back to the boat with a slow retrieve. His cardinal rule was to be absolutely quiet. "If you get hung up, break your line rather than go to the bank," cautioned Grizzle. Today, the lake still produces a few largemouth bass up to 26 inches long.

Other fish species include rainbow trout, bluegill, smallmouth bass, black crappie, and channel catfish. There are also small populations of longear sunfish and pumpkinseed (*Lepomis gibbosus*). "Greenbo Lake is the only lake I know of that has a population of pumpkinseed," said Al Surmont, assistant fishery biologist in the northeastern district. The native sunfish species, which resembles a redear sunfish, thrives in bodies of water which have rooted aquatic vegetation. It is uncertain how pumpkinseeds got into Greenbo Lake.

Since 1989 grass carp have been stocked in the lake to control nuisance rooted aquatic vegetation. Grass carp cannot be kept by anglers and must be returned to the lake immediately if caught.

There are two important regulations of which anglers need to be aware: first, outboard motors must be operated at idle speed only, and second, the possession and use of shad for bait is prohibited.

There are fish attractors in Pruitt Hollow and on the main lake near the boat ramp. Beavers have felled trees in some areas of the lake, providing additional wood cover along the shoreline.

Rainbow Trout   The rainbow trout fishery is rated excellent, and the outlook is for numerous 9- to 12-inch fish. In recent years rainbow trout have become Greenbo Lake's most sought-after species. More trout are creeled in March and April than any other months because cold

Delbert Grizzle with the mount of a 13-pound, 8 ounce largemouth bass he caught from Greenbo Lake on the night of August 3, 1966. It was the Kentucky state record for over seventeen years.

water brings the fish up shallow, where they are more accessible to anglers. In a creel survey conducted from January through April 1993, 88 percent of all anglers interviewed were fishing for trout. During that period 7,049 fishermen harvested 11,752 rainbows. Rainbow trout now make up 40.5 percent of the total pounds of fish harvested from the lake.

"It's a relatively new fishery that a lot of people don't know about," said district fishery biologist Lew Kornman. "There's potential for big fish because trout can carry over from year to year." Trout have been stocked since the early 1990s. "It's a dense stocking rate," said Kornman. "The lake is stocked once a year, in January, with about 15,000 9-inch trout." The trout being caught range from stocking size to about 17 inches, with reports of a few fish being taken that are about 20 to 24 inches long. "The biggest trout I've personally seen was a 16- to 17-incher, weighing between a pound and a half and 2 pounds," said Kornman.

Most of the fishing is being done at the dam, and in the tailrace, an arm of the lake next to the dam. Bank fishermen are using nightcrawlers, bits of marshmallow, kernel corn, cheese, and power baits, which are scented, dough-like synthetics. Kornman said some larger trout are being caught by trolling or casting small crankbaits on light line. Night fishing over lights is catching on during the summer months.

Catfish The catfish fishery is rated good, and the outlook is for numerous 10- to 14-inch fish. Channel catfish are stocked annually (about 4,500), and the best times to fish are late spring on the flats in the upper end of the lake, and in July, down by the dam. Large fish (up to 24 inches) are present.

Largemouth Bass The largemouth bass fishery is rated fair, and the outlook is for a stable population of keeper-size (12- to 15-inch) fish. Greenbo Lake's reputation for producing lunkers is still intact. The summer of 1996 marked the thirtieth anniversary of Delbert Grizzle's 13-pound, 8-ounce fish that held the Kentucky state record for almost eighteen years. "The percentage of large bass [in the population] is impressive," said Surmont. "We've sampled bass up to 10 pounds. They are fat, chunky fish."

Growth rates are typical for an eastern Kentucky lake. Surmont said largemouth bass in Greenbo Lake reach 12 inches by age three and 15 inches by age five. "Most of the bass are in the 10- to 15-inch size range, but there's quite a few 20- to 26-inch bass, too." According to the 1993 creel survey, the average bass harvested was a 12.5-incher. "In 1993, anglers caught about 24,971 bass and harvested 784." Since there are no shad in Greenbo Lake, Surmont believes that the larger bass may be feeding on rainbow trout. Statewide regulations are in effect on largemouth bass—a 12-inch minimum size limit and a six-fish daily creel.

In recent years, two factors have combined to make bass fishing more difficult. In 1989, grass carp were introduced into the lake to clean up nuisance rooted aquatic vegetation. As a result, bass have had to locate on less visible structure—stumps, submerged logs, and bottom features such as channels and humps. "Anglers aren't catching bass like they should," said Surmont. "They're having trouble finding fish." And since Greenbo Lake is no longer being fertilized, it stays clear year-round, which causes bass to locate in deeper water.

Here are a few tips for landing largemouth bass at Greenbo. Some top bass lures at the lake are Silver Buddy, a sinking, vibrating metal "blade" bait; deep-diving crankbaits; and plastic worms which are Carolina-rigged, or fished on the surface at night without any weight. Since bass may be suspending, anglers should try trolling or casting trout-colored crankbaits in open water. Pruitt Hollow is one of the best areas on the lake for bass fishing. "April and May are the best fishing months, followed far behind by September and October," said Surmont. "Fishing pressure is extremely heavy on bass on the weekends." On rainy spring days, bass will locate where creeks empty into the lake, seeking warm water. Fish spinnerbaits in the murky water conditions.

Smallmouth Bass The smallmouth bass fishery is rated fair, and the outlook is for a small population of 8- to 12-inch fish. Smallmouth bass were stocked in the lake periodically from 1987 through 1994. "We stocked two different sizes, 2- to 3-inch fish in the 1980s, and 5- to 6-inch fish from 1992 through 1994," said Surmont. "What we don't understand is why we aren't seeing larger fish, because we're certain some natural reproduction is occurring." The fishery is now being evaluated. A few smallmouth bass are being caught each year, but the fishery is very limited.

Crappie The black crappie fishery is rated fair, and the outlook is for small numbers of 8- to 11-inch fish. The average crappie being harvested is an 8.8-incher, according to the 1993 creel survey. A one-time stocking was made in 1993, when a hatchery surplus of 845 black crappie were released in the lake. "Black crappie have a much lower reproductive rate [than white crappie]," said Surmont. "So we aren't worried about any [overpopulation] problems."

Bluegill The bluegill fishery is rated poor, and the outlook is for a gradually improving population. Most fish are 3 to 5 inches long, but size is improving. A few 7- to 9-inch fish are being taken by anglers who fish deep banks on the main lake during the spring with crickets, meal worms, and wax worms.

Tailwater Fishing Opportunities

The dam is earthen fill, with a concrete spillway. The tailwaters are too small to support game fish.

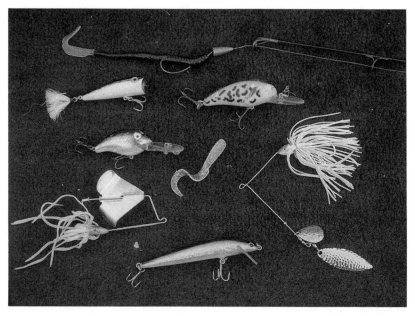

This selection of bass lures includes crankbaits, a spinnerbait, a buzzbait, topwater lures, a plastic worm, and a curlytail grub.

GREEN RIVER LAKE

Bluegill ⬥⬥	Smallmouth Bass ⬥⬥⬥
Catfish ⬥⬥⬥⬥	Spotted Bass ⬥⬥
Crappie ⬥⬥⬥	Walleye ⬥⬥
Largemouth Bass ⬥⬥⬥	White Bass ⬥⬥⬥⬥
Muskellunge ⬥⬥⬥⬥	Tailwaters ⬥⬥⬥

Location Green River Lake is about 90 miles southeast of Louisville in Taylor and Adair Counties, east of Ky. 55 between Campbellsville and Columbia. The dam is 26 miles upstream of Greensburg, and 305.7 miles above the mouth of Green River. Drainage area above the dam is 682 square miles. The main access highways are Ky. 55, Ky. 551, Ky. 372, Ky. 1061, and Ky. 76. Construction began in April 1964, and the lake was completed in June 1969.

Anglers are reminded that there are six no-wake embayments—Robinson Creek, Stone Quarry Creek, Butler Creek, White Oak Creek, Snake Creek, and Casey Creek—in addition to about 20 miles of the main river above the Ky. 551 bridge.

Size At summer pool (elevation 675), the 8,210-acre lake stretches 25 miles and has 147 miles of shoreline. The average depth is about 25 feet, and at its deepest point, just above the dam, the lake is 65 feet deep. The winter drawdown reduces the lake to 6,650 acres and an elevation of 664 feet. There is a big island in the bend of the lake below Smith Ridge.

Trophic State Index (TSI) Green River Lake has a TSI of 48, which ranks it as a mesotrophic lake (moderate fertility).

Lake Manager's Office U.S. Army Corps of Engineers, Resource Manager's Office, Green River Lake, 544 Lake Road, Campbellsville, KY 42718-9805, telephone (502) 465-4463.

Managing Fishery Biologist Kentucky Department of Fish and Wildlife Resources, Southwestern Fishery District, B.D. Laflin, District Biologist, 4800 Nashville Road, Bowling Green, KY 42101, telephone (502) 842-3677.

Lake Level/Fishing Report Line There is no lake information line.

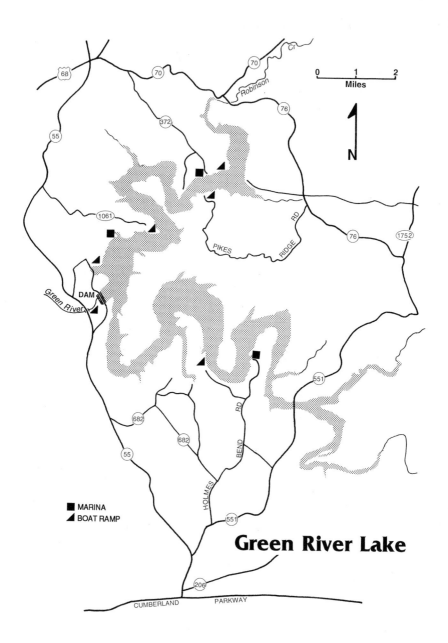

Green River Lake

■ MARINA
▲ BOAT RAMP

Marinas   There are three marinas on the lake. *Holmes Bend Marina*, open seasonally (April 1 through October 31), is 6 miles north of Columbia, off Ky. 551. The address and telephone numbers are Box 353, Columbia, KY 42728, (502) 384-4425 or toll free (800) 801-8154. *Emerald Isle Marina*, open seasonally (March 1 through November 30), is 5 miles southeast of Campbellsville, off Ky. 372. The address and telephone numbers are Smith Ridge Road, Box 282, Campbellsville, KY 42719, (502) 465-3412 or toll free (888) 815-2000. The cost to launch a boat is $3. *Green River Marina*, open seasonally (March 1 through October 31), is 8 miles south of Campbellsville, off Ky. 1061. The address and telephone numbers are 2892 Lone Valley Road, Campbellsville, KY 42718, (502) 465-2512 or toll free (800) 488-2512.

Boat Launching Ramps   There are five boat launching ramps on the lake in addition to the ramps at the marinas. *Smith Ridge* boat ramp is 5 miles southeast of Campbellsville, off Ky. 372. There is a $2 fee to launch at the boat ramp, $25 for an annual pass, with discounts available to senior citizens. *Pike Ridge* boat ramp is 8 miles southeast of Campbellsville, off Ky. 76. There is a $2 fee to launch at the boat ramp, $25 for an annual pass, with discounts available to senior citizens. *Dam* (Site 1) boat ramp is 6 miles south of Campbellsville, off Ky. 55. There is a $2 fee to launch at the boat ramp, $25 for an annual pass, with discounts available to senior citizens. *State Park* boat ramp (at Lone Valley) is 7 miles south of Campbellsville, off Ky. 1061. *Butler Creek* boat ramp is 5 miles north of Columbia, off Ky. 682.

Local Tourism Information   Taylor County Tourist Commission, 211 Court Street, Box 4021, Campbellsville, KY 42719, telephone (502) 465-3786 or toll free (800) 738-4719.

Fishing   Green River Lake is a wishbone-shaped impoundment with broad flats along the old river channel and a backdrop of rolling hills. A few embayments are filled with standing timber.

Because of its close proximity to Lake Cumberland and Dale Hollow Lake, Green River Lake has been overlooked by many anglers. This is hard to understand considering the lake's quality and diverse fisheries. The muskie fishery is outstanding, and many anglers believe it rivals Cave Run Lake. There is great anticipation about the future of walleye fishing ever since a stocking program began in 1993 and keeper fish started being creeled in 1995. The smallmouth bass fishery does not get the accolades it deserves, despite its track record of producing fish up to

9 pounds. Other fish species present in the lake include largemouth and spotted bass, bluegill, channel catfish, crappie, and white bass. Threadfin shad are present in the lake but were never stocked by the department.

Muskellunge The muskie fishery is rated good to excellent, and the outlook is for numerous legal size (30-inch) fish, and a fair number of 40-inch and larger fish. In the last decade, Green River Lake's muskie fishery has bloomed. "It's gotten progressively better," said southwestern district fishery biologist B.D. Laflin. Green River Lake is yielding

Owen Chelf of Lebanon caught and released this 33-inch muskie in Green River Lake in June 1990.

both large numbers of legal size fish and trophy muskies up to 30 pounds. A 1994 creel survey found that the average muskie harvested was 36.3 inches long and weighed 11.9 pounds, with 738 muskies kept from more than 2,300 caught. "A lot more fish are being released," Laflin said.

Compare those numbers with the previous creel survey, conducted in 1991. At that time the average muskie being harvested was a 33-incher that weighed about 9 pounds. An estimated 570 muskies were harvested in 1991, but only 729 harvestable-size fish were released by anglers.

Laflin said the number of muskie anglers has increased only slightly in recent years despite the fact that the lake's muskie harvest has eclipsed the muskie harvest at Cave Run Lake. The peak months of muskie harvest at Green River Lake in 1994 were March, July, and August. "Catches are being made all over the lake. No one area is yielding more muskies," said Laflin.

According to department records, muskie were first released in Green River Lake in 1977. The lake's muskie fishery really started to take off in the mid-1980s. The reason was the higher survival rate of 13-inch sub-adult fish that were first stocked in the fall of 1982. The 13-inch muskies have been stocked exclusively since 1989. The stocking rate is typically one fish per acre or less. In 1995 for example, about 2,700 13-inchers were stocked. Before that, 9-inchers were stocked in the summer in alternating years. "The smaller muskies just didn't survive as well. I think they were being preyed upon by big bass," Laflin said.

The rationale behind stocking Green River Lake with muskie has always been to restore a native fishery that was destroyed when the lake was impounded. However, there is no evidence of muskie spawning in the lake. It takes about three years for a 13-inch muskie to reach the minimum legal size of 30 inches.

The Bill Norman crankbait, which has an enticing wobble like an injured shad, has been a favorite with many muskie anglers at Green River Lake for a long time, although the lure is not fished as much today as it was in the late 1980s and early 1990s. Silver and black is the most productive color pattern. Some muskie anglers modify the Bill Norman crankbait by adding larger hooks and replacing the metal snap to increase the action.

"I think muskie have a tendency to attack a lure from the side rather than engulfing it from the rear," said Hugh Glasscock, who has fished for muskie in Green River Lake since the early 1980s. "They almost always are hooked in the mouth with the middle treble hook, that's why it's the hook I replace with a larger one. Most times the front and rear treble hooks are foul hooked in the fish's head or gills."

Glasscock, who lives in Lebanon, said May and June are his favorite months to fish for muskies. "The fish are on their postspawn feeding spree, and if you can find a flooded treetop in 10 to 15 feet of water you better be holding on real tight when you bring your bait through it," he said.

At Green River Lake, muskie seem to prefer deadfalls in the deep hollows or slide sites on channel points where whole trees, as well as rocks and stumps, are piled up. Glasscock said that "generally speaking, smaller muskie are caught more often in shallow water, and the bigger fish will hold tight to structure that's near the deep water of the old river channel." Robinson Creek is one of the top muskie-producing embayments on the lake because it has so much deep-water structure

The best time of the year to fish is a matter of opinion. Muskie guide Bill Jarboe knows from experience that he is likely to see more big fish in the fall. He believes muskie fishing is at its best from late September through mid-December. "A lot of people would probably disagree, but I think fall fishing is better," said Jarboe, who lives just a few minutes' drive from the boat launching ramp at the state park. "There's a lot more stable weather."

Early December can be especially productive. "When the lake gets to winter pool, about a week after that, the fishing can get real serious." Jarboe said if there's high water, and they keep pulling the lake, the good fishing can be delayed a week or two.

The best fishing in the fall occurs when muskies move up onto shallow structure in coves and slides on main lake bluffs. "They relate to channels and the edges of flats that extend out into the lake. That's when I catch a lot of muskies on twitch and jerk baits running about 6 to 8 feet deep." Green River Lake has flooded timber in a few coves, but the deeper, V-shaped side hollows do not hold muskies like they do at Cave Run Lake, Jarboe said.

Shad are the key to finding fish. "Basically, if you know what the shad are doing, then you can find the muskies," said Jarboe, noting that Green River Lake has a big forage base of gizzard and threadfin shad. "The shad are constantly moving, in and out of coves." In the fall, muskies are likely to be feeding on 4-inch threadfin shad, Jarboe said, but "later they'll be going after larger prey, 14-inch shad and suckers, when they go on their prewinter feeding binge."

Jarboe said the biggest muskie he has seen caught from Green River

Lake was 49 inches long and weighed 42 pounds. It was caught in March on a Bagley DB2 crankbait. "We have some awfully heavy fish here."

When Jarboe finds a big fish, he camps out. "A big fish will stay in the area. You have to stay on him day and night until he bites and you can put the steel to him." He suggested casting an area thoroughly, changing baits, even leaving for awhile, then coming back to fish the bank again.

"In the fall a lot of times it's a patience game," said Jarboe. "You have to fish the same bank over and over if you know where the fish is." The ideal fall day for muskie fishing is partly cloudy and a little bit windy, with water temperatures in the mid-60s, Jarboe said. "Wind is a big help at finding muskies anytime. A day after a big blow is good fishing."

When water temperatures fall into the low 60s, Jarboe begins slowing up his retrieve, allowing crankbaits and jerk baits to float up. "I like a stop-and-go retrieve," he explained. "When the bait floats up, the muskie thinks it's trying to get away, and he'll blow up on it."

His favorite muskie baits are Suick, a jerk bait, and three crankbaits— the 6-inch Swim Whiz, Bill Norman, and the 1/2- to 1-ounce A.C. Shiner (00). "I like bright colors on almost anything," said Jarboe. "White, white and chartreuse, orange and black, and red. When it's cloudy I fish more subtle colors." He has not had much luck fishing bucktails on Green River Lake. "I guess it's because there aren't any weed beds," he said.

Jarboe has caught several muskies over 30 pounds and believes the next state record muskie could come from Green River Lake. "These are fatter, healthier fish [than are in Cave Run Lake] and they seem to jump a lot more."

Largemouth Bass The largemouth bass fishery is rated good, and the outlook is for numerous 10- to 16-inch fish. "The population is stable and continues to produce larger fish [over 20 inches]," said Laflin. This is despite a 12-inch minimum size limit and fishing pressure that has increased since the early 1990s. Largemouth bass were the third most harvested fished (46,780), behind white crappie and bluegill, according to the 1994 creel survey. Laflin estimated that 68 percent of the black bass in the lake are largemouths.

Fishing guide Tommy Hall has two important tips for bass anglers at Green River Lake. "Downsize your lures and fish red crankbaits in the spring," said Hall, who runs Fish Finder Guide Service.

Bait and site selection vary with the season. Hall fishes shallow coves in the spring. He prefers fishing spinnerbaits in murky water and Sluggo jerk baits or suspending crankbaits like the Rattlin' Rogue or

Thunderstick when the water is clear or clearing. Early in the summer Hall switches to Carolina-rigged lizards, which he fishes on points and drop-offs. "You can also catch largemouth early in the morning on surface lures—Rebel Pop-R, Lunker Lure buzzbait, or Storm Chug Bug—but once the sun comes up it's over," said Hall. He prefers to fish the west shore of the lake, and especially likes Robinson Creek. Other good bass fishing areas are Holmes Bend and Lone Valley. There appear to be more largemouth bass mid-lake. During the dog days of summer, it's best to fish at night, Hall said. "The fishing gets awfully tough." In late summer, look for schooling shad up on flats in Robinson Creek. "In the fall, I fish fast-moving, small baits that correspond to the smaller shad," said Hall. "Also, the water's usually clear and you don't want the bass to get a good look at what you're throwing." The lures of choice are small spinnerbaits and a 1/4-ounce Rat-L-Trap. The upper lake is not that good in the summer. "It's real shallow and the water is much too clear," said Laflin. "Cover is sparse on the flats."

Smallmouth Bass   The smallmouth bass fishery is rated good, and the outlook is for numerous 8- to 12-inch fish and potential trophy fish. The population is centered in the lower lake, with good fishing in early spring in the vicinity of the dam. As water temperatures approach 60 degrees and the lake is on the rise, smallmouth move up into the shallows to spawn.

"Green really has an unsung smallmouth fishery," said Hall. Some of the top fishing areas are the riprap along the face of the dam, the gravel flat on the east shore of the lake, across from the dam, and the riprap dike on the north side of the emergency spillway. Another good spot is a rock hump across from the dam. It is submerged in about 6 or 8 feet at summer pool.

Live bait anglers prefer minnows rigged on a light wire hook, 8-pound test line, and just a split shot of lead cast to the banks. Minnows are great bait in the late fall, throughout the winter, and into early spring.

In early spring, Hall suggested casting a red Model A Bomber crankbait. "Later I fish suspending jerk baits—Rattlin' Rogue or Thunderstick." Warm spring nights, when air temperatures are in the 50s and low 60s, are an excellent time to fish.

Smallmouth make up about 9 percent of the black bass harvest. In an eight-month creel survey in 1994, the average smallmouth harvested was a 13.6-incher, and 1,003 smallmouth were taken. By comparison, the largemouth bass harvest was 8,098. Smallmouth up to 21 inches long were collected by electrofishing in the spring of 1994.

Walleye   The walleye fishery is rated fair, and the outlook is for an expanding population of harvestable fish. Walleye fingerlings were first stocked in Green River Lake in 1993. They began reaching the 15-inch minimum in 1995. Ted Crowell, assistant director of fisheries, said it takes two years for the walleye to grow to keeper size from fry (about 1 1/2 inches long) when stocked. "Our goal has been to develop a self-sustaining population that will contribute to fishing at the lake," Crowell said. "We'd like to see 1 pound of walleye harvested per surface acre of water." Male fish are likely to reach 15 inches before females, said B.D. Laflin. Reports of nice catches of walleye started coming in in 1996, when 3-pounders began showing up.

An estimated 798,501 walleye were stocked the first year of the study. "The strategy was to have a strong initial stocking," Crowell said. "We planned to stock about 450,000, but we had a banner year at the hatchery." The stocking rate for the lake is 50 fish per surface acre of water. The 1994 stocking class numbered 448,000, and 400,000 were stocked in 1995.

Biologists are monitoring walleye reproduction efforts. A spawning run has materialized, and walleye are being caught in the river above the lake and from numerous gravel-bottomed tributary streams. Some of the best fishing in late February, March, and April has been in Robinson Creek.

During the summer, look for walleye in 20 to 30 feet of water off main lake points. Drift spinner rigs baited with live nightcrawlers.

Crappie   The crappie fishery is rated good, and the outlook is for numerous 8- to 10-inch fish, with a few larger fish present (up to 13 inches). Fishing pressure is heavy. More crappie are caught from Green River Lake than any other species. They account for the bulk of the harvest. Based on the 1994 creel survey, Green River Lake yielded 133,124 white crappie, of which anglers harvested 51,028. The white crappie harvest represented 37.41 percent of all fish taken in 1994. B.D. Laflin said the crappie fishery of the mid-1990s is much improved. A 9-inch minimum size limit took effect March 1, 1995. It takes a crappie between three and four years to reach harvestable size. May is the top month for crappie harvest, followed by June and September.

In March most crappie are in submerged creek channels. They move into shoreline deadfalls as the water warms into the 60s. "There's some standing timber in the lake, but it's not attractive to crappie. Almost all of it is in coves. It's stickups or stumps, the limbs have rotted away."

White crappie are by far the predominate species. "There are a very few black crappie, maybe one in a thousand. It's never been more than a remnant population," said Laflin.

White Bass   The white bass fishery is rated excellent, and the outlook is for numerous 10- to 15-inch fish. The lake supports a large population, with some large fish, said Laflin. White bass are largely ignored and only fished for seasonally—during the spring run and in the summer when jumping. "It's a very good population." White bass up to 18 inches have been taken. The spring spawning run occurs in the Green River arm of the lake, and to a lesser extent in Robinson Creek, the lake's largest tributary. A few fish also run up Wilson Creek.

In the summer white bass are easy to catch. They usually start jumping in early July, if temperatures are seasonal. Jump action starts when swarms of recently spawned shad school up and head for open water. Small crankbaits, spinners, and plunker and fly rigs are top lures for casting the jumps.

Night fishing for white bass is less popular with anglers, but there is some trolling done during the day. "Troll along the sides of submerged roadbeds," Laflin said, "and across long, sloping points." A good area is the submerged roadbed between the boat launching ramps at Pike Ridge and Smith Ridge. Small spinners, streamer flies, and plastic curlytail grubs trolled behind deep-diving crankbaits are effective. The main lake mudflats (adjacent to the river channel) and the big rock pile above the dam are also good places to find white bass in the summer.

No hybrid striped bass have ever been stocked in Green River Lake.

Bluegill   The bluegill fishery is rated fair, and the outlook is for a large population of 6-inch fish, with a few 7- to 8-inch fish. The bluegill fishery is largely ignored by anglers.

Spotted Bass   The spotted bass fishery is rated fair, and the outlook is for abundant 8- to 12-inch fish, with very few larger fish present. Laflin estimates that 23 percent of the black bass in the lake are spotted bass. Fish with live minnows, small plastic grubs, and deep-diving crankbaits in the lower lake on rocky banks.

Channel Catfish   The fishery is rated excellent, and the outlook is for numerous 1- to 4-pound channel catfish throughout the lake, and some big flatheads. Be cautioned, however, that Green River Lake is under a fish consumption advisory for catfish (and carp) because of polychlorinated biphenyls (PCBs) contamination. "It's a localized problem," said Laflin. The contaminated area is a 10-acre cove off Ky. 55, about 2 miles above the dam on the Green River arm of the lake. The cove is marked with warning buoys.

Flesh samples showed PCBs above the Food and Drug Administration action level of 2 parts per million. The PCBs came into the lake from a Tennessee Gas pipeline compressor station about a quarter mile uphill from the lake, according to the Kentucky Division of Water. The problem was discovered in the mid-1990s. PCBs had either been disposed of improperly or had been leaking from a compressor. PCBs, banned in the 1970s, were sometimes added to lubricating and cooling oils as a fire retardant. They have been found to work their way up the food chain and accumulate in the eggs and fatty tissue of fish.

Frequent consumption of even low levels of fish contaminated with PCBs may increase the long-term risk of cancer. Persons who decide to eat contaminated fish should take precautions to minimize PCB intake. Only skinless, boneless fillets should be consumed. Roast or bake fillets so the fat melts away. Discard fatty juices. They should never be reused for cooking other foods.

The advisory was issued for the entire lake since fish travel between coves and the main lake seasonally, but the risk is minimal outside the contaminated area. "As far as I know we've never had a fish consumption advisory issued on a major lake," said Wayne Davis, chief of the environmental section for the Kentucky Department of Fish and Wildlife Resources. The site is being studied for a future clean-up.

Tailwater Fishing Opportunities

The tailwaters support what is generally considered a cool-water fishery of smallmouth bass, walleye, and muskie, but spotted bass, drum, catfish, sauger, largemouth bass, redear sunfish, and bluegill are also taken. Because of regulated discharge from the lake, water temperatures in the tailwaters have a maximum of 70 degrees. At normal flow, the tailwaters can easily be waded or fished from a float tube, canoe, or cartop (10- or 12-foot) johnboat. In 1995 the Kentucky Department of Fish and Wildlife Resources built a boat launching ramp just below the dam, off Ky. 55. There is no fee to launch.

Both walleye and sauger are native to the Green River basin. Walleye have been stocked in the river below Green River Dam since the early 1990s. "There's always been walleye in the Green River," said Laflin. "We're seeing good numbers of walleye in the tailwaters, with 4- to 7-pound fish being taken." Laflin said there is some good walleye fishing in the Green River as far downstream as Lock 5, 10 miles north of Bowling Green, off Ky. 185, on the Warren/Edmonson County line.

Muskies are also taken frequently from the tailwaters. The best fishing is in Taylor County section of the river, but there are muskies all throughout the upper Green River system, down to pool number four, near Morgantown, Laflin said.

Green River Lake Dam.

HERRINGTON LAKE

Bluegill ●◄ ●◄ ●◄   Largemouth Bass ●◄ ●◄ ●◄
Catfish ●◄ ●◄ ●◄   Spotted Bass ●◄ ●◄ ●◄
Crappie ●◄ ●◄ ●◄   White Bass ●◄ ●◄ ●◄
Hybrid Striped Bass ●◄ ●◄ ●◄   Tailwaters ●◄ ●◄ ●◄

Location   Herrington Lake, about 30 miles south of Lexington, forms the boundary between Mercer, Garrard, and Boyle Counties. The main access highways are U.S. 27, Ky. 33, and Ky. 152.

For several reasons, Herrington Lake is very different from the other reservoirs profiled in this book. Herrington Lake is open to the public for recreation, but is privately owned. It was constructed by Kentucky Utilities Company (KU) for the generation of hydroelectric power. KU does not own or operate any boat launching ramps or marinas on the lake, disseminate information (brochures or maps) about the lake to the public, or play any role whatsoever in the tourism promotion of the lake or its recreational opportunities. This is ironic since Herrington Lake was the state's first large-scale impoundment and years ago produced some of the finest reservoir fishing the state has ever known.

Herrington Lake filled in the spring of 1925. Very little timber was cut from the lake bed. When the gates of the dam were closed, an immense, forested valley was flooded. Over the years, most of the wood cover has rotted away.

The waters are held back by a 287-foot-high dam on the Dix River, about 3 miles above the confluence with the Kentucky River at High Bridge. The lake's shoreline is developed with vacation homes, boat docks, and fishing camps. KU owns to elevation 760. There are two large no-wake areas—Cane Run Branch and a mile of the main lake from just below Sunset Marina to Kennedy Bridge.

Size   At summer pool (elevation 735-740), the 35-mile lake ranges in size from 2,410 to 2,580 acres and has about 92 miles of shoreline. The winter drawdown reduces the lake to about 2,250 acres at elevation 725. One of the deepest reservoirs in Kentucky, Herrington Lake has an average depth of 78 feet and is 249 feet deep just above the dam. The

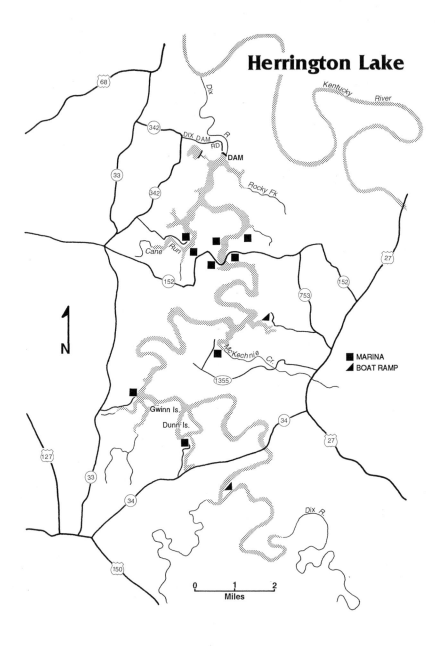

Herrington Lake

68
Dix
Kentucky River
342
DIX DAM RD
R
33
DAM
342
Rocky Fk
Cane Run
152
27
152
753
McKechnie Cr.
1355
■ MARINA
▲ BOAT RAMP
Gwinn Is.
Dunn Is.
34
27
127
33
34
Dix R.
150

```
0        1        2
        Miles
```

N

lower lake has a rugged shoreline, with steep rock walls and long, sloping bedrock points. There are two islands—Gwinn and Dunn—in the midsection of the reservoir.

Trophic State Index (TSI)   Herrington Lake has a TSI of 54, which ranks it as a eutrophic lake (high fertility).

Lake Manager's Office   Kentucky Utilities Company, 1 Quality Street, Lexington, KY 40507, telephone (606) 255-0394.

Managing Fishery Biologist   Kentucky Department of Fish and Wildlife Resources, Central Fishery District, Kerry Prather, District Biologist, 1 Game Farm Road, Frankfort, KY 40601, telephone (502) 564-5448.

Lake Level/Fishing Report Line   To obtain the lake level and anticipated daily hydroelectric power generation schedule, which affects discharges into the tailwaters, call the KU dispatch office at Dix Dam at (606) 748-5221.

Marinas   There are nine marinas. *Chimney Rock Marina*, open year-round, is 4 miles east of Burgin, off Ky. 152. The address and telephone number are 250 Chimney Rock Road, Box 508, Burgin, KY 40310, (606) 748-9065. The launch fee is $5. *Sunset Marina*, open year-round, is 6 miles east of Burgin, off Ky. 152. The address and telephone number are 2040 Kennedy Bridge Road, Lancaster, KY 40444, (606) 548-3591. The launch fee is $5. *Sims Mid-Lake Marina*, open seasonally (April 1 to October 31), is 4 miles south of Burgin, off Ky. 33. The address and telephone number are 238 Cedar Lane, Harrodsburg, KY 40330, (606) 748-5520. The launch fee is $5. *Kamp Kennedy Marina*, open year-round, is 5 miles east of Burgin, off Ky. 152. The address and telephone number are Box H, Burgin, KY 40310, (606) 548-2101. The launch fee is $5. *Pandora Marina*, open year-round, is 4 miles east of Burgin, off Ky. 152. The address and telephone number are 1 Pandora Drive, Box 624, Burgin, KY 40310, (606) 748-9121. The launch fee is $5. *Herrington Marina*, open seasonally (April 1 to November 1), is 4.5 miles south of Camp Nelson, off U.S. 27 and Ky. 1355. The address and telephone number are Herrington Marina, 136 Homestead Lane, Lancaster, KY 40444, (606) 548-2282. The launch fee is $5. *Gwinn Island Marina*, open year-round, is 5 miles north of Danville, off Ky. 33. The address and telephone number are 1200 Gwinn Island Road, Danville, KY 40422, (606) 236-4286. The launch fee is $5. *Royalty's Fishing Camp*, open year-

Herrington Marina.

round, is 3 miles east of Burgin, off Ky. 33 and Curdsville Road. The address and telephone number are 940 Norman's Camp Road, Harrodsburg, KY 40330, (606) 748-5459. The launch fee is $5. *Cane Run Fishing Camp* is 4 miles east of Burgin, off Ky. 152. The address and telephone number are 335 Cane Run Fishing Camp Road, Harrodsburg, KY 40330, (606) 748-5487. The launch fee is $5.

Boat Launching Ramps   There are two boat launching ramps on the lake in addition to the ramps at the marinas. *Red Gate* boat launching ramp is 2 miles west of Bryantsville, off Ky. 27. The launch fee is $5. *Bryant's Camp* boat launching ramp is 5 miles northeast of Danville, off Ky. 34. The launch fee is $5.

Local Tourism Information   Harrodsburg/Mercer County Tourist Commission, 103 South Main Street, Box 283, Harrodsburg, KY 40330, telephone (606) 734-2364 or toll free (800) 355-9192.

Fishing   Herrington Lake, built in a rocky gorge with plateau land above, is one of the most fertile reservoirs in the state. The watershed drains limestone-rich agricultural land, and numerous septic systems from recreation homes around the lake provide additional nutrients. Also, treated sewage from Danville is discharged into the lake headwaters. This influx of nutrients enables the lake to support a huge forage base of gizzard and threadfin shad.

In the early 1960s there were so many adult shad in the lake that an eradication program was undertaken, using rotenone, an organic fish toxicant made from derris root. When added to water, rotenone makes fish gills hemorrhage, causing death by suffocation. The treatment was successful, but it also killed off a remnant smallmouth bass fishery. There also have been numerous winter kills of shad through the years, but the populations always bounce back. For years, threadfin shad were trap netted from Herrington Lake and stocked in lakes across the state.

Since Herrington Lake was the state's first large scale impoundment and was built before fishery science became so sophisticated, the lake has been stocked with just about every predator fish imaginable. Over the years, rainbow trout, walleye, northern pike, striped bass, and smallmouth bass were stocked, but all of these introductions failed to meet project goals.

Today, more than seventy years after the lake was built, the fishery includes largemouth and spotted bass, white bass, hybrid striped bass, bluegill, catfish, and crappie. There is also a large population of longnose gar, which grow up to 3 feet in length. During the spring (late April to early June), schools of gar congregate in coves throughout the lower lake.

"Despite its age, Herrington is stable in terms of fish production," said central district fishery biologist Kerry Prather. "If there are some concerns, it's blue-green algae from increased nutrient loads."

Largemouth Bass   The largemouth bass fishery is rated good, and the outlook is for numerous keeper fish (over 12 inches). Herrington Lake's largemouth bass fishery is one of the five best in Kentucky. "The fish are in excellent condition, and growth is good," said Prather. "In age and growth studies in 1995 we found that largemouth bass reach keeper size before age three. There's more fish over 12 inches than under 12 inches." Herrington Lake is a bass factory, a real producer, Prather said. Typically, bass reach 6.6 inches the first year of growth. By age five, they are 15.3 inches long. Prather said the 1996 creel survey data showed that anglers harvest about 3.96 pounds of largemouth bass per acre and release another 1.69 pounds. "The average fish harvested is a 14.4-incher."

There is trophy fish potential, too. In March and April, large bass

Debbie Wiener with a largemouth bass she caught from Herrington Lake.

are found around shoreline cover in shallow coves and main lake cuts, where drift has collected. "In our sampling we see lots of big fish up to 22 inches. Prespawn that's a 7-pounder, and 5- and 6-pounders are not uncommon at all." Prather said a 20-inch largemouth bass is likely to be about ten years old.

Herrington Lake's bass population is closely monitored. "We check the population each spring," said Prather. "There's a lot of catch-and-release bass fishing; we don't see the harvest impact [found at other lakes]."

Herrington is one of only four major lakes in Kentucky (the others are Dale Hollow, Green River, and Martins Fork Lake) that still has a 12-inch minimum size limit on largemouth bass. "If we go to a 15-inch minimum size limit, it will be because of added tournament pressure brought on by the lower size limit," said Prather.

The best fishing is in the upper lake, above Gwinn Island. "There's more nutrients, and bass are more accessible to anglers [in shallower water]," said Prather. "Numbers increase as you go up the lake. There's a higher density of bass."

Several lower sites are also particularly good for largemouth bass. Some of the best bass fishing embayments in the lower lake are Rocky Fork, Cane Run Branch, McKecknie Creek, and Spears Creek. The mudflats immediately above and below Chenault Bridge (Ky. 34) hold bass in the spring, and "The Hogback," a rock hump on the north end of Dunn Island, is a postspawn bass magnet.

In the spring, Lexington professional angler Alex Thomasson fishes spinnerbaits. He also uses a suspending Smithwick's Rattlin' Rogue, a 5 1/2-inch crankbait with a blue back, silver sides, and an orange belly. "I put some Storm SuspenDots [adhesive-backed lead strips] on the belly of the lure to make it stay down longer," said Thomasson.

Other good lure choices are the jig and pork rind combination, topwater lures, plastic lizards, and tube jigs. "I like to swim the lizards and tube jigs back to the boat rather than bouncing them off the bottom," said Thomasson. "Topwater poppers such as the Rebel Pop-R are best when the fry are in the bushes."

During the summer, most of the bass fishing occurs at night when

Dwight Fugate fishes for bass near Herrington Lake's Gwinn Island.

Texas-rigged plastic worms are fished with success on shelf rock banks. There is some submerged timber left in the lake on deep, main lake points. Bass suspend over this cover in deep water and are very difficult to catch.

Hybrid Striped Bass   The hybrid striped bass fishery is rated good to excellent, and the outlook is for increased numbers of 18- to 20-inch fish. Herrington Lake continues to have the potential to produce a state record hybrid striped bass. "There's a lot of forage and cool water," said Prather. "Three- to five-pounders are common, and the lake produces fish in excess of 15 pounds." It takes about three years for a hybrid striped bass to reach 15 inches. At Herrington Lake there is a twenty-fish daily creel limit for white bass and their hybrids, but no more than five fish may be 15 inches or longer.

Hybrid striped bass have been stocked in Herrington Lake since 1979, after the lake's fabled white bass run went into decline and efforts to establish a population of purebred striped bass failed to meet project goals. "The hybrid is more versatile [than the purebred striped bass]," said fishery biologist Benjy Kinman. "Adult hybrids don't have a preference for cold water and have about the same temperature and oxygen requirements as a white bass." In late summer hybrids can live in the upper levels of the thermocline (a transitional zone where water temperatures drop about a degree a foot). They are tolerant of water in the 70s.

In the past, Herrington Lake has been stocked at the rate of about 20 fish per surface acre of water. Based on 2,500 surface acres of water, that is about 50,000 fish a year. Actual numbers stocked have varied with hybrid availability. For example, in 1993, 65,430 were stocked; in 1994, 80,817; in 1995, 47,000; and in 1996, 60,367. "In the last four years, the stocking rate has varied from 19 to 32 fish per acre," said Prather.

Hybrid fry, hatched at the Frankfort Hatchery in mid-May, are raised on a plankton diet and are stocked at about 1 1/2 inches long in June. "We usually stock what's called the reciprocal cross—a male striped bass and a female white bass," said Prather. The growing hybrids feed predominately on shad. They can consume fish that are about one-third their body length. Thus, a 24-inch hybrid can swallow an 8-inch shad.

At Herrington Lake, hybrids are caught by casting, trolling, or stillfishing live bait at night over lights. A good trolling rig can be made using a deep-diving crankbait, a three-way swivel, and a small lure trailing on an 18-inch leader. A good choice is a white marabou jig or unweighted curlytail grub. Hybrids can also be caught on chicken livers and live crayfish fished on the bottom off points. Fathead minnows, shiners, and live shad drifted at night in open water are other winning combinations. When still-fishing with live bait at night, it is best to just drift. Do not anchor or tie the boat to anything, because if you hook a hybrid, he will find a way to get you hung up. Use your electric motor to position the boat so you will drift out of coves around deep points.

The best months for fishing for hybrids at Herrington Lake are May through August. Rainy, overcast days are prime for hybrid fishing. In early summer there is usually some jump action when schools of hybrids chase swarms of newly spawned shad. A plunker and fly rig is ideal for casting the jumps—a surface plug with a hair jig trailing behind on an 18- to 24-inch leader.

A hot spot on the lower lake is Curds Branch, a cove just above the dam. The small embayment is where hot water discharges from the E.W. Brown Generating Station. There is a submerged hump at the mouth of the embayment, where hybrids often suspend. A rock point extends out into the lake about 75 yards. It is about 16 feet deep over the hump, but the depth drops off sharply to 70 feet. The idea is to position the boat atop the hump and cast a small spoon or spinner out into the deeper water surrounding it. Strip out line and let the lure fall toward the bottom before beginning your retrieve. Hybrids seldom hit the lure on the way down, but the sudden change in direction and speed when you start reeling can trigger a strike. Another hot spot on the lake is McKecknie Branch. Fish the rocky, stair-stepped points.

If there is a drawback to hybrids, it is their downstream migration when the lake is high. "Whenever water goes over the emergency spillway, we lose fish out of the lake," said Prather.

Crappie   The crappie fishery is rated good, and the outlook is for numerous 8-inch fish. "There was a low harvest during the spring of 1996 because of high water," said Prather. "There should be a good carryover of crappie."

In the deep, rocky lake, finding crappie has never been easy, but the quality of fish is high. "We see 10- to 11-inch crappie, they're real chunks," said Kerry Prather. "There's an excellent growth rate for crappie, with no stunting." Herrington Lake supports both white and black crappie. "Most of the harvest is made by local anglers," said Prather. "Fishing pressure is rather low and seasonal." The most recent creel survey in 1996 showed a crappie harvest of about 3 pounds per surface acre of water. "The average length of the white crappie harvested [in 1996] was 9.3 inches, and 10 inches for black crappie." The best crappie fishing is typically during the spring, when the fish move up shallow.

The narrow, winding lake is as difficult for biologists to manage as it is for anglers to master. "It's not conducive to crappie sampling," said Prather. "We've tried trap netting but the lake is too deep so we've had to rely on electrofishing." Many of the same obstacles hinder anglers. It is easier to find crappie in the upper lake, where there are more deadfalls and other downed wood cover. Prather said the dominant species in the upper lake is white crappie. The lower lake has steep, rocky shores. In places there are "forests" of submerged standing timber, but often the treetops aren't visible at the surface. Black crappie are more abundant in the lower lake. "We've seen some fish up to 12 inches," said Prather.

Use a depth finder to locate submerged structure—root wads, stumps, and sunken tree tops. During high water there are enormous drift piles in many of the shallow coves. Sometimes black crappie suspend under this floating debris. Also, do not overlook manmade cover, such as old boat docks, fish attractors, and brush piles tied to standing timber. In the spring expect crappie to be holding in 4 to 6 feet of water. On shallow cover, crappie will often be facing into the wind to intercept food drifting their way, or facing into the sun so that food on the surface is silhouetted by the back lighting.

Successful crappie anglers develop a "milk run" of cover where they have taken crappie before. In a typical day of fishing they may make fifteen to thirty stops while on the water. Small jigs, 1/32- or 1/16-ounce, fished on ultralight tackle and 6-pound test monofilament line are the preferred tackle and lures for spring crappie fishing. White, pearl, chartreuse, and pink are top colors. Curlytail, tube, and marabou jigs work equally well. Cast toward the cover and count down the lure as it falls to find the depth at which the crappie are holding.

White Bass   The white bass fishery is rated good, and the outlook is for stable numbers of 11- to 13-inch fish. According to the 1996 creel survey, the average white bass being harvested is a 10.4-incher.

There is still a spring spawning run, which usually begins in early April, but there are not nearly as many white bass as there were before the mid-1970s. Provided that water levels are adequate, the run extends up the Dix River in the vicinity of the U.S. 27 bridge (between Stanford and Lancaster). Two factors contributed to the decline in white bass: drought, which limited spawning, and increased fertility of the water. "White bass did well in the past, when the lake was less fertile," said Prather.

Three fishing strategies work well in the lake—trolling in the upper lake in March prior to the spring run, still-fishing live minnows at night over lanterns in May, and casting the jumps in June. The "plunker and fly" rig, perfected at Herrington Lake in the 1950s, is a good choice for casting the jumps. A tuft of white hair, tied on a treble hook, is fished on an 18- to 24-inch leader behind a floating, lipped stick bait. The "plunker" gives the rig weight so it can be cast long distances to jumps or blind cast into areas where fish have recently surfaced. The retrieve is rapid and erratic, simulating surface feeding action, and white bass strike the trailing, unweighted "fly" jig.

The daily creel limit is twenty white bass or their hybrids, but no more than five may be 15 inches or longer.

Spotted Bass   The spotted bass fishery is rated good, and the outlook is for numerous small fish. "We see lots of fingerlings and subadult fish when we shock [take samples by electrofishing]," said Prather. Spotted bass are more common in the lower lake. "The average fish being harvested is a 10.8-incher," said Prather. "We don't see many fish over 14 inches." The harvest of spotted bass under 12 inches is encouraged because it lessens competition for food and improves largemouth bass growth rates. Fishing pressure is low on spotted bass, and most catches are incidental. Fishing live minnows or tube jigs is a proven strategy for spotted bass on Herrington's numerous rocky banks.

Bluegill   The bluegill fishery is rated good, and the outlook is for numerous 6- to 8-inch fish. "Heavy predation and restricted spawning areas in the lower lake help to keep bluegill size up, despite the presence of shad," said Prather. There is excellent fishing in late spring drifting crickets along steep rock walls in the lower lake in 10 to 30 feet of water. "If you look in the heads of shallow coves, you'll find colonies of bedding bluegills in May and June," said Prather. Fishing pressure is heavy, and the average bluegill being taken is a 6.1-incher.

Catfish   The catfish fishery is rated good, and the outlook is for numerous fish in the 2- to 4-pound range. Herrington Lake supports both channel and flathead catfish. "No stocking is being done," said Prather. "Both populations are self-sustaining, and there's not much fishing pressure."

Flatheads range in size up to 25 inches, with most fish in the 15- to 18-inch size range. "The average flathead being harvested is a 16.5-incher, according to the 1996 creel survey," Prather said. "And the average channel catfish being taken is 15.4 inches long."

Tailwater Fishing Opportunities

There is no public access by automobile or on foot to the Herrington Lake tailwaters. Fishing in the tailwaters is restricted to artificial lures only. No live bait or organic bait (corn or cheese) is allowed. Anglers must enter the tailwaters by boat from ramps on the Kentucky River, near High Bridge in Jessamine County, off Ky. 29. Canoes, small johnboats, and float tubes are best. Shallow riffles and large rocks make the stream too hazardous for bass boats, especially at low water.

The water being discharged from the tailwaters is ideal for trout but supports only limited populations of warm-water fish (largemouth bass, crappie, and sunfish) within a mile of Dix River's confluence with the Kentucky River. Autumn is one of the best times to fish for trout in the Herrington Lake tailwaters. "The browns get real active in September and October," said trout guide Hagan Wonn. "They congregate below riffles and line up in the chutes." An early start is not necessary when fishing during the summer, Wonn said. "I've had better luck here in the afternoons and evenings." Fishing can be excellent at night, too. "The insect activity really picks up around the dam because of the lights."

Most of the tree-canopied stream can be waded, but there are some deep holes. "At low water, trout tend to congregate below riffles, and in deeper eddies around wood structure." Since water is drawn off the bottom of Herrington Lake, the water temperature in the tailwaters is fairly constant. Waders are recommended because water in the 50s is a bit uncomfortable for "wet legging."

Anglers can expect the average rainbow and brown trout to be 10 to 13 inches long, however holdover trout up to 18 inches are taken from the Dix River every season. Wonn fishes with a 9-foot, 4-weight Sage fly rod. "Four to six-weight is fine here." He recommended a floating, weight-forward fly line and 6X tippet leader when fishing small flies. A 6X tippet is about 3 1/2-pound test.

Dry fly patterns he prefers are the Adams, Elk Hair Caddis, and Royal Trude. Sinking flies (wet flies and nymphs) include the Bead Head Mayfly, San Juan Worm, Wolly Bugger, and Sow Bug. When fishing tandem (two wet flies) or a nymph, he uses a strike indicator, a small, adhesive-backed piece of foam that is attached to the line to help the angler detect a subtle bite when a fly is drifting in the current. It works like a bobber because it allows a sinking fly to be fished at any desired depth.

The 2-mile stretch of the scenic river below Dix Dam was desig-

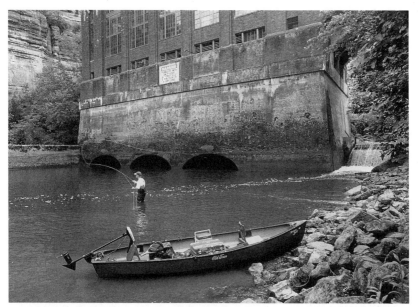

Trout guide Hagan Wonn fly fishes in the tailwaters below the dam at Herrington Lake.

nated as Kentucky's first blue ribbon trout stream in the spring of 1990, in hopes of producing a trophy fishery. But Dix River has never reached the potential biologists envisioned. Several factors might have been at work. First, the stream is so small and so isolated that law enforcement is difficult. Periodically, the stream is hit by violators—fishermen exceeding the creel limit and fishing with bait. Second, several years ago the river was lowered when repairs were made to leaks in Dix Dam, and rocks and other debris were cleared from the base of the dam's emergency spillway. That affected the depth of the pool above the stream's largest riffle and temporarily reduced insect life.

The department's trout specialist, fishery biologist Jim Axon, said he also thought that stocking rates were too high for such a small area, about 2 miles of water. "We were putting in too many fish," he said. "We lowered the stocking rate for browns to increase their size and promote better growth." Initially, only brown trout were stocked. "We started stocking rainbows to provide more fishing opportunities," Axon said. Each year the tailwaters is stocked with about 600 7- to 8-inch brown trout. Some years as many as 4,000 9- to 10-inch rainbow trout are also stocked. There is a 15-inch minimum size limit on brown trout, with a daily creel limit of eight trout, but only three may be brown trout. There is no minimum size limit on rainbow trout.

During summer, assuming the lake is at normal pool, a typical generation schedule is noon to 6 P.M. Heavy rains or a higher demand for electricity might lengthen each day's hours of power generation. A sign on the hydroelectric generating plant below the dam warns fishermen that they have two minutes after the alarm sounds before heavy discharges of water will come through the dam. Hazardous currents can wash boats downstream if they are not securely tied to the bank. "The water only comes up about a foot, but it gets really swift," said Wonn, creating a potentially dangerous situation for anglers.

KENTUCKY LAKE

Bluegill ◄◄◄◄◄◄

Catfish ◄◄◄◄◄◄◄◄

Crappie ◄◄◄◄◄◄◄◄

Largemouth Bass ◄◄◄◄◄◄◄◄

Redear Sunfish ◄◄

Sauger ◄◄◄◄◄◄

Smallmouth Bass ◄◄◄◄◄◄

Spotted Bass ◄◄◄◄◄◄

White Bass ◄◄◄◄

Tailwaters ◄◄◄◄◄◄◄◄

Location Kentucky Lake is 15 miles southeast of Paducah in Trigg, Lyon, Marshall, and Calloway Counties in Kentucky, and extends into Tennessee. The massive reservoir was impounded from the Tennessee River, the Ohio River's largest tributary, which drains 40,569 square miles in parts of seven states. Kentucky Dam is 25 miles upstream of the Tennessee River's confluence with the Ohio River. As many as five thousand men worked on the project, which was six years in construction, between July 1938 and August 1944.

Built by the Tennessee Valley Authority, Kentucky Lake was the first of two "sister" lakes (the other is Lake Barkley) that surround Land Between the Lakes, TVA's 170,000-acre national recreation and demonstration area authorized by President John F. Kennedy in 1964.

Interstate 24, U.S. 68, Ky. 58, and Ky. 962 are the main access highways to the west bank of the lake.

Size Kentucky Dam, a 20-story, 8,422-foot-long structure, impounds the nation's fifth largest river. The 160,300-acre lake (49,511 acres in Kentucky) is 184 miles long. Kentucky Lake reaches summer pool at elevation 359, with a 3-foot drawdown to winter pool, elevation 356. It is connected to Lake Barkley by a canal at Grand Rivers, Kentucky. The canal was completed in 1966.

Trophic State Index (TSI) Kentucky Lake has a TSI of 53, which ranks it as a eutrophic lake (high fertility).

Lake Manager's Office Tennessee Valley Authority, Paris Land Management Office, Box 280, Paris, TN 38242, telephone (901) 642-2041. Ask for *Fish Attractor Map*, a free brochure which details the location of fish attractors in Kentucky Lake and Lake Barkley.

Managing Fishery Biologist Kentucky Department of Fish and Wild-

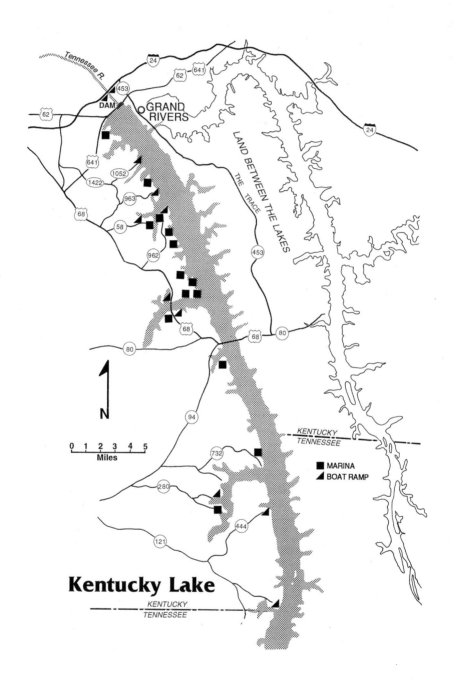

Kentucky Lake

Kentucky Lake.

life Resources, Western Fishery District, Paul Rister, District Biologist, Route 4, Box 785, Murray, KY 42071, telephone (502) 753-3886.

Lake Level/Fishing Report Line   The Marshall County Chamber of Commerce Fishing Hotline is (502) 527-5952. The LBL Fishing Report is (502) 924-2000, ext. 2. The TVA lake information line is (800) 238-2264.

Marinas   There are 14 marinas on the Kentucky portion of the lake. Boat launching is free for guests at private resorts, but a fee (which varies greatly) is charged for other visitors. Parking may be limited at some private marinas, so it is best to call first. *Kentucky Dam Marina*, open year-round (weather permitting), is in Gilbertsville, adjacent to Kentucky Dam Village State Resort Park, off Ky. 62/U.S. 641. The address and telephone number are Box 126, Gilbertsville, KY 42044, (502) 362-8386. There is no fee to launch a boat. *Moors Resort and Marina*, open year-round, is 9 miles south of Kentucky Dam, off Ky. 963. The address and telephone numbers are 570 Moors Road, Gilbertsville, KY 42044, (502) 362-8361 or toll free (800) 626-5472. *Malcolm Creek Resort Marina*, open seasonally (April 1 to October 1), is 5 miles east of Briensburg, off Ky. 58. The address and telephone numbers are 325 Gutherie Drive, Benton, KY 42025, (502) 354-6496 or toll free (800) 733-6713. *Big Bear Resort Marina*, open seasonally (March 1 to October 1), is 8 miles northeast of Fairdealing, off Ky. 58. The address and telephone number are 30 Big Bear Resort Road, Benton, KY 42025, (502) 354-6414. From out of state you may call toll free (800) 922-BEAR. *King Creek Resort and Marina*, open seasonally (March 1 to October 31), is 5 miles southeast of Briensburg, off Ky. 58. The address and telephone numbers are 972 King Creek Road, Benton, KY 42025, (502) 354-8268 or toll free (800) 733-6710. *Hester's Spot in the Sun Marina*, open seasonally (March 15 to November 1), is 3 miles east of Fairdealing, off Ky. 962. The address and telephone number are 350 Hester Road, Benton, KY 42025, (502) 354-8280. *Southern Komfort Marina*, open seasonally (March 1 to November 1), is 3 miles east of Fairdealing, off Ky. 962. The address and telephone numbers are 460 Southern Komfort Road, Benton, KY 42025, (502) 354-6422 or toll free (800) 526-4946.

Shawnee Bay Resort Marina, open seasonally (March 1 to November 30), is 3 miles east of Fairdealing, off Ky. 962. The address and telephone numbers are 1297 Shawnee Bay Road, Benton, KY 42025, (502) 354-8360 or toll free (800) 272-4413. There is no public access to the ramp. *Lakeside Camping Resort Marina*, open seasonally (March 1 to October 31), is adjacent to the U.S. 68 bridge over the Jonathan Creek embayment. The address and telephone numbers are 12363 Highway U.S. 68E, Benton, KY 42025, (502) 354-8157 or toll free (800) 842-9018. *Sportsman's Anchor Marina*, open seasonally (March 15 to November 1), is adjacent to the U.S. 68 bridge over the Jonathan Creek embayment. The address and telephone numbers are 12800 U.S. Highway 68E, Benton, KY 42025, (502) 354-6568 or toll free (800) 326-3625. *Town and County Resort Marina*, open year-round, is 1 mile east of the U.S. 68 bridge over the Jonathan Creek embayment. The address and telephone numbers are 1425 Gardner Road, Benton, KY 42025, (502) 354-6587 or toll free (800) 347-1470.

Kenlake Marina, open year-round, is in Aurora, adjacent to Kenlake State Resort Park, off U.S. 68. The address and telephone numbers are 888 Kenlake Marina Road, Hardin, KY 42048, (502) 474-2245 or toll free (800) 624-4124. There is no fee to launch a boat. *Paradise Resort Marina*, open year-round, is 13 miles east of Murray, off Ky. 972. The address and telephone numbers are 1024 Paradise Drive, Murray, KY 42071, (502) 436-2767 or toll free (800) 340-2767. *The Blood River Campground and Marina*, open seasonally (March 1 to November 15), is 10 miles north of Murray, off Ky. 280. The address and telephone number are 274 Tackle Box Lane, Murray, KY 42071, (502) 436-5321.

Boat Launching Ramps   There are nine boat launching ramps on the western shore of Kentucky Lake in addition to the ramps at the marinas. There is no fee to launch at any of these ramps. *Rocky Point* boat ramp is off Ky. 693, at the mouth of Little Bear Creek. *Bear Creek* public boat ramp is off Ky. 58, adjacent to Big Bear Resort. *Buckhorn Bay Public Recreation Day Use Area* boat ramp is off Ky. 963, adjacent to Moors Resort. *Barge Island* boat ramp is at the mouth of Bear Creek, off Ky. 962. *Marshall County Water Access Area* is off U.S. 68, across the road from Lakeside Camping Resort and Marina, in the Jonathan Creek embayment. *Harry L. Waterfield boat* ramp is off U.S. 68, across the road from Sportsman's Lodge, on the Jonathan Creek embayment. *The Thoroughbred Recreation Area* boat ramp is in the Blood River embayment, off Poplar Springs Church Road (Ky. 614). *Boyds Branch* boat ramp is north of Hamlin, off Ky. 444. *Patterson* boat ramp is at the mouth of Shannon Creek, off Fort Heiman Road.

There are four boat launching ramps on the eastern shore of Kentucky Lake in Land Between the Lakes. There is no fee to launch a boat at any of these ramps. For a map, write to Land Between the Lakes, 100 Van Morgan Drive, Golden Pond, KY 42211-9001, or telephone (502) 924-2000.

Local Tourism Information   Kentucky's Western Waterland, 721 Complex Drive, Grand Rivers, KY 42045, telephone (502) 928-4411 or toll free (800) 448-1069. Marshall County Tourist Commission, 105 Administration Avenue, Box 129, Gilbertsville, KY 42044, telephone (502) 362-4128 or toll free (800) 467-7145. Cadiz/Trigg County Tourist Commission, Box 735, Cadiz, KY 42211, telephone (502) 522-3892. Lyon County Tourist Commission, Box 1030, Eddyville, KY 42038, telephone (502) 388-5300 or toll free (800) 355-3885.

Fishing   A classic flatland reservoir, Kentucky Lake is arguably the state's top fishing reservoir, both in quality of fish and species diversity. Its reputation was made on slab-sized crappie, but in the early 1990s the bass population blossomed into a nationally recognized fishery, attracting considerable attention in the outdoors media. Several professional bass fishing tournaments held on the lake also touted its bass fishery. Excellent populations of largemouth bass and smallmouth bass are present, as well as numbers of larger than average spotted bass. But all fish populations are cyclic, and Kentucky Lake's bass fishery appears to be declining to more normal levels. Sauger, striped bass (in the Tennessee River tailwaters), catfish, white bass, bluegill, and redear sunfish are also present.

Kentucky Lake is clearer than Lake Barkley, with the clearest water found in the embayments on the south end of the reservoir. During the drought years of the late 1980s, Eurasian water milfoil invaded Kentucky Lake due to the extreme clarity of the water, but a return to more normal rainfall levels in the mid-1990s caused the aquatic vegetation to all but disappear. The extensive weed beds were responsible for the bass boom, and also encouraged other species like black crappie and shellcrackers.

Crappie   The crappie fishery is rated excellent, and the outlook is for numerous 10-inch fish and a large year class of sublegal fish to follow. Crappie populations have risen throughout the mid-1990s with the return to normal rainfall levels, which have been responsible for improved spring fishing conditions.

The spring spawning run usually offers the best fishing of the year, provided waters levels are adequate. Low water means clearer water, which makes crappie in the shallows easier to spook. During low water the best fishing is early and late, when light levels are subdued.

Crappie cover in Kentucky Lake includes brush piles, stake beds, stumps, and logs in the backs of bays, where crappie might be in just a foot or so of water. Years of intensive mussel brailing on the main lake has destroyed a lot of the natural cover.

Crappie season can start as early as March if there is unseasonably warm weather. "I've caught crappie in 2 feet of water on the banks in March," said Dick Hudson, who fishes in Bear Creek. In March and early April crappie are usually staging in creek channels, waiting to make their spawning run to the banks. "When they're in deep water, they're so scattered they're hard to catch [in numbers]."

Black crappie spawn before white crappie—at 62 degrees. They thrive in clear lakes. Their numbers have increased significantly since the drought years in the late 1980s. Today, about 30 percent of the crappie in Kentucky Lake are black crappie, and during the spring run numerous quality fish—1 1/2 to 1 3/4-pounders—are caught by anglers.

Hudson prefers to fish with live minnows rather than jigs. He uses a 12-foot crappie pole, rigged with 12-pound test monofilament line, a No. 2 bronze crappie hook, No. 5 split shot, and a cork float. An old-timer who has fished Kentucky Lake for decades, Hudson fishes from a

14-foot johnboat, sitting on the bow, with a crappie pole in one hand and a scull paddle in the other. "Sculling is so much quieter than an electric motor," said Hudson, who can move in close to the bank in the small boat, where he can ease the bait down between gaps in the submerged brush.

In the late 1980s, when Kentucky Lake became so clear, casting artificials on ultralight spinning tackle came into wide use. "Most days a fisherman casting jigs will catch twice as many crappie as the guy using minnows," said crappie guide Jim Pool. "There's no question in my mind that fishing jigs is the most productive method for catching crappie." Pool said he switched to light tackle because of changing fishing conditions. "The clearer water makes the crappie harder to approach. They're warier. If you get your boat too close to the brush pile you're fishing, you'll run the fish right off."

As a general rule, the clearer the water the deeper the spawn. In clear water crappie may spawn in 10 to 12 feet of water and never come to the banks. In murky to muddy water, crappie may be taken from the tops of submerged cover in 3 to 5 feet of water. They may even move up onto the banks, where they are so shallow their dorsal fins are almost out of the water.

Pool has several suggestions for crappie fishermen. Use 6-foot graphite spinning rods, open-face spinning reels, 6- or 4-pound test monofilament line, and 1/16- or 1/32-ounce jigs. The longer rod is helpful in casting farther. Position the boat so you can cast to the edges of the brush pile, Pool said. In the spring, when the water is stained, fish with a 1/16-ounce Roadrunner jig tipped with a lime green curlytail. Other productive color patterns are chartreuse and red, and yellow and white. "You'll catch 90 percent more fish [with lime green]. I prefer to fish with the Roadrunner jig because the flash from its blade makes a big difference when the water is stained."

The retrieve is important, too, Pool said. "Cast over or to one side of the brush pile. After the jig hits the water, raise your rod tip to twelve o'clock [straight up] and reel forward just enough to close the bail. Then begin a slow retrieve. You want the jig to drift slowly over the branches of the brush pile."

Strikes usually happen when crappie dart out of the center of the cover, although fish often suspend on the fringes, so be sure to cast out from the cover a few times. "I keep the rod tip high so that the jig will run shallow as I begin my retrieve," Pool said. "If you let the jig sink too much before you start the retrieve, you'll get hung up in the brush."

Pool suggested "counting down" the lure to assure proper depth once the level at which the fish are located has been determined.

Another productive method is vertical jigging over brush piles or stump rows along drop-offs. The lure of choice for this technique is a 1/16-ounce tube jig, fished on a fly rod or a 12-foot telescopic fiberglass pole.

Some of the top crappie fishing embayments on the west bank are Taylor Creek, Bear Creek, Jonathan Creek, Ledbetter Creek, Blood River, and Cypress Creek. On the east bank, bordering Land Between the Lakes, some of the top crappie-producing embayments are Pisgah Bay, Vickers Bay, and Barnett Creek.

Largemouth Bass The largemouth bass fishery is rated excellent, and the outlook is for numerous 14- to 16-inch fish, and for fish over 18 inches. On March 1, 1997, a 15-inch minimum size limit took effect. Prior to the regulation change, there was a 14-inch minimum size limit, but one fish in the daily creel of six could be under 14 inches. According to a 1995 creel survey, the one bass below the 14-inch minimum size limit accounted for 37 percent of the bass harvest at Kentucky Lake. Biologists sought a more restrictive size limit because they were concerned that declines in 14-inch or smaller bass combined with lower year class production would reduce the number of 15-inch bass by at least 40 percent by the year 2000. Largemouth bass make up about 80 percent of all black bass in Kentucky Lake.

Fishing guide Bill Craig said some of his favorite embayments to fish in late March, April, and early May are Pisgah Bay, Sledd Creek, Big Bear Creek, and Moss Creek. "In the spring I'm mostly fishing coves and shallow water," said Craig. "Water clarity makes it difficult to sight fish. If I can, I fish a jerk bait like a Sluggo." He also floats a plastic worm, hooking it as if it were going to be rigged Texas style, but fished without any weight. Postspawn, after the bass move off the banks, Craig fishes the drop-offs with black and blue jig and pork rind combinations or Carolina-rigged lizards. "I let my pig and jig sink, then I jerk it off the bottom [to trigger a strike]." Craig prefers to fish watermelon- or pumpkinseed-colored lizards on a 4-foot monofilament leader behind a 1-ounce egg sinker. "I can feel the bottom better with the heavier weight." His favorite fall pattern is casting a white spinnerbait or a medium-running shad-colored crankbait in coves and secondary points.

Smallmouth Bass The smallmouth bass fishery is rated good, and the outlook is for few fish over 14 inches. But the population also contains some big fish. The best fishing is along rocky shorelines on the east shore of the lake, especially pea gravel points in the spring.

In the early 1990s, smallmouth bass became something of a bonus fish for Kentucky Lake anglers. Populations increased significantly during the drought years of the late 1980s because of improved water clarity. "There's probably more smallmouth in Kentucky Lake than any of the other lakes, except for Cumberland and Dale Hollow," said Ted Crowell, assistant director of fisheries for the Kentucky Department of Fish and Wildlife Resources. "Smallmouth are all over the lake now, not just the lower few miles." Some top embayments are Higgins Bay, Big Bear, Blood River, Jonathan Creek, and the Kentucky Lake–Lake Barkley canal, where there are miles of riprap (crushed stone) along the banks. The east bank of the lake has more smallmouth habitat because prevailing winds have whipped up waves, which have cleared the banks of dirt, exposing cliffs and piles of chert, reddish-orange chunk rock, which smallmouth seem to prefer.

The potential for a trophy fish is good. Smallmouth up to 9 pounds are being taken. Fishery biologist Paul Rister said night electrofishing surveys in July 1995 showed large numbers of smallmouth on the rocky, main lake points on the eastern shore of Kentucky Lake, which borders Land Between the Lakes. "In 8 1/2 hours we sampled 542 smallmouth," Rister said. "The average harvestable fish was a 14- to 15-incher. The largest smallmouth we got was 21 inches long." Smallmouth now make up about 5 percent of all black bass in Kentucky Lake. They feed primarily on shad and crayfish.

Retired fishery biologist Bill McLemore said autumn fishing is good. "When the water temperature hits 60 degrees, smallmouth react real positive to the banks [during the day]." Fall is also a good time to scout for areas to fish during the summer. "When the lake is down [to winter pool, elevation 354] you can see the fish-holding structure," said McLemore. "The ideal spot is where a creek channel mouth has a rock cliff on one side and a flat with stumps on the other. You're looking for about 20 feet of water [at summer pool]. The availability of deep water nearby is very important to smallmouth."

During the summer months, smallmouth action is strictly early and late in the day, and during the night. When smallmouth are shallow during the warm-weather months a top lure is a chrome Cordell Crazy Shad, a propeller surface bait. A good choice for night fishing is a black buzzbait. Top lures for smallmouth when they are suspended in the channel during the day are a black and blue jig and pork rind combination and Carolina-rigged plastic baits. Good color choices are fire and ice (red and blue) or grape and blue. Cranking river ledges with a Poe's

400 series crankbait or Bagley DB3 will also catch smallmouth in deep water.

Channel Catfish The channel catfish fishery is rated excellent, and the outlook is for numerous 3- to 4-pound fish. The best fishing is in the spring along rocky shorelines and riprap, near boat ramps and bridge abutments. Some of the top areas to fish are Taylor Creek, Ledbetter Creek, and the U.S. 68 bridge near the Fenton boat ramp on the east shore of the lake. Rister said a collapse of the local commercial market for catfish has caused populations to soar.

Blue Catfish The blue catfish fishery is rated excellent, and the outlook is for numerous 3- to 4-pound fish. The best fishing is in the summer on the flats along an old river channel where creek channels intersect in about 20 feet of water. Drift shad cut bait on a bottom-bouncing rig.

White Bass The white bass fishery is rated fair, and the outlook is for moderate numbers of 12- to 14-inch fish. August is one of the best months for white bass fishing. Fishing guide Bobby Leidecker said fishing success is dependent on how much water goes through Kentucky Dam. "The higher the discharge rate, the swifter the current in the river channel, and the more likely that schools of shad will be drawn onto the tops of submerged islands."

The high discharge rates are a result of the drawdown of the lakes to winter pool and the increased electric power demands caused by hot weather.

Late summer is also a prime time for white bass jumps, Leidecker said. Gulls often provide clues to where jumps are taking place. "In mid-September, when cold fronts start to hit, we get a lot of gulls migrating through," Leidecker said. "If you see a bunch of gulls diving down into the water, you better get there fast, because it means the white bass are tearing up the water."

Over the years Leidecker has found that three spots—two on the lower end of Kentucky Lake and one on the Barkley Lake side of the canal that connects the twin reservoirs—consistently produce good catches of white bass. "On a scale of one to ten, these spots are tens," said Leidecker. One of his favorites near the dam has been dubbed "The Goldmine." Another is the submerged island at river mile 27, which is about 5 miles up the lake from the dam.

On top of the island, the water is about 20 feet deep. Move off a few boat lengths, and it plummets to 60 feet. Usually, Leidecker positions the boat so he's casting out into the deeper water of the drop-off. "I

Catfish can be found below Kentucky Dam in the Tennessee River tailwaters of Kentucky Lake.

guess when the current picks up, it alerts the white bass," Leidecker said. "It's like turning on a light switch. One minute you're not catching a fish, the next you're getting a strike on almost every cast." When the fish are right below the boat it is not uncommon to get several jolting hits before a fish is hooked. Sometimes huge jumps erupt, with shad scattering every which way, and the surface of the water is thrashed into a froth. "I've looked down and have seen the water black with fish. Big schools, boiling up," Leidecker said.

Despite the feeding frenzy, some lures work better than others, and not just any retrieve will trigger a strike from the suspended white bass. The lure of choice at Kentucky Lake is a white 1/4-ounce Roostertail spinner. When the fish are deeper, Leidecker fishes a heavier 1/2- to 3/4-ounce Little George. "Cast out as far as you can and count to twenty [while the lure sinks]," Leidecker said. "Then start reeling so the blade is turning steadily. You can't reel too fast. Strikes usually come just as you start your retrieve." If Leidecker does not get a strike right away, he stops reeling and opens the bail of his spinning reel, letting the lure free fall to the bottom. "You've got to bring your lure right up through the middle of them to draw a strike."

A spinner moving at high speed imitates a nervous shad trying to escape, Leidecker explained. "They see it and instinctively go for it. They think it's a shad that's being chased and is trying to get away." A 6-foot spinning rod and open-face spinning reel spooled with 6- to 8-pound test monofilament are ideal for this type of white bass fishing. You need to be able to cast out about 20 yards, to reach jumps, and fish as much water as possible.

"Early in the season, white bass are congregated around the water intakes on the dam," Leidecker said. "The water is about 90 feet deep, but the fish are suspended at about 15 to 20 feet." The trick is to position the boat next to the dam. Then cast out, allowing your Roostertail spinner to sink down (while counting to about fifteen), and drift in toward the water intakes. "Most of the fish you catch will grab the lure right under the boat as you start reeling up," Leidecker said.

By the second week in June, the white bass have moved away from the dam, out into the main river channel, as the shad begin to school up in open water. This main lake pattern continues throughout the summer into early October, when water temperatures drop into the 60s. "About that time, white bass get hard to find. There is a noticeable drop in surface action," Leidecker said. But those last few days of fall fishing for white bass in the jumps sometimes are the best.

Most of the white bass caught from Kentucky Lake run about 3/4 of a pound to 2 pounds. "About 3 pounds is as big a white bass as I've caught out here on the lake," said Leidecker. Occasionally, hybrids or striped bass are caught along with the white bass.

Sauger   The sauger fishery is rated good, and the outlook is for moderate numbers of 14-inch fish. Sauger populations fluctuate and have made a comeback from low levels in the late 1980s during the drought years when the lake was extremely clear. A 14-inch minimum size limit became effective on March 1, 1995. The best fishing begins in October, when sauger begin moving up and down the lake on the river channel flats and ridges where they can be caught by trolling crankbaits or drifting jigs tipped with minnows.

Spotted Bass   The spotted bass fishery is rated good, and the outlook is for moderate numbers of 8- to 13-inch fish. Fish chunk rock and pea gravel banks in the lower lake. Tube jigs, 4-inch plastic worms, and small crankbaits are excellent lures to fish.

Bluegill   The bluegill fishery is rated excellent, and the outlook is for numerous 6- to 8-inch fish. The peak of fishing occurs in May, when bluegills swarm the gravel flats in shallow water to spawn.

Mayfly hatches throughout the summer bring bluegill to the surface, providing plenty of action for fly rod and ultralight enthusiasts. The hatches are most likely to occur on banks that have stands of willows, sweet gum, and sycamore trees.

Heavy predation by largemouth bass may have helped increase the size of bluegill in recent years. Threadfin shad were lost to winter kill in 1994-95 and 1996-97, so bass started feeding more on the large number of 3- to 5-inch bluegill in the lake.

Redear Sunfish (Shellcrackers)   The redear sunfish fishery is rated poor to fair, and the outlook is for fewer numbers of quality fish. "Beginning in 1995 anglers started taking lots of shellcrackers up to 10 inches," said retired district fishery biologist Bill McLemore. "[By 1997] there wasn't a decline in the adult fish [10-and 11-inchers] harvested," said Rister. "But we're seeing fewer smaller fish."

With the disappearance of aquatic vegetation, growth and survival of shellcrackers is not as good as it was in the early 1990s. "A major food source [tiny crustaceans in the weed beds] was lost," said Rister. "And with the weeds gone, it's hard to key on them [locate schools], so fishing has become hit or miss." Fish in the coves on the east shore of the lake. Live bait (crickets, red worms, and wax worms) works best for catching shellcrackers, but you have to fish on the bottom.

Tailwater Fishing Opportunities

There is a very strong argument that the Kentucky Lake tailwaters is the best warm-water tailwaters in the state. The species anglers catch from the Tennessee River include channel and blue catfish, crappie, sauger, and striped bass. A fishing pier just below the dam creates an eddy, offering bank fishermen a good opportunity to cast out into the tailwaters or fish in the quiet water. The "boils," water churned up by the generation of hydroelectric power, are a favorite place to snag spoonbill catfish.

Discharge rates through the dam and the presence of large numbers of shad play major roles in fishing success, particularly for mobile fish species like sauger and striped bass. "We tried to correlate discharge with fish harvest and found that harvest increased the most when the No. 5 generator was on," said Rister. "There's a bigger eddy and more shad tend to move up into the tailwaters to feed on algae."

There are two boat launching ramps in the tailwaters below Kentucky Dam on TVA property. The ramp on the west bank of the Tennessee River is off Ky. 282, and the ramp on the east bank of the Tennessee River is off Peaceful Valley Road, adjacent to the Sanders Archaeological Interpretive Area. There is no fee to launch at either ramp.

Striped Bass The striped bass fishery is rated fair to good, and the outlook is for declining numbers of fish. "The fishery has declined drastically," said Rister. "There are fewer 5- to 7-pound fish, and most fish are about 5 pounds. . . . The striped bass aren't as concentrated as they used to be. A lot of fish seem to have migrated to the Smithland Dam tailwaters on the Ohio River."

The striped bass fishery got started in the early 1990s when huge schools of fish began migrating up the Tennessee River from the Ohio River to feed on shad and skipjack herring. Most of the stripers caught at that time were believed to have been from natural reproduction that occurred during the drought in 1988 when the Ohio River was very low and flowing at a much faster rate. Current is necessary for striped bass to spawn in the wild since the buoyant eggs must drift for several days to hatch. If a striper egg sinks to the bottom, it dies.

As a result of heavy catches and fear that the fishery would go into rapid decline, a supplemental stocking program began in 1992 and the daily creel limit was lowered to three fish (with a 15-inch minimum size limit). Each year 100,000 stripers are stocked in the tailwaters. The fishery peaked in 1993, and the striped bass fisheries in the Kentucky Lake and

Lake Barkley tailwaters are about equal in size and quality. Crankbaits, live shad, jigs (Sassy Shad), and topwater lures are top baits for these tailwater stripers.

Catfish   The catfish fishery is rated excellent, and the outlook is for numerous 3- to 4-pound fish. The Kentucky Lake tailwaters is the state's best catfish hole, and one of the best in the southeastern United States.

During the summer months, channel catfish and blue catfish (*Ictalurus furcatus*) are drawn to the tailwaters in unbelievable numbers to feed on forage fish sucked through the dam and disabled by the turbines. There is a constant chumming of shad, skipjack herring, and minnows.

Thus cut bait, the viscera and gills of gizzard shad, is very effective. Use a small pocketknife to disembowel the shad by making a cut from its anus to the base of the gills. Skipjack herring, which also make good bait, are very aggressive predators and can be caught by casting tiny hair jigs into the boils. Except for days when it is bitterly cold, or very sunny, gizzard and threadfin shad can be captured with long-handled dip nets and cast nets as they school around the riprap and fishing pier, which is an old bridge abutment with guardrails. Some anglers fish chicken livers, catalpa worms, or prepared dough baits. Catalpa worms, 2-inch green caterpillars found on catalpa trees during the summer months, are particularly effective on channel cats.

A bottom-bouncing rig is the best choice for fishing in the current because snags are a problem. Use a three-way swivel, with the 4-ounce lead weight on the bottom, and a 1/0 hook suspended on a 12-inch leader so it will trail to the side in the current and not hang up on the rocks.

Fishing 20- to 30-pound monofilament line on a heavy rod is recommended since huge catfish are present. Catfish suspend on the tops of rock piles, humps, and ledges along the river channel. The best fishing is from a boat.

The blue catfish, often absent from other major lakes in Kentucky, is the dominant species. This catfish thrives in current and is native to the lower Ohio and Mississippi Rivers and their major river tributaries, including the Tennessee, Cumberland, and Green. The blue is similar in appearance to the channel catfish. The most obvious difference is the channel catfish's rounded anal fin.

Blue catfish can attain enormous sizes, with 25-pounders being fairly common. Guess where Kentucky's state record blue catfish was caught. The monster Kentucky Lake catfish weighed 100 pounds and was caught on August 21, 1970, by J.E. Copeland of Benton, Kentucky.

Sauger   The sauger fishery is rated fair to good, and the outlook is for increasing numbers of keeper fish. "Sauger are coming back slowly," said Rister. "There's lots of 10-inch fish in the population now." Sauger populations went into decline during the drought years. There is a 14-inch minimum size limit. Some of the best fishing is at the end of the lock wall, which angles out and creates an eddy.

"Sauger arrive in late fall and stay there all winter," said Rister. "February fishing is best, provided there isn't high water." Fish jigs tipped with minnows or troll deep-diving crankbaits along the ledge of the river channel. Another good way to fish minnows are on a bottom-bouncing rig made with a bell sinker, a light wire hook, and a three-way swivel. It is critical in sauger fishing that the bait or lure bounce off the bottom or remain within a foot or so of the bottom.

Crappie   The crappie fishery is rated good, and the outlook is for numerous 8- to 12-inch fish. "It's a hit or miss situation," said Rister. "If you can catch it when the crappie are there, fishing can be excellent." Cast Roadrunner jigs or fish live minnows on a slip cork set at about 1 to 3 feet deep when crappie are up shallow in the spring.

LAKE BARKLEY

Bluegill ➤➤➤➤	Sauger ➤➤
Catfish ➤➤➤➤	Smallmouth Bass ➤
Crappie ➤➤➤➤	Spotted Bass ➤
Largemouth Bass ➤➤➤➤	White Bass ➤➤➤➤
Redear Sunfish ➤➤➤➤	Tailwaters ➤➤➤➤

Location Lake Barkley, named by Congress to honor the late Senator and Vice President Alben W. Barkley, is 30 miles southeast of Paducah, in Trigg, Lyon, and Livingston Counties. Impounding the Cumberland River, Barkley Dam is located at river mile 30.6. The 7,985-foot-long earthen and concrete dam includes a navigation lock, canal, and hydroelectric plant. Construction began in June 1957 and was completed in July 1966. The main access highways are Interstate 24, the Western Kentucky Parkway, U.S. 62, and Ky. 139.

Size At summer pool (elevation 359), the 57,920-acre lake (42,020 of the acres are in Kentucky) is 118 miles long and has 1,004 miles of shoreline. The lake headwaters end at Cheatham Lock and Dam in Montgomery County, Tennessee. The winter drawdown reduces Lake Barkley to 45,210 acres at elevation 354. Lake Barkley is connected to Kentucky Lake by a canal at Grand Rivers.

Trophic State Index (TSI) Lake Barkley has a TSI of 61, which ranks it as a eutrophic lake (high fertility).

Lake Manager's Office U.S. Army Corps of Engineers, Resource Manager's Office, Lake Barkley, Box 218, Grand Rivers, KY 42045, telephone (502) 362-4236.

Managing Fishery Biologist Kentucky Department of Fish and Wildlife Resources, Western Fishery District, Paul Rister, District Biologist, Route 4, Box 785, Murray, KY 42071, telephone (502) 753-3886.

Lake Level/Fishing Report Line The U.S. Army Corps of Engineers lake information line is (800) 261-5036. The LBL Fishing Report is (502) 924-2000, ext. 2. Another option is (800) 261-LAKE. Follow the recorded instructions to receive reports on the automated information line.

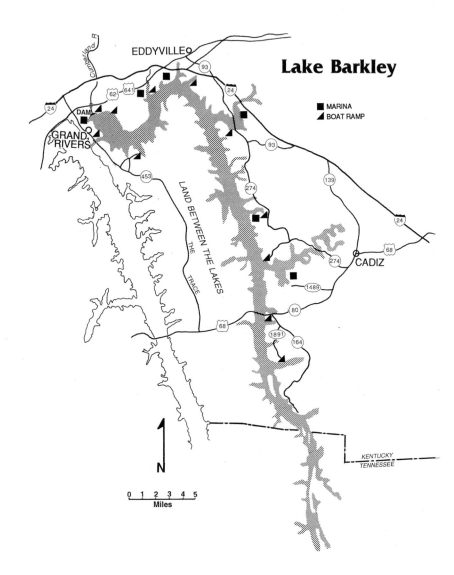

Lake Barkley

■ MARINA
◢ BOAT RAMP

EDDYVILLE

Cumberland R

GRAND RIVERS
DAM

LAND BETWEEN THE LAKES

THE TRACE

CADIZ

KENTUCKY
TENNESSEE

N

0 1 2 3 4 5
Miles

Marinas   There are six marinas on the Kentucky portion of the lake. *Green Turtle Bay Marina*, open year-round, is near the dam, off Ky. 453. The address and telephone numbers are Box 249, 265 Nautical Drive, Grand Rivers, KY 42045, (502) 362-0121 or toll free (800) 844-8862. *Buzzard Rock Marina*, open year-round, is 1 mile west of Kuttawa, off U.S. 62. The address and telephone number are Box 130, Kuttawa, KY 42055, (502) 388-7925. *Kuttawa Harbour*, open year-round, is 1 mile east of Kuttawa, off U.S. 62. The address and telephone number are 1709 Lake Barkley Drive, Kuttawa, KY 42055, (502) 388-9563. *Eddy Creek Marina*, open year-round, is 3 miles south of Eddyville, off Ky. 93. The address and telephone numbers are Ky. 93 South, Eddyville, KY 42038, (502) 388-2271 or toll free (800) 626-2300. *Prizer Point Marina*, open year-round, is 4 miles north of Cadiz, off Ky. 274. The address and telephone number are 1777 Prizer Point Road, Cadiz, KY 42211, (502) 522-3762. *Lake Barkley State Resort Park Marina*, open year-round, is 3 miles west of Cadiz, off U.S. 68/Ky. 80. The address and telephone numbers are Box 790, Cadiz, KY 42211, (502) 924-1131 or toll free (800) 325-1708.

Boat Launching Ramps   There are ten boat launching ramps on the eastern shore of Lake Barkley in addition to the ramps at the marinas. *Canal* boat ramp is off Ky. 453, 1/2 mile south of the Kentucky Lake/ Lake Barkley Canal. There is a $2 fee to launch at the boat ramp, $25 for an annual pass, with discounts available to senior citizens. *Eureka* boat ramp is just above the dam, on Eureka Ferry Road, off U.S. 62. *Boyd's Landing* boat ramp is 5 miles south of Kuttawa, off Ky. 810. *Kuttawa* boat ramp is at Kuttawa, 3 miles off U.S. 62. *Eddyville* boat ramp is 2 miles south of Eddyville, off Ky. 93. *Eddy Creek* boat ramp is 10 miles south of Eddyville, off Ky. 274. *Hurricane Creek* boat ramp is 10 miles north of Cadiz, off Ky. 274. *Cadiz* boat ramp is on the Little River in Cadiz, off Ky. 139. *Devil's Elbow* boat ramp is 6 miles west of Cadiz, off U.S. 68. *Linton* boat ramp is in Linton, just north of the Tennessee line, off Ky. 164.

There are eight boat launching ramps on the western shore of Lake Barkley in Land Between the Lakes. For a map, write to Land Between the Lakes, 100 Van Morgan Drive, Golden Pond, KY 42211-9001, or telephone (502) 924-2000. There is no fee to launch a boat at any of these ramps.

Local Tourism Information   Kentucky's Western Waterland, 721 Complex Drive, Grand Rivers, KY 42045, telephone (502) 928-4411 or toll free (800) 448-1069. Cadiz/Trigg County Tourist Commission, Box 735, Cadiz, KY 42211, telephone (502) 522-3892. Lyon County Tourist Commission, Box 1030, Eddyville, KY 42038, telephone (502) 388-5300 or toll free (800) 355-3885.

Fishing   Lake Barkley is a classic flatland reservoir with a wide variety of structure, from roadbeds, stump rows, and brush piles in shallow embayments to river channel islands, rock bluffs, and gravel points. There are some definite drop-offs along the old river channel, whereas on Kentucky Lake there are a lot of gradually sloping points.

Lake Barkley has the second highest fertility ranking of the reservoirs profiled in this book. A high exchange rate of nutrient-rich waters has made the lake a fish factory. The reservoir's reputation was built on its excellent largemouth bass fishery, but Lake Barkley also offers excellent crappie, white bass, bluegill, and catfish angling opportunities. To a lesser extent, there are populations of spotted and smallmouth bass, sauger, and striped bass (in the tailwaters).

Lake Barkley is a younger lake than Kentucky Lake and has more wood cover. There are extensive mudflats in the mid and upper lake. Also, much shallower than Kentucky Lake, Lake Barkley muddies up more quickly when the wind blows and can produce dangerous waves. The western shore of the reservoir, which borders Land Between the Lakes, has more chunk rock and gravel, and thus clearer water.

Largemouth Bass   The largemouth bass fishery is rated excellent, and the outlook is for numerous 14- to 16-inch fish, with a large population of sublegal fish (9- to 13-inches). On March 1, 1997, the minimum size limit on largemouth and smallmouth bass was raised to 15 inches. Largemouth make up 90 percent of all black bass in Lake Barkley.

Spring fishing is lunker time. Just ask Les Horton of Lexington, who caught a 10-pound, 7-ouncer one afternoon in late April while prefishing for a club tournament. "The bass was on a bush in about 18 inches of water," said Horton. "As soon as I set the hook it took off for deep water." Horton caught the 29 1/4-inch bass on an 8-inch electric blue firetail worm while fishing a pea gravel bank adjacent to the old river channel.

Bill Craig, who guides on both lakes, said big largemouth bass are taken from Barkley every spring as the lake begins to rise and fish move up on the flats. Craig said a good spring strategy is to develop a milk run of spots to fish, based on the water level. "Bass move up and down with the water."

In the spring he likes to fish chartreuse and white spinnerbaits over submerged roadbeds, which Lake Barkley has in abundance. He rigs his spinnerbaits with Colorado or Indiana blades for a slower roll. "I start fishing Barkley when the water warms up to 61 to 62 degrees," he explained, "because I think bass are a little more aggressive over there."

Some of his favorite embayments in April and May are Crooked Creek, Little River, Eddy Creek, and Mammoth Furnace. Carmack and Demumber's Bay also have classic structure, roadbeds, and stump-lined creek channels that snake through broad flats. Try fishing Carolina-rigged lizards postspawn.

In early fall, as the water begins to cool down, bass begin to move up shallow again. Craig's top fall pattern is casting secondary points with pumpkin or orange and red Rat-L-Trap crankbaits.

With the drawdown to winter pool, bass leave the flats and head for 16 to 24 feet of water, where major tributary channels intersect the old river channel. Jig and pork rind combinations or deep-diving crankbaits work well on the bluffs along the old river channel. Position the boat so you can cast parallel to the bank. Try fishing Money Cliff, at river mile 39, for a late fall "wallhanger."

Crappie   The crappie fishery is rated excellent, and the outlook is for a large population of keeper-size fish (10-inchers). Many anglers think Lake Barkley consistently produces fewer crappie and smaller crappie than its sister impoundment, Kentucky Lake, but Bill McLemore said that is not necessarily the case. "Lake Barkley is the second best crappie lake in Kentucky [behind Kentucky Lake]," said McLemore, who retired as western fishery district biologist in January 1997. "But we've had times in the past when the crappie harvest from Lake Barkley exceeded the crappie harvest from Kentucky Lake."

Lake Barkley has good crappie cover. "It's a much younger lake than Kentucky Lake," said McLemore. "The creek channels are well-defined and there's more wood structure on the flats. Mussel brailing activity on Kentucky Lake has destroyed a lot of good crappie habitat."

Lake Barkley's black crappie population has expanded steadily since the late 1980s. "A lot of the bays on the western shore of Lake Barkley are spring fed, so the water is much clearer, to the black crappie's liking," said McLemore. "And you'll find black crappie on the rock and pea gravel points on the eastern shore, too."

But, McLemore said, Kentucky Lake continues to produce more 2-pound crappie than Lake Barkley. "At Kentucky and Barkley a 10-inch crappie weighs about a half pound, a 12- to 13-inch crappie is a 1-pound

Black crappie come to the banks to spawn earlier than white crappie, when water temperatures reach 62 degrees.

fish, and a 15- to 16-inch crappie weighs about 2 pounds." There is a 10-inch minimum size limit on crappie at Lake Barkley, with a thirty-fish daily creel.

"In a way the crappie fishery at Lake Barkley is underutilized. . . . Fishing pressure on crappie in Lake Barkley is considerably less [compared to Kentucky Lake]," especially in the upper end, which is a maze of channels and islands. "I think anglers are intimidated by the rapid changes in depth and are afraid of running aground." You can find crappie on brush piles in submerged creek channels throughout the fall. In winter, crappie move to the main lake channel drop-offs.

Growth rates are similar for both species of crappie in Lake Barkley, but vary from year to year, McLemore said. Sampling of the crappie population by trap netting in 1994 revealed that 83 percent of the population were white crappie. The remaining 17 percent were black crappie. The study revealed that crappie were reaching harvestable size (10 inches) in their third or fourth growing season, but the growth rates of crappie sampled in October 1995 were markedly improved. "Crappie spawned in the spring of 1994 had a mean length of 8 inches, and two-year-old fish had a mean length of 11 inches," McLemore said.

White Bass The white bass fishery is rated excellent, and the outlook is for a large population of fish up to 17 inches in length. White bass in Lake Barkley are on the rise after nearly a decade in decline. "Populations have increased to more normal levels with the return to more seasonal rainfall levels," said McLemore. "During the drought years of the late 1980s there was low flow and less migration." The Little River, the largest tributary to Lake Barkley, didn't have its usual spring spawning runs during the periods of low water, thus white bass reproduction dropped and populations dwindled. Now, "numbers are good and they're chunky fish," said McLemore.

The flow of current from Kentucky Lake through the canal into Lake Barkley is a magnet for white bass. The fishing action heats up in July and August when discharges of water through the two dams increase as electricity demand peaks. "There's a big flat on the Barkley Lake side of the canal where they seem to jump every fall. The water comes through the canal and circles left at the point where a creek enters the lake. [The current] pins the shad up against the [submerged] river bank," said fishing guide Bobby Leidecker. Increased flow pushes forage onto flats around islands and submerged humps. Schools of white bass are usually found along the Cumberland River channel from the mouth of Nickell Branch to the north side of the canal. Trolling and casting the jumps are the preferred fishing methods. Some good artificial lure choices are white roostertails, chrome slab spoons, and shad-colored Rat-L-Trap crankbaits.

Channel Catfish The channel catfish fishery is rated excellent, and the outlook is for numerous 1- to 4-pound fish. The best fishing is in May and June on rocky shorelines and on riprap around the U.S. 68 bridge. Also try shoreline developments such as marinas and vacation homes. Later in the summer, fish at the mouth of Devil's Elbow Creek in about 20 feet of water where the creek channel joins the river channel.

Blue Catfish The blue catfish fishery is rated excellent, and the outlook is for numerous 1- to 4-pound fish. There is good potential for 25-pounders. The best fishing is during the summer where creek and river channels intersect in deep water. Fish cut shad on heavy tackle and hang on.

Bluegill The bluegill fishery is rated excellent, and the outlook is for numerous 6- to 8-inch fish. It is an underutilized, stable population that produces larger bluegill than Kentucky Lake. The best fishing is in May in shallow embayments around willow trees. The Little River embayment is a bluegill hotspot because it has lots of riprap and shallow water. "Bluegills also like small embayments on the Land Between the Lakes shoreline," said Rister. "Where they can bed on the gravel, out of the wind." Fish tiny poppers and foam spiders on a fly rod, or use live bait—crickets, red worms, or wax worms—on ultralight spinning tackle.

Redear Sunfish (Shellcrackers)   The redear sunfish fishery is rated excellent, and the outlook is for 9- to 10-inch fish. In May and June, fish in the backs of bays on the western shore of the lake on pea gravel banks.

Sauger   The sauger fishery is rated fair, and the outlook is for low numbers of 12- to 16-inch fish. There is a small population, but most fish are above 12 inches. A 14-inch minimum size limit took effect on March 1, 1995. Sauger are caught by trolling crankbaits on main lake ridges along the river channel. The best fishing is in the fall.

Smallmouth Bass   The smallmouth bass fishery is rated poor, and the outlook is for low numbers of fish. "We're getting reports of smallmouth bass being caught by anglers drifting live shad around the mouth of the canal where there's lots of ridges and ledges," said Rister. "We're going to sample the area by electrofishing at night. There's lots of chunk rock and gravel on the Land Between the Lakes side of Barkley Lake, and that's where we'll be looking for smallmouth." A 15-inch minimum size limit took effect on March 1, 1997. Smallmouth bass represent about 1 percent of all black bass in the reservoir.

Spotted Bass   The spotted bass fishery is rated poor, and the outlook is for low numbers of fish. An occasional 15-inch fish is caught. Spotted bass make up about 9 percent of the black bass in the reservoir. Fish jigs and other plastic baits on the rocky banks. Kentucky Lake has better spotted bass habitat and a much larger population.

Tailwater Fishing Opportunities

The Lake Barkley tailwaters are very similar to the Kentucky Lake tailwaters in fish species availability and quality. The Cumberland River yields channel and blue catfish, striped bass, crappie, and sauger, plus a bonus fishery—largemouth bass. There is a boat launching ramp in the tailwaters off U.S. 62. There is no fee to launch.

The best fishing is when water is discharged through Barkley Dam's No. 1 and No. 2 generators, which are on the east side of the dam. At certain discharge levels, water is deflected by riprap on the east bank of the river, creating a huge eddy which attracts striped bass and other fish.

There are steps and sidewalks down to the water, but no fishing pier. Bank anglers must stand on the rocks when they fish.

Striped Bass   The striped bass fishery is rated fair to good, and the outlook is for declining numbers of fish. "The fishery has declined drastically," said Rister. "There are fewer 5- to 7-pound fish, and most fish are about 5 pounds. . . . The striped bass aren't as concentrated as they used to be. A lot of fish seem to have migrated to the Smithland Dam tailwaters on the Ohio River."

As a result of heavy catches and fear that the fishery would go into rapid decline, a supplemental stocking program began in 1992 and the daily creel limit was lowered to three fish (with a 15-inch minimum size limit). Each year 100,000 stripers are stocked in the tailwaters. The fishery, which peaked in 1993, is about equal to that of the Kentucky Lake tailwaters in size and quality. Crankbaits, live shad, jigs (Sassy Shad), and topwater lures are top baits for these tailwater stripers.

Catfish   The catfish fishery is rated excellent, and the outlook is for numerous 1- to 4-pound fish. "About 70 percent of the fish caught in the tailwaters are catfish," said Rister. Catfish are smaller and not as numerous as in the Kentucky Lake tailwaters.

Catfish suspend on the tops of rock piles, humps, and ledges along the river channel. The best fishing is from a boat. Cut bait, the viscera and gills of gizzard shad, is the most effective bait, and a bottom-bouncing rig is the best choice for fishing in the current. Use a three-way swivel, with the 4-ounce lead weight on the bottom, and a 1/0 hook suspended on a 12-inch leader so it will trail to the side in the current and not hang up on the rocks. Fishing 20- to 30-pound monofilament line on a heavy rod is recommended since huge catfish are present. Blue catfish, the dominant species, can attain an enormous size, with 25-pounders being fairly common.

Sauger   The sauger fishery is rated fair to good, and the outlook is for increasing numbers of keeper fish. "Sauger are coming back slowly," said Rister. "There's lots of 10-inch fish in the population now." Sauger populations went into decline during the drought years. There is a 14-inch minimum size limit.

"Sauger arrive in late fall and stay there all winter," said Rister. "February fishing is best, provided there isn't high water." Fish the ledges of the old river channel with deep-diving crankbaits or live minnows on a bottom-bouncing rig made with a bell sinker, a light wire hook, and a three-way swivel.

Crappie   The crappie fishery is rated poor to good, and the outlook is for numerous 8- to 12-inch fish. However, crappie are less numerous than in the Kentucky Lake tailwaters. Cast Roadrunner jigs or fish live minnows on a slip cork set at about 1 to 3 feet deep when crappie are up shallow in the spring.

Largemouth Bass   The largemouth bass fishery is rated good, and the outlook is for numerous 12- to 16-inch fish. "Downstream of the Interstate 24 bridge [over the Cumberland River] there is a long stretch of bedrock and chunk rock on the east side of the river," said Rister. "At times there are lots of bass on this bank." Bass fishing could get even better in the future, Rister said, if the U.S. Army Corps of Engineers puts riprap on 4 miles of the river bank as planned. "It would help stabilize the banks from further erosion."

LAKE CUMBERLAND

Catfish ◄●◄ ◄●◄ ◄●◄   Striped Bass ◄●◄ ◄●◄ ◄●◄
Crappie ◄●◄ ◄●◄   Walleye ◄●◄ ◄●◄ ◄●◄
Largemouth Bass ◄●◄ ◄●◄ ◄●◄   White Bass ◄●◄ ◄●◄ ◄●◄
Smallmouth Bass ◄●◄ ◄●◄ ◄●◄   Tailwaters ◄●◄ ◄●◄ ◄●◄ ◄●◄
Spotted Bass ◄●◄ ◄●◄ ◄●◄

Location   Lake Cumberland is about 100 miles south of Lexington in McCreary, Whitley, Laurel, Pulaski, Wayne, Russell, and Clinton Counties. The Cumberland River, more than 700 miles long with a drainage basin of 18,000 square miles in Kentucky and Tennessee, was named in honor of William Augustus, the Duke of Cumberland, by pioneer explorer Dr. Thomas Walker on April 17, 1750. Wolf Creek Dam was built at river mile 460.9, 10 miles south of Jamestown. Construction began on Lake Cumberland in August 1941 but was delayed for three years during World War II. The project, built at a cost of $80.4 million, was opened to the public in August 1952. The main access highways are U.S. 127, Ky. 90, Ky. 192, U.S. 27, and the Cumberland Parkway. The headwaters of the lake extend to the mouth of the Rockcastle River, in Daniel Boone National Forest. The rocky, scenic lake, which is dotted with islands and waterfalls, is one of Kentucky's most significant tourism attractions, drawing swarms of out-of-state boaters and fishermen.

Size   Lake Cumberland has more surface acres of water in Kentucky than any other reservoir, 50,250. Kentucky Lake and Lake Barkley, which extend into Tennessee, are larger overall, but only 49,511 acres of Kentucky Lake are in Kentucky, and only 42,020 acres of Lake Barkley are in Kentucky. Lake Cumberland has 1,255 miles of shoreline at summer pool (elevation 723). One of the state's deepest impoundments, the lake has an average depth of 90 feet. It is about 180 feet deep just above the dam. The winter drawdown reduces the lake to 35,823 acres at elevation 673.

Trophic State Index (TSI)   Lake Cumberland has a TSI of 38, which ranks it as an oligotrophic lake (low fertility). However, the Pitman Creek embayment, 256 acres, has a TSI of 54; the Lily Creek embayment, 144 acres, has a TSI of 59; and the Beaver Creek embayment, 742 acres, has

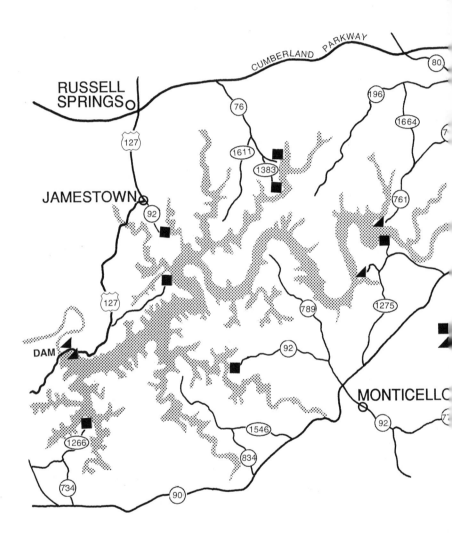

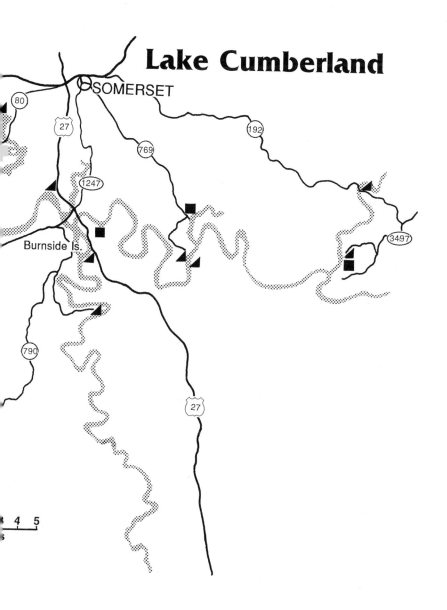

Lake Cumberland

SOMERSET

80
27
192
769
1247
Burnside Is.
3497
790
27

4 5

a TSI of 57. All of these embayments are ranked as eutrophic (high fertility).

Lake Manager's Office   U.S. Army Corps of Engineers, Resource Manager's Office, Lake Cumberland, 855 Boat Dock Road, Somerset, KY 42501, telephone (606) 679-6337.

Managing Fishery Biologist   Kentucky Department of Fish and Wildlife Resources, Southeastern Fishery District, Doug Stephens, District Biologist, 2073 N. Highway 25 West, Williamsburg, KY 40769, telephone (606) 549-1332.

Lake Level/Fishing Report Line   The U.S. Army Corps of Engineers lake information line is (800) 965-5253. Another option is (800) 261-LAKE. Follow the recorded instructions to receive reports on the automated information line.

Marinas   There are eleven marinas on the lake. Boat launching is free for guests at private resorts, but a fee is charged for other visitors. Also, parking may be limited at some private marinas, so it is best to call first. *Grider Hill Dock*, open seasonally (March 30 to October 31), is 12 miles south of Wolf Creek Dam, off U.S. 127. The address and telephone number are Route 4, Box 800, Albany, KY 42602, (606) 387-5501. *Beaver Creek Resort Marina*, open year-round, is 8 miles northwest of Monticello, off Ky. 92. The address and telephone number are Box 377, Monticello, KY 42633, (606) 348-7280. *State Dock at Lake Cumberland*, open year-round, is adjacent to Lake Cumberland State Resort Park, 10 miles south of Jamestown, off U.S. 127. The address and telephone numbers are 6365 State Park Road, Jamestown, KY 42629, (502) 343-2525 or toll free (800) 234-DOCK. *Jamestown Resort and Marina LTD*, open seasonally (April 1 to October 31), is 4 miles south of Jamestown, off Ky. 92. The address and telephone number are 3677 South Highway 92, Jamestown, KY 42629, (502) 343-5253. *Alligator Dock No. 1*, open year-round, is 13 miles southeast of Russell Springs, off Ky. 76. The address and telephone number are 6959 South Highway 76, Russell Springs, KY 42642, (502) 866-3634. *Alligator II Marina*, open year-round, is 13 miles southeast of Russell Springs, off Ky. 1383. The address and telephone number are 2108 Highway 1383, Russell Springs, KY 42642, (502) 866-6616. The fax is (502) 866-4410.

Conley Bottom Resort Marina, open year-round, is 9 miles north of Monticello, off Ky. 1275. The address and telephone number are Route 5, Box 5360, Monticello, KY 42633, (606) 348-6351. The fax is (606)

348-4125. *Lee's Ford Marina Resort*, open year-round, is 5 miles west of Somerset, off Ky. 80. The address and telephone number are Box 753, Somerset, KY 42502, (606) 636-6426. *Burnside Marina*, open year-round, is in Burnside, off U.S. 27. The address and telephone number are West Lakeshore Drive, Burnside, KY 42519, (606) 561-4223. *Buck Creek Dock*, open seasonally (April 1 to December 1), is 7 miles southeast of Somerset, off Ky. 769. The address and telephone number are 9700 Rush Creek Road, Somerset, KY 42502, (606) 382-5542. *London Boat Dock*, open seasonally (April 1 to November 1, weather permitting), is at the mouth of the Rockcastle River, 26 miles southeast of Somerset, off Ky. 192. The address and telephone number are 6779 London Dock Road, London, KY 40744, (606) 864-5225.

Boat Launching Ramps   There are twelve boat launching ramps on the lake in addition to the ramps at the marinas. *Halcomb's Landing* boat ramp is adjacent to the dam, 10 miles south of Jamestown, off U.S. 127. There is a $2 fee to launch at the boat ramp, $25 for an annual pass, with discounts available to senior citizens. *Fall Creek* boat ramp is 8 miles north of Monticello, off Ky. 1275. *Cumberland Point* boat ramp is 8 miles south of Nancy, off Ky. 761. *Pulaski County Park* boat ramp is 3 miles east of Nancy, off Ky. 80. *Fishing Creek* boat ramp is 5 miles west of Somerset, off Ky. 80. There is a $2 fee to launch at the boat ramp, $25 for an annual pass, with discounts available to senior citizens. *Waitsboro* boat ramp is 5 miles south of Somerset, off Ky. 27. There is a $2 fee to launch at the boat ramp, $25 for an annual pass, with discounts available to senior citizens. *Burnside Island State Park* boat ramp is 2 miles south of Burnside, off U.S. 27. *Omega* boat ramp is 12 miles south of Somerset, off Ky. 769. *Cave Creek* boat ramp is 13 miles southeast of Burnside, off U.S. 27. *Bee Rock* boat ramp is 15 miles east of Somerset, off Ky. 192. *Rockcastle* boat ramp is 23 miles southeast of Somerset, off Ky. 192. *Echo Point* boat ramp is on the Big South Fork of the Cumberland River, 8 miles south of Burnside, off Ky. 90.

Local Tourism Information   Russell County Tourist Commission, Box 64, Russell Springs, KY 42642, telephone (502) 866-4333. Somerset/ Pulaski County Tourist Commission, Box 622, Somerset, KY 42502, telephone (502) 679-6394 or toll free (800) 642-6287.

Fishing   Tree-covered hills are the backdrop for this scenic impoundment, which is a favorite with houseboaters. Rocky points and islands give the lake fjord-like grandeur from the air. But Lake Cumberland is not just beautiful. It is also rich in cool-water fisheries. The lake's deep, highly oxygenated waters support the state's best striped bass fishery, the state's largest walleye fishery, and a smallmouth bass fishery that at times offers fishing comparable to Dale Hollow Lake and Kentucky Lake. Other significant fisheries include largemouth bass, crappie, white bass, and catfish. The lake's forage base is composed primarily of threadfin and gizzard shad and alewives, a nonnative species.

Striped Bass   The striped bass fishery is rated good, and the outlook is for numerous 8- to 12-pound fish, with occasional catches of 20-pounders. In the mid-1980s Lake Cumberland was full of huge striped bass, but nobody knew how to consistently catch them. Then, in a surprisingly short time, anglers discovered that fishing with live bait was the key to success, and reality interrupted what had become a dream come true. By the early 1990s the lake's previously unexploited striped bass fishery was reeling from the crush of heavy fishing pressure. Catch rates plummeted and the average size striper being taken declined to 7 or 8 pounds. The 25- to 30-pound fish which had become so commonplace simply disappeared from the creel. But as anglers have seen happen before, a fine tuning of regulations, combined with a few strong year classes coming on, can turn fishing around almost as quickly as a population can go bad.

The fine tuning of the regulations affected both minimum size and daily creel limits. Throughout the 1970s and early 1980s, the limit had been a five-fish daily creel with a 15-inch minimum size limit, then in September 1988 the daily creel was reduced to three fish. On March 1, 1994, the striped bass regulations at Lake Cumberland were further tightened to a 24-inch minimum size limit with a two-fish daily creel. A 24-inch striper is about a three year-old fish.

The striped bass fishery at Lake Cumberland will never be what it was in the 1980s, but it has come a long way back. "Striped bass are coming on big time," said striper guide Tim Tarter. "It was a hot lake back then, but the hype is off now. It's gone through that stage and levelled off [in popularity]."

"There was a decline in harvest but the fishery didn't bottom out," said Ted Crowell, assistant director of fisheries for the Kentucky Department of Fish and Wildlife Resources.

Stripers are currently being stocked at a rate of five fish per acre. One downside of the 24-inch minimum size limit might be that fish have three years instead of two before they can be harvested. During this time, they are subjected to more mortality factors such as disease and stress from being hooked and released, especially during the warm-weather months.

Crowell said the minimum size and creel limits on stripers have been accepted by anglers "as a viable savior for the fishery. There's no indication of widespread violations."

Tarter believes strong year classes in the late 1980s is the reason more 20- to 30-pound stripers are showing up now than in recent years. "Why those year classes, which are now eight- to nine-year-old fish, did better is unknown," said Crowell.

There are even a few trophy fish still being caught from Lake Cumberland, fish in the 40-pound range. "People are starting to fish for stripers in areas of the lake that haven't received much fishing pressure in the past," said Tarter. "I think these areas offer the best chance to catch a trophy fish."

The presence of alewives, a nonnative forage fish, is already having the effect of less surface feeding by the lake's striper fishery. Tarter said alewives have become the number one live bait for stripers at Lake Cumberland. "People who think the fishing is still down aren't adapting to changing fishing techniques."

A guide at Lake Cumberland since 1984, Tim Tarter pioneered live bait fishing on Lake Cumberland using planer boards. He knows that when the water warms in the spring stripers scatter out over the flats at the heads of creeks. In April, stripers are usually cruising shallow flats, or laying on the bottom in the channels, looking up for prey swimming along the lip of the drop-off.

A slip-sinker bottom rig is an excellent choice when stripers are in the channels. Tarter ties a No. 2 treble hook to a 2-foot leader, then attaches the other end of the leader to a barrel swivel. The line from the reel is then threaded through a 2-ounce egg sinker and tied to the other end of the barrel swivel. "A half ounce of lead would hold the bait on the bottom, but I use more to get casting distance," explained Tarter.

Alewives are the bait of choice. "Hook them through one nostril and out the other," said Tarter. He catches alewives with a cast net over lights at night. When the stripers are up shallow he drifts live alewives on planer boards, hooking them up through the chin, using a 3/0 Kahle hook.

As the days warm, stripers move out to deeper water (below 30 feet) where down lines work best. "Mark the fish on the graph, drift over them, and drop the bait into them on a straight line."

Tarter said fishing year-round you have got to be versatile. "One fishing method might not be as exciting, but a striper will fight the same when he's hooked. . . . The whole secret is finding fish. You've got to read the signs."

Striper guide Rick Holt agrees that changing fishing strategies is the key to success, especially in the late summer and early fall, when water temperatures start to drop and striped bass move toward shallower water. "[Unseasonably hot] weather makes the fish go deeper earlier in the summer," said Holt, a striper guide on Lake Cumberland for the past fourteen years. "During the summer we were fishing with live bait at night." In the severe heat of August he caught one fish on the main lake in 90 feet of water. By September, with surface water temperatures still in the mid 70s, stripers may still be in about 65 feet of water at the mouths of major tributaries. "That's why Cumberland is such a good striper lake. There's plenty of [dissolved] oxygen down deep, even when the surface temperatures are high," Holt said. "[In early fall] stripers are typically in water that's about 65 to 67 degrees." In the early fall, Holt switches to fishing plastics on downriggers. The top lures are anything that imitates 5- to 6-inch forage. This includes Sassy Shad and Rat-L-Trap crankbaits and doll flies tipped with curlytail grubs. Chartreuse is a top color. He said the artificials are effective because they have an erratic action that triggers strikes. Early fall is about the only time of the year that Holt fishes this way. "About 90 percent of the time I fish live bait out of a center-console boat."

Trolling is effective, Holt said, because when the thermocline starts to break up, the fish scatter. "When you're trolling you can cover so much more water." After the early morning bite is over, the stripers usually school back up. "This time of year stripers use creek channels as superhighways," Holt said. "They come up from the channels to feed on the drop-offs."

An excellent place to fish for stripers is where the creek channel meets the bank, especially where there are high rock walls. "Wind direction is important, too, when you're fishing open water," Holt said. "The wind pushes plankton and bait to one side. That's the bank you want to fish."

Alewives have altered striper behavior in another way. "The stripers are much deeper because the alewives prefer colder water," said Holt. Later in the fall, when the surface water temperature drops into the 60s, stripers will move into the tributaries in about 20 feet of water, making nighttime feeding forays in the shallows at the heads of creeks.

Actually, the winter pattern might be the most predictable of all because the fish are schooled up tight and will not be far from shad in search of the warmest water, usually over mud flats in the backs of bays.

Striped bass are scattered all over Lake Cumberland, but the best fishing seems to be in the lower lake. Some of top embayments are Beaver, Otter, Wolf, and Lily Creeks.

Smallmouth Bass The smallmouth bass fishery is rated good, and the outlook is for numerous 16- to 17-inch fish. Lake Cumberland is one of the top three smallmouth bass lakes in the state (with Dale Hollow and Kentucky Lake) because of its immense size and large numbers of high-quality fish. "We've had a lot of reports of good catches from anglers in the last two years," said fishery biologist Doug Stephens. "And some big fish, over 20 inches, have been taken."

Smallmouth bass now account for about 20 percent of the black bass harvest by number and 30 percent by weight. According to 1994 creel survey data, the average smallmouth being harvested was a 16.7-incher that weighed 2.23 pounds. "Smallmouth populations have been steady and consistent, maybe slightly improving," said John Williams, assistant district fishery biologist. Williams said fishing pressure on smallmouth bass has remained constant in recent years. There is a 15-inch minimum size limit.

"The best catch and harvest months (for all black bass species) on Lake Cumberland are October, May, September, and November," said Williams. In the late fall, winter, and early spring, fishing activity is concentrated in the lower lake, especially the rocky points close to the old river channel. Jigs, crankbaits, and live minnows are top lures for cold-weather smallmouth bass fishing.

"In the spring when we do electrofishing we see a lot of smallmouth in the Harmon Creek area," said Stephens. Harmon Creek is on the south side of the lake, between Beaver Creek and Camp Earl Wallace (near Monticello).

The best fishing usually occurs in the late fall, between Thanksgiving and Christmas, unless a severe cold snap hits, when water temperatures drop into the 50s. Guide Rick Holt said the best fishing only lasts a few weeks and that the winning strategy is pitching live minnows on light spinning tackle. Holt fishes a 6-foot, graphite spinning rod, with his reel spooled in 6- to 10-pound test monofilament line. He uses a No. 1 Eagle Claw bait hook, which has tiny barbs to keep the minnow from sliding up the shank of the hook. It is important to have lots of hooks and sinkers on hand because hangups are frequent.

Usually Holt fishes without any weight on his line or uses a 1/32-

ounce split shot if the fish are no deeper than 15 feet. "If the fish are over 15 feet deep, I prefer a 1/8-ounce sinker." Split shot are attached to the line about a foot above the hook. "If there's a bluebird sky [a high pressure system] you may have to back off [the banks] and fish as deep as 30 feet."

Lively minnows are important. Hook the minnow up through the lower jaw and into the snout. Cast your bait underhand to the bank and allowed it to sink. "The presentation has to look natural [like a swimming minnow]," said Holt. "You bring the minnow back to the boat slowly, pumping the rod and then letting the minnow sink back down to the next rock shelf below." You'll get hung up a lot if your retrieve is too slow because the minnow will swim into cracks in the rocks.

Bites are pretty obvious. "Most of the time the fish is going to grab the bait and run with it," said Holt. "When the run stops, pick up the slack and set the hook." When the smallmouth are acting finicky, Holt sometimes opens the bail of his reel to give more line to the fish on a run. This prevents the fish from feeling the angler through tension on the line.

But bites are not always so subtle. "Sometimes the fish tries to jerk the rod out of your hand." Smallmouths that are serious about taking the bait do not fool around. If you feel a heavy tug on the line, it is best to set the hook immediately, Holt said.

"The ideal water temperature is 58 to 50 degrees, " Holt said. "The cooler the water, the slower the presentation." In November the bait of choice is a 3- to 4-inch shiner minnow. "When water temperatures drop into the low 50s, I switch to sucker minnows," said Holt. "They give you more action in cold water." Holt said minnows are the best live bait in the fall because smallmouth bass are primarily feeding on shad. "The water is so cool that crayfish and hellgrammites [an aquatic insect] have gone [into the mud for the winter]."

The best banks to fish are those that adjoin the old river channel. "Be sure to fish the insides of points." Banks with big rocks and stair-step shelves are also good bets for smallies, but do not overlook mud or gravel banks with creek channel drop-offs nearby.

Borrowing a trick from striper fishing, Holt said when he fishes a long bank he sometimes puts a second line out to try to catch deep, suspended fish. He puts a shiner out on the deep side of the boat about 30 feet down, then ties the line to a balloon. This allows the bait to drift behind the boat. "A lot of trips you'll catch the biggest fish that way. . . . You don't catch many largemouth bass fishing this way but we do pick up some nice spots [spotted bass]."

Walleye The walleye fishery is rated good, and the outlook is for numerous 18-inch fish. Lake Cumberland is home to the state's largest walleye fishery, with a reputation for producing high numbers of walleye, but few trophy-size fish.

In September 1995, the North American Walleye Anglers (NAWA) "Quest" Championship was held on Lake Cumberland. The professional tournament, won by Dave Hanson with a catch of 42.63 pounds of walleye, focused national attention on the fishery and showed local anglers how to catch the elusive fish. But for the most part, the lake's walleye fishery remains untapped. According to data collected in a creel survey in 1994, about 10,000 walleye (25,000 pounds) were taken from Lake Cumberland. "There's a lot of potential for fishermen," said Ted Crowell, assistant director of the Fisheries Division for the Kentucky Department of Fish and Wildlife Resources. "The opportunity is not really being taken advantage of."

Since the mid-1980s about 350,000 1 1/2-inch walleye fingerlings have been stocked in the lake annually to supplement the natural reproduction that is occurring. "Lake Cumberland has always been the number one priority [in stocking] walleye," said Crowell. "[The lake] gets any excess the hatchery produces."

"Walleye are spawning in several areas around the lake," said Stephens. "On the riprap on the face of the dam, in the lake headwaters, and windswept, rocky points. They run up tributary arms too."

Stephens said walleye are caught all over the lake. "A majority of the fish are being taken [mid-lake] from Fishing Creek down to Harmon Creek," said Stephens. "There seems to be more fish concentrated there."

Vary your strategy according to the season. February through April there is good fishing in the Big South Fork and Cumberland River arms of the lake. In May, the best fishing is off main lake points. "An awful lot of walleye are caught at night," said Stephens. Live nightcrawlers and jigging spoons are top baits when fishing over lights. During the summer months, trolling and drifting spinner rigs are the most effective fishing methods. "During the daytime when there's heavy boat traffic a good number of walleye are caught [on crankbaits] along mudlines," said Stephens. Since walleye have eyes that are very sensitive to light they seem to prefer the muddy water, where they wait in ambush for passing forage. Some anglers use planer boards so they can fish crankbaits far away from engine noise and the shadow cast by the boat.

The summer pattern, which ends when the lake begins to cool down in late September, is the most dependable, if the weather cooperates. "A stable weather pattern is what you want," said walleye guide Fletcher Wise. "What I like is several days of hot, humid weather, with a light south wind." The late summer walleye bite might be as good as it gets off gravel and clay banks in about 25 to 30 feet of water. The best summer strategy is to develop a milk run of fishing spots and try to find active fish. "They move in and out [on the banks]," said Wise. "If you fish an area long enough, you'll trigger a strike." When Wise finds walleye, he sticks with them, methodically fishing an area, back and forth along the depth contour. "Boat control is 80 percent of walleye fishing," said Wise. "You want to go down the bank at the depth they're feeding." If he is marking fish and does not get a strike, he will change the blades on his spinner rig until he finds what color combination they want.

Most of the walleye Wise finds during the summer are right at 30 feet off long, sloping main lake points. The fish are right on the bottom, or suspended just a foot or so up in the water column. Wise said the depth at which you first mark fish on the depth finder in the morning is the depth at which you will find most of the fish that day. Walleye are most likely to be found on drop-offs or near humps or rock piles. Banks with huge slabs or chunks of rock are good too.

Lively bait is important. "I like a fresh, solid nightcrawler," said Wise. "Whenever they get mushy, I put on a new worm." Wise said a spinner rig baited with a live nightcrawler is the lure of choice for catching walleye during the summer. The nightcrawler is rigged on a double hook harness and trails behind a 1 1/2- to 3-ounce lead bottom bouncer, depending on the depth being fished. "I like to fish a 3-ounce bottom bouncer at 30 feet," said Wise.

Wise spools his casting reels in 30-pound braided line (Cabela's Rip Cord), which is tied to the bottom bouncer. The leader is made from 16-pound test Magna Thin monofilament line, and a snap swivel is used to connect the leader to the bottom bouncer, to keep the leader from twisting. Most of the time Wise fishes a 40-inch leader. "Longer snells [leaders] are used when the bottom is smooth. If there's lots of rocks longer leaders tend to hang up too much."

Two No. 4 Cabela's live bait hooks are snelled to the leader about 2 inches apart. "The hooks have short shanks and turned out eyelets," said Wise. A snell knot is used so the hooks will be in line on the leader, allowing the nightcrawler to drift naturally. To snell a hook, thread one end of the leader through the hook's eyelet, then wrap the line around the hook shank eight times. Bring the other end of the leader through the hook eyelet from the opposite side, then pull the line tight. Repeat the process for the front hook. To complete the spinner rig thread four plastic beads on the leader ahead of the front hook. Next, add a quick change blade clip (clevis), also available from Cabela's, which offers the option of using different colored blades without having to retie the spinner rig. The final step is adding another bead and tying a loop into the end of the leader.

"I like to match the color of the blades with the beads," said Wise. "The standard [plastic] bead is a 4 mm salmon egg red." Colors that Wise uses to catch walleye on Lake Cumberland are silver, red and white, chartreuse, pink, gold, and orange. He usually fishes a No. 2 or No. 3 Colorado or Indiana style blade. "When it's real dark or in early morning I use gold or fluorescent blades," said Wise. "The brighter the [light conditions], the lighter [the lure color] I fish."

In late September, after the lake turns over, walleye move out from structure on the banks to deeper water for a couple of weeks, Wise said. "You'd think they would move shallower, but they don't. I've caught walleye as deep as 72 feet." Just after the fall turnover, Wise gives up using nightcrawlers and fishes 4- to 7-inch chub minnows. "You won't catch very many fish during that period, but they'll be good ones, 5 pounds and up." Later in the fall Wise switches from live bait to jigging spoons.

Largemouth Bass   The largemouth bass fishery is rated good, and the outlook is for numerous 12- to 17-inch fish. In the past five years, there has been a noticeable improvement in the largemouth bass fishery. "There's definitely more 12- to 14-inch fish being caught and released," said district fishery biologist Doug Stephens. "Conservation officers are getting quite a few comments about the improved size of fish." Stephens said the reason for the improvement is the 15-inch minimum size limit, instituted in 1989.

The higher-quality bass fishery has led to more angler interest. The hours spent fishing for black bass has increased since 1990 from 80,781 hours to 96,298 in 1994, according to creel data. "In 1994 about 40 percent of the anglers at the lake fished for black bass."

Largemouth bass are more plentiful in the upper lake for several reasons. "There's a little more nutrients available for the production of plankton, more shallow water and associated structure, better spawning cover, and more suitable forage areas."

Bass movements can be tracked according to the seasons. From late March into mid-April, when water temperatures reach into the 60s, fish spinnerbaits around wood structure—logs, deadfalls, and flooded brush—

on mud or gravel banks, and flip jig and pork rind combinations into drift piles at the heads of bays. Postspawn, bass move out to deeper water on rocky banks and are caught on plastic worms, tube jigs, and crankbaits. During the fall and winter, as the lake is falling to winter pool, bass tend to relate more to creek channels.

Tournament angler Ronnie Grant, who lives in Columbia, said fishing the flats is the most reliable fall pattern. "The main lake and the large creeks in the lower lake get better as the fall progresses." A slight rise in water temperature brings bass out of creek channels and scatters them across the sun-warmed mudflats, chasing shad, Grant explained. In the fall and winter (into February, weather permitting) he fishes jig and pork rind combinations. He also uses 4-inch grubs and tube jigs. Sometime Grant puts a piece of foam in the body of his tube jigs to make them float up higher and sink slower. "The colder the water, the lighter jig I fish."

Brush and stumps near deep water should be fished thoroughly because they usually hold bass that are waiting to ambush shad. "Sometimes I start out fishing a spinnerbait because the flashing metal blades resemble scurrying bait fish. Then I switch to a jig."

In clear water, Grant prefers to fish a brown jig, with a brown or orange pork frog. Other favorite color combinations are black with blue and black with chartreuse.

Humps and flats are main targets in the fall. Sometimes Grant casts Carolina-rigged worms, salt craws, or lizards to cover as much water as possible, trying to locate a concentration of bass. "Position the boat in the channel and cast to the hump so the lizard drifts over the drop-off." Grant uses a 1-ounce egg sinker when fishing a Carolina rig.

Rain is a trigger for fall bass at Lake Cumberland. "If the lake rises a foot or two, the bass will really turn on," said Grant. "Look for creek tributaries where stained or dark water is entering the lake. That causes bass to really stack up."

Lake Cumberland produces largemouth bass up to 8 pounds. Some of the top bass fishing embayments are Fishing Creek, Wolf Creek, Beaver Creek and Lily Creek.

Spotted Bass   The spotted bass fishery is rated good, and the outlook for 1997 is for more 12- to 14-inch fish. Heavy fishing pressure on spotted bass has been a factor in helping to boost largemouth bass quality. "Lots of spotted bass have been removed, and that means less competition with largemouth bass," Stephens said. "That's exactly what we wanted [removing the size limit] to do." There has also been a steady decline in spotted bass harvest, reflecting a drop in the population, from 13,411 in 1990 to 1,531 in 1994. The good news is that more large spotted bass are being taken by anglers, with occasional 2- to 3-pounders.

In the fall, fish grubs and tube jigs around wood structure on steep, rocky points in large embayments. When water temperatures fall close to 50 degrees, spotted bass can get real aggressive.

Crappie   The crappie fishery is rated fair, and the outlook is for improved numbers of 10-inch fish. Crappie density is increasing, and there is a strong year class (1994) waiting in the wings. Both white and black crappie are present in the lake. A 10-inch minimum size limit took effect on March 1, 1993.

Adjust your fishing to the season. Top crappie embayments in the spring are Fishing Creek, Pumpkin Creek, and Wolf Creek, above Erv Popplewell's Alligator Marina No. 1. In the summer crappie are scattered and hard to catch, but in the fall they begin schooling up again. However, they can be deep, in 20 to 35 feet of water, over mudslide banks and beech tree deadfalls in deep coves.

Several other areas are also noted for their attraction of crappie. Caney Fork, off Wolf Creek, has quite a bit of good cover, including submerged treetops that are consistent crappie producers. In the past there has been a great deal of fish attractor work, aimed primarily at crappie, in the Conley Bottom area of the lake. At winter pool anglers have created crappie "holes" by sinking cedar trees off channel points.

White Bass   The white bass fishery is rated good, and the outlook is for numerous 12- to 14-inch fish. Some of the best fishing of the year is at night in May and June, when anglers still-fishing live minnows over lights can make big catches on main lake points near the old river channel. Good areas to fish are the channel banks around Lowgap Island.

Catfish   The catfish fishery is rated good, and the outlook is for numerous 14- to 20-inch channel catfish. Flathead catfish are also present and grow to enormous size. Catfish receive little fishing pressure.

Tailwater Fishing Opportunities

The Cumberland tailwaters is arguably the state's best cool-water tailwaters because of its length and the cool-water species it supports—brown and rainbow trout, striped bass, and walleye. It is about 75 miles from Wolf Creek Dam to the Kentucky-Tennessee line. There is a boat launching ramp at Kendall Recreation Area. The launch fee is $2, or $25 for an annual pass, with discounts available to senior citizens.

Trout   On March 1, 1997, trout regulations changed to reflect brown trout being featured as a trophy fish, with a 20-inch minimum size limit and a one-fish daily creel. For rainbow trout, there is no minimum size limit and an eight-fish daily creel.

Ted Crowell, assistant director of fisheries, said the change in trout regulations prompts a shift in the stocking strategy. "We're shifting emphasis to the brown trout, with stockings downstream, to Helms Landing, Winfreys Ferry, Crocus Creek, and Burkesville. And we plan to stock an equal number of rainbow trout closer to the dam." Rainbow trout will also be stocked below Burkesville. "The quality rainbow trout fishery that exists [in the lower river] now is a result of low fishing pressure and rainbows that have migrated into the area," said Crowell. April through November a total of 82,500 rainbow trout and 30,000 brown trout are stocked in the tailwaters.

Trout grow fast in the Cumberland River, which has excellent water quality and abundant food organisms. The dam pumps a fresh supply of cool, oxygenated water into the river daily. Without question, the Cumberland is Kentucky's premier trout river. It has been producing high-quality trout for years, including the state record brown and rainbow. However, there is no conclusive evidence of natural reproduction in the Cumberland tailwaters or tributary streams.

Trout can be caught from the tailwaters year-round. During high flow conditions in winter, trout move around quite a lot and are harder to catch than during the late summer and early fall. Anglers should concentrate on casting the banks with crankbaits fished on light spinning tackle (4- to 8-pound test monofilament).

Fishing guide Randell Gibson has several suggestions. Fish a No. 7 or No. 9 Shad Rap crankbait (gold, silver, or firetiger pattern), a floating/diving crankbait such as a Rapala, or spinners like the Blue Fox or Mepps. Another option is to try to dig out a big fish that is suspended over something. "You've got to fish boiling water," said Gibson, "where a trout is buried down out of the main current, holding to a stump, rock, or log." Gibson also fishes slack water at the mouths of creeks.

Fly fisherman take to the river in summer, when levels stabilize into a daily routine of discharge and slack water. Steve Woodring, of Louisville, who has fished the Cumberland tailwaters for years, said fall is his favorite time to fish for trout below Burkesville because of low water and near-minimum power generation. During low water in the fall, a lot of the river can be waded.

Water-level fluctuation is keyed to rainfall and power generation, which decreases as the lake level drops. The river level normally fluctuates as much as 20 feet throughout the year. "Most years we have fishable river levels by May or June," said Woodring. "The rise and fall of the river dictates the best times to fish, and the fishing strategy. Fishing is good when the river is falling to slack water, and for the first few minutes of the rise when there's a feeding frenzy." Anglers must remember that changes in the river level are delayed the farther downstream you are. For example, there is a ten- to eleven-hour difference from the dam to Cloyd's Landing.

Trout are often concentrated at gravel bars, where creeks enter the river, or at islands. They also locate behind rocks in riffles and in depressions on the bottom. Woodring said trout hide behind rocks on the outside of bends in the river, waiting in ambush for food to drift by; likewise, the drop-offs where eddies meet swift current consistently hold trout.

At low water, the river is a series of shallow pools and riffles, ideal for rafts, canoes, float tubes, and johnboats. Large boats are not recommended because of the shallow water.

Woodring fishes the Cumberland with a 9-foot fly rod, floating line, and a 9-foot leader, tied with a 2X tippet (about 10-pound test line), when fishing sinking flies. "Actually, you could fish with a shorter leader, but I'd use a lighter leader when fishing dry flies." He generally fishes upstream as he wades, casting across the current and letting the fly drift. "If the line stops, you're either hung or you've got a fish."

Some suggested flies:

Japanese beetle. This is a 1/2-inch imitation of an insect that emerges in mid-June and dies by early August after laying eggs. "It is one of my favorite times, when big fish are on the surface," Woodring said.

Stone fly nymph. Tied on a size No. 6 hook, it imitates a large black and brown aquatic insect.

Wolly Bugger. This black fly with a marabou tail imitates an aquatic insect.

Streamers. These 1- to 1 1/2-inch flies tied on No. 4 or No. 6 hooks imitate minnows. Woodring's choice is the Clouser Minnow, with a color preference for brown and white, with metallic tinsel.

Scuds. These flies imitate freshwater shrimp, are tan, gray, or olive, and are tied on a No. 14 hook.

Walleye Spring and fall walleye congregate below Wolf Creek Dam, and many of the walleye that show up in the tailwaters in the fall stay all winter until the spring run. Guide Fletcher Wise will never forget what happened to him on December 27, 1977. "I was walleye fishing for only the second time and I caught a 16-pound, 12-ouncer," said Wise. "And I've been chasing them ever since." Jigs tipped with minnows, crankbaits, and spinner rigs baited with nightcrawlers, or nightcrawlers drifted in the current with just BB split shot will catch walleye in the tailwaters.

Striped Bass   It is the consistent temperature and year-end flow that makes the Cumberland River so appealing to striped bass. "The water temperature doesn't vary by 15 degrees throughout the year," said Randell Gibson, a Cumberland County native and licensed guide who has been fishing the Lake Cumberland tailwaters since the 1960s. "Usually it stays in the mid-50s." For that reason, striper fishing in the tailwaters varies little throughout the year. There is no time of the year when fishing is markedly better, with one exception. When the lake reaches summer pool in the early summer, the discharges into the tailwater become more predictable and consistent. Gibson said the stripers get in synch with the flow regime. "The river goes up and down to certain levels. It's almost on a pattern like tides in the ocean."

The winter months are the toughest to fish because high discharge rates make it difficult to locate the mobile, elusive fish. "High water scatters the shad and the stripers," said Gibson. "Stripers could be anywhere. They key on the shad and really don't concentrate in any certain area."

When discharge rates are high there are also dangerous water conditions to deal with; the river is full of rocks and snags. "This is no place for a small boat when the water is up," said Gibson, who fishes out of a 21-foot, center console aluminum boat powered by a 200-horsepower Yamaha jet drive.

The Cumberland tailwaters yields large stripers. The average striper boated from the river will be considerably larger than the average striper caught from the lake. "Most fish from the river average over 20 pounds. These are trophy head hunting waters. Forty-pounders are a reality." In July 1993, Gibson boated a 51-pounder from the Cumberland tailwaters.

It is the swift current in the river that fishery biologists suspect is drawing stripers into the Cumberland tailwaters from Cordell Hull, a 11,900-acre Tennessee reservoir that has been stocked with stripers since 1984. "Usually there's heavy discharges all through the winter and spring into May," said Gibson. The dam at Cordell Hull is 72 miles downstream of the Kentucky/Tennessee line. "It's fairly typical of stripers [to travel that far]," said Benjy Kinman, statewide fishery coordinator for the Kentucky Department of Fish and Wildlife Resources. "There's also some level of escapement from Lake Cumberland," said Kinman. "I'm convinced young-of-the-year stripers can make it through the turbines." Kinman said the department has never stocked any stripers in the Cumberland tailwaters. Natural reproduction may be occurring in the river in Tennessee.

The most consistent fishing strategy is roaming the tailwater searching for concentrations of shad. "The larger concentrations are usually within 8 to 10 miles of the dam." Gibson fishes in the boils below the dam, at the mouths of creeks, and in areas along the banks littered with submerged trees. A lot of times he motors above the area he is going to fish and drifts through it, casting to both sides of the bank. "Changes in the river level causes them to relocate," said Gibson. "Sometimes when the water comes on they go crazy, and when the flow shuts off they can quit biting. The fishing is very dependent on what happens at the dam."

Gibson mostly casts crankbaits and jigs. His favorite crankbaits are the Super Shad Rap and Cisco Kid, series 600. "I like to crank the Shad Rap and use a stop-and-go finesse retrieve on the Cisco Kid." He sticks with basic colors—usually black and silver or gold and silver. In the boils he fishes chartreuse bucktail jigs and several styles of plastic grubs (straight, curlytail, and eel tail), from 1/2 to 2 ounces, depending on how heavy the current is. "Let it fall, then rip it, so it hops several feet off the bottom." Twenty-pound clear monofilament line spooled on a casting reel and a heavy-action casting rod is the standard striper outfit Gibson fishes.

Anglers wait for the start of a bass tournament on Lake Cumberland. Photograph courtesy of Breck Smither.

LAKE MALONE

Bluegill ⊷ ⊷ ⊷	Largemouth Bass ⊷ ⊷ ⊷
Catfish ⊷ ⊷ ⊷	Redear Sunfish ⊷ ⊷ ⊷
Crappie ⊷ ⊷ ⊷	

Location   Lake Malone is a rocky, scenic lake about 18 miles north of Russellville, in Muhlenberg, Todd, and Logan Counties. The main access highways are U.S. 431, Ky. 973, and Ky. 1293. Built by the Kentucky Department of Fish and Wildlife Resources, in cooperation with the U.S. Soil Conservation Service, the lake opened in 1963. The state-owned lake was impounded from Rocky Creek, a tributary to the Mud River.

Size   The 10-mile, wishbone-shaped reservoir has 692 surface acres and 34 miles of shoreline. A deep, flat-bottomed lake, Lake Malone has a mean depth of 20.8 feet, with a maximum depth of about 35 feet. There is very little fluctuation in the lake's level. Excess water simply spills over the earthen and concrete dam into a small tailwater area.

Trophic State Index (TSI)   Lake Malone has a TSI of 56, which ranks it as a eutrophic lake (high fertility).

Lake Manager's Office   Lake Malone State Park, Highway 973, Dunmor, KY 42339, telephone (502) 657-2111.

Managing Fishery Biologist   Kentucky Department of Fish and Wildlife Resources, Northwestern Fishery District, David Bell, District Biologist, 1398 Highway 81 North, Calhoun, KY 42327, telephone (502) 273-3117.

Lake Level/Fishing Report Line   Anglers can call the Lake Malone Country Store for current fishing conditions at (502) 657-2624.

Marinas   There are two marinas. *Lake Malone State Park Marina*, open May 1 to Labor Day, is 1 mile west of Dunmor, off Ky. 973. The address and telephone number are Highway 973, Dunmor, KY 42339, (502) 657-2110. There is no fee to launch a boat. *Shady Cliff Resort*, open year-round, is 4 miles southwest of Dunmor, off Ky. 1293. The address and

Lake Malone

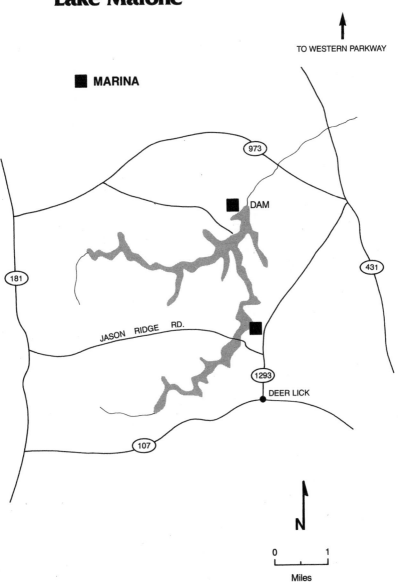

TO WESTERN PARKWAY

■ MARINA

973

DAM

431

181

JASON RIDGE RD.

1293

DEER LICK

107

N

0   1
Miles

telephone number are 530 Lake Malone Road, Lewisburg, KY 42256, (502) 657-9580. There is a $1 fee to launch a boat.

Boat Launching Ramps   There are no boat launching ramps other than the ramps at the marinas.

Local Tourism Information   Logan County Chamber of Commerce, 116 S. Main Street, Russellville, KY 42276, telephone (502) 726-2206.

Fishing   In terms of its size, Lake Malone certainly cannot be considered a major reservoir. But its diverse panfish populations and the fact that Lake Malone offers the best fishing in westcentral Kentucky (an area six counties wide from Bowling Green to Cadiz) are reasons enough to include the reservoir in this book.

According to a 1994 creel survey, there were 31,668 fishing trips per acre (for all species), with an average of 4.1 hours per trip. Anglers harvested 11.31 pounds of panfish per acre out of a total harvest of 44.92 pounds per acre. About 44 percent of the panfish harvest was bluegill, followed by white crappie at 16 percent and channel catfish at 15 percent. There are eight species of panfish in Lake Malone: two species of catfish (channel catfish and yellow bullheads), green sunfish, warmouth, bluegill, longear sunfish, redear sunfish (shellcrackers), and white crappie.

In 1976, 14,000 striped bass fry were stocked in the lake, but few survived to become adults and project goals were never met, so the stockings were discontinued.

Scattered beds of rooted aquatic vegetation are present in the upper end of the lake, and in Bradley Hollow, which is near the dam. A few coves have small stands of flooded timber. Gizzard shad are present, and the lake is fertilized April through June.

Boats are limited to 18 feet, and pontoons are limited to 22 feet. Outboard motors may not be larger than 150 horsepower. There is a ski zone in the lower lake, but outside the ski zone, boats must be operated at idle speed when passing anglers. Buoys mark no-wake areas near the state park and in the Shady Cliff embayment, which has numerous privately owned cabins and small boat docks along the shore.

Largemouth Bass   The largemouth bass fishery is rated good, and the outlook is for increasing numbers of 12- to 15-inch fish since the change to a slot limit. "We're already seeing a tremendous change," said Tom Culton, an avid angler and the Muhlenberg County conservation officer since 1981. "I think we're going to see some excellent fishing this fall or next spring [1998]." Culton said the number of fish in the slot, 12- to 15-inchers that must be released, has increased since the regulation took effect on March 1, 1996.

Lake Malone has a reputation for yielding a few lunker largemouth bass in March when the fish first come up shallow from their winter haunts. "The jig and pork rind is the big fish lure," said Culton. "But the plastic worm is still the most popular, and a very effective lure." Early in the year you should fish run-ins, small tributaries, and wet-weather streams, where warm water enters the lake after spring rains. Largemouth bass up to 8 pounds are caught each spring, and the lake record is thought to be an 11-pound, 4-ouncer caught in December 1981.

Some anglers find Lake Malone difficult to fish because it is deep (the mean depth is 20.8 feet) and steep sided.

"When the bass are in their spawning mode, the secondary points are good fishing because the bass stage there before coming up shallow," said Culton. Later, in the summer, there are lots of jumps when schools of small bass head for open water to chase shad. "That's when a Rat-L-Trap or Tiny Torpedo are very effective," said Culton. "There are also a lot of bass up in the weed beds at that time of year. The Sluggo [a soft plastic jerk bait] catches a lot of fish."

Largemouth bass receive moderate to heavy fishing pressure, and growth is average. It takes a largemouth bass about three and a half years to reach the legal harvestable size. More bass are harvested in May than any other month. There are no spotted bass or smallmouth bass in Lake Malone.

Bluegill   The bluegill fishery is rated good, and the outlook is for numerous 6- to 8-inch fish. More bluegill were caught than any other species, 75,155, according to the 1994 creel survey, and the average bluegill harvested was 6.63 inches long. Drifting meal worms, wax worms, or crickets in 8 to 15 feet of water off deep rock banks is a good way to catch large bream.

Redear Sunfish (Shellcrackers)   The redear fishery is rated good, and the outlook is for numerous 8- to 10-inch fish. "The redear fishing is outstanding," said fishery biologist Robert Rold. "There's a lot of big redear in Lake Malone." In 1994, anglers harvested 5,645 shellcrackers, with an average size of 8.30 inches.

The best fishing of the year is in May and June. Culton suggested working the banks into the heads of coves until a colony of redear spawning beds is located. "I like to fish a popeye [a small jig] tipped with a wax worm," said Culton. A cork or clear casting plug is attached to the line from the reel, and the popeye jig is tied on a 12- to 18-inch leader. This gives the rig enough weight to be cast on light spinning tackle. Retrieve the cork erratically, and the jig will entice strikes from aggressive fish.

Crappie   The crappie fishery is rated good, and the outlook is for increasing numbers of 8- to 10-inch fish. White crappie have good growth and size, but low density. According to 1994 creel survey data, anglers harvested 13,753 crappie, with an average size of 9.84 inches. A lack of spawning habitat in the steep-sided lake may be a limiting factor to crappie populations.

Submerged deadfalls in 10 to 15 feet of water offer the best opportunity for finding schools of crappie. "In the fall I like to fish minnows on a slip cork, drifting the banks around flooded treetops," said Culton. "You can't go wrong."

Channel Catfish   The channel catfish fishery is rated good, and the outlook is for increasing numbers of 12- to 16-inch fish. The population is sustained by natural reproduction and annual stockings. In 1994, anglers harvested 13,299 catfish, with an average size of 13.34 inches. Catfish up to 25 inches are taken by anglers.

Culton said he catches catfish on chicken livers, making underhanded casts with spinning tackle to rock bluffs and around boat houses. "There's also a great deal of limb lining and jug fishing for catfish," said Culton. "At the state park there's plenty of room to fish from the banks."

Tailwater Fishing Opportunities

The tailwater area is a very small creek and supports only limited spring fishing for bluegill.

LAUREL RIVER LAKE

Bluegill ⋈ ⋈ ⋈	Spotted Bass ⋈ ⋈ ⋈
Catfish ⋈ ⋈ ⋈	Trout ⋈ ⋈ ⋈ ⋈
Crappie ⋈	Walleye ⋈ ⋈ ⋈
Largemouth Bass ⋈ ⋈	White Bass ⋈ ⋈ ⋈
Smallmouth Bass ⋈ ⋈	Tailwaters ⋈ ⋈

Location   Laurel River Lake is about 100 miles south of Lexington, in Laurel and Whitley Counties. The dam is about 20 miles east of Corbin, off Ky. 1193, about 1 1/2 miles above the Laurel River's confluence with the Cumberland River. One of the state's most scenic lakes, Laurel River Lake is surrounded by Daniel Boone National Forest and has tree-covered hills and rocky cliffs along the shoreline. The Craig's Creek embayment is spectacular in the fall, when colored leaves are the backdrop for rugged islands and waterfalls. The main access highways are U.S. 25W, Ky. 1193, and Ky. 192.

Size   The 5,600-acre reservoir, which opened in 1974, has 205 miles of shoreline and is 19.2 miles long at summer pool. The summer pool elevation is 1,012 feet. The lake is 206 feet deep just above the dam and has an average depth of 75 feet, making it one of the deepest in the state. Winter pool elevation is 982 feet, reducing the lake to 4,200 surface acres.

Trophic State Index (TSI)   Laurel River Lake has a TSI of 38, which ranks it as oligotrophic lake (low fertility). But the Laurel River embayment, 754 acres, has a TSI of 43, which ranks it as mesotrophic (moderate fertility), and the headwaters of the Laurel River embayment, 316 acres, has a TSI of 52, which ranks it as eutrophic (high fertility).

Lake Manager's Office   U.S. Army Corps of Engineers, Resource Manager's Office, Laurel River Lake, 1433 Laurel Lake Road, London, KY 40744-9739, telephone (606) 864-6412.

Managing Fishery Biologist   Kentucky Department of Fish and Wildlife Resources, Southeastern Fishery District, Doug Stephens, District Biologist, 2073 N. Highway 25 West, Williamsburg, KY 40769, telephone (606) 549-1332.

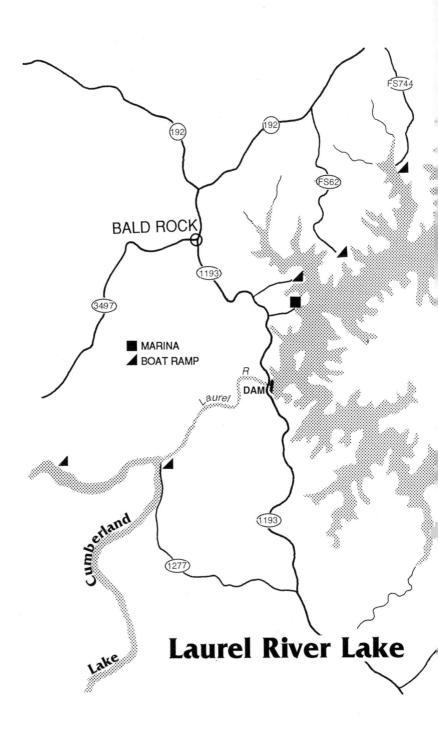

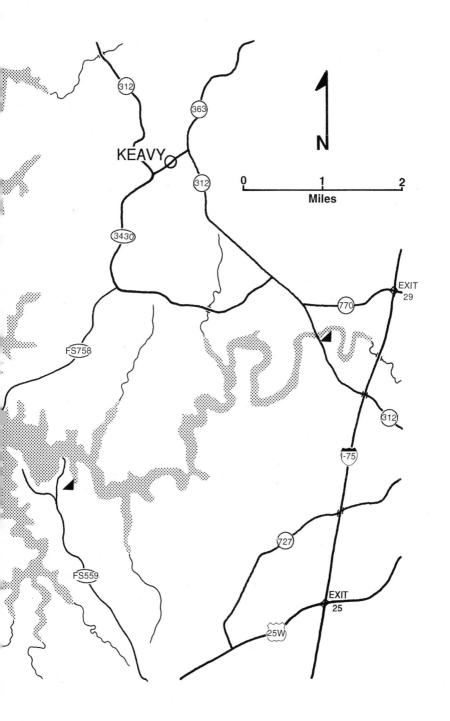

Lake Level/Fishing Report Line   The U.S. Army Corps of Engineers lake information line is (800) 261-5037. Another option is (800) 261-LAKE. Follow the recorded instructions to receive reports on the automated information line.

Marinas   There are two marinas. *Holly Bay Marina*, open year-round, is 18 miles southwest of London, off Ky. 1193. The address and telephone number are Box 674, London, KY 40741, (606) 864-6542. *Grove Marina*, open year-round, is 11 miles west of Corbin, off Forest Service Road 558. The address and telephone number are Box 1483, Corbin, KY 40702, (606) 523-2323.

Boat Launching Ramps   There are seven boat launching ramps on the lake in addition to the ramps at the marina. There is no fee to launch a boat at any of these ramps. *Grove Recreation Area* boat ramp is off Forest Service Road 558, about 10 miles east of Corbin. *High Top* boat ramp is off U.S. 25W, about 7 miles west of Corbin. *Laurel Bridge* boat ramp is at the headwaters of the lake, off Ky. 312, about 2 miles northwest of Corbin. *Flatwoods* boat ramp is off Ky. 3430, about 7 miles northwest of Corbin. *Marsh Branch* boat ramp is off Forest Service Road 744, about 13 miles southwest of London. *Craig's Creek* boat ramp is off Forest Service Road 62, about 15 miles southwest of London. *Holly Bay Campground* boat ramp is off Ky. 1193, about 17 miles southwest of London.

Local Tourism Information   London/Laurel County Tourist Commission, 140 W. Daniel Boone Parkway, London, KY 40741, telephone (606) 878-6900 or toll free (800) 348-0095.

Fishing   Laurel River Lake is a deep, steep-sided highland reservoir with numerous coves filled with flooded timber and many species. Cool-water species—rainbow trout, brown trout, walleye, and smallmouth bass—thrive in the lake's deep, clear waters. Other significant fisheries are largemouth bass, spotted bass, white bass, bluegill, and catfish. Crappie and longear sunfish are also present, along with a small population of shellcrackers (redear sunfish) established between 1988 and 1991 when 450,000 excess 1- to 2-inch fish were stocked. The main forage fish is gizzard shad, and there is a remnant population of threadfin shad from stockings that occurred between 1986 and 1988. In 1996 there was a severe winter kill of shad, but generally threadfin shad overwinter in Laurel River Lake. There are isolated patches of muskgrass, a rooted algae.

Cane Branch, marked by buoys and cable stretched across the mouth of the embayment, is open to fishing, but gasoline motors are prohibited in an effort to cut down on noise and wake. The embayment is a waterfowl management/refuge area, with numerous Canada goose nest boxes and shoreline fields planted in food plots.

For most of the year, Laurel River Lake is extremely clear, especially the lower half of the reservoir.

Rainbow Trout   The rainbow trout fishery is rated excellent, and the outlook is for numerous 10- to 14-inch fish. Occasional catches of 3- to 5-pound fish are made. Laurel River Lake is Kentucky's top trout lake, considering the size and number of trout the lake is able to support. Only three other major impoundments in Kentucky—Greenbo Lake, Paintsville Lake, and Dale Hollow Lake—are stocked with trout. Each February, about 125,000 rainbow trout, reared at the Wolf Creek National Fish Hatchery, are placed in the lake at various locations. Many of the trout become "holdovers," surviving for a year or more, growing at the surprisingly fast rate of an inch a month. They can reach 3 to 5 pounds. A 4-pound rainbow trout is about 20 inches long.

Fishery biologist Doug Stephens said the deep, clear lake is an ideal habitat. "Laurel has what we call a two-story fishery," said Stephens. "There's lots of oxygen below the thermocline, which is uncommon in Kentucky reservoirs." This enables cool-water species like trout and walleye to thrive in the lower depths of the lake, while warm-water species like largemouth bass, white bass, bluegill, and catfish live in the upper few feet. "Rainbow trout prefer water temperatures in the 60s but can take temperatures up to the low 70s."

Fishing depth is greatly affected by water temperature. A lot of trout, including a high percentage of holdovers, are caught in the late fall, winter, and early spring by anglers trolling crankbaits in open water on the main lake. The trout begin to move up in late November when water temperatures drop into the 50s. At times they are as shallow as 5 feet from the surface, suspended over 50 to 60 feet of water. Troll with shallow- to medium-running crankbaits such as A.C. Shiner, Original Rapala, Rapala Husky Jerk, or Shad Rap. Fish with light monofilament line (4- to 8-pound test), either flat line trolling with the lure about 100 yards behind the boat or using planer boards. In late spring and summer a popular way to catch trout is over lights at night, still-fishing with kernel corn, cheese, nightcrawlers, and Berkley Power Baits, a scented dough. When water temperatures are below 68 degrees trout like to suspend over channels in 10 to 20 feet of water, near points, rock walls, and humps that are close to the channel's deep water. Later, in the summer, rainbow trout may go as deep as 20 to 35 feet and concentrate in the lower half of the lake, where there is more oxygen at their preferred temperature range.

Some of the top areas of the lake for trout fishing are Craig's Creek, the rock wall at the mouth of Line Creek, the large peninsula at the mouth of Quaker Branch, and Indian Camp Creek.

Brown Trout   The brown trout fishery is rated excellent, and the outlook is for numerous 10- to 14-inch fish. Occasional catches of 3- to 5-pound fish are made. Eighty thousand brown trout have been stocked in Laurel River Lake since 1995. "This was the first time brown trout have been stocked in a major lake in Kentucky," said Stephens. Brown trout grow faster and much larger than rainbow trout, and are not stressed as much by warm water during the peak of summer's heat. "The brown are an added opportunity," said Stephens. Evaluation of age and growth, plus catch rates, will determine if the stockings will continue in the late 1990s.

Walleye   The walleye fishery is rated good, and the outlook is for lower numbers of 16- to 20-inch fish than in the early 1990s. But the lake still has trophy potential, offering the best opportunity in Kentucky to land a "wall hanger."

Rick Markesbery of Florence, Kentucky, is credited with pioneering the fishery in September 1994. He was the first person to ever fish a spinner rig in the lake and catch large numbers of walleye. "I really believe one of the fish I lost was a 40-incher that weighed over 20 pounds," he said. "Maybe even a state record." His biggest catch was a 35-inch, 15-pounder. Markesbery's discovery led to several newspaper features and national magazine articles, which put Laurel River Lake's walleye fishery on the map.

The fishery is sustained by stocking. Since 1986 more than 2.8 million walleye have been stocked in Laurel. The annual stocking rate is fifty fish per acre, or 280,000 a year. Biologists are not sure if walleye natural reproduction is occurring in Laurel River Lake to supplement the stocking program. All of the stocked walleye are northern strain fish, who normally spawn in lake environments. The southern strain of walleye, like those found in the Cumberland River basin, were river spawners, who needed gravel substrate and current to reproduce. It is uncertain if native walleye were present in the Laurel River when the lake was impounded.

Fishery biologist John Williams's radio telemetry study, completed in 1996, answered a lot of questions about walleye movement in Laurel

River Lake. "A spring run occurs in March, with fish migrating all the way up the Laurel River arm of the lake to the Corbin City Dam," said Williams. "By the end of May, walleye have moved out, and there aren't many fish up the Laurel River arm of the lake."

During the summer, walleye spend most of their time in timbered coves in the lower lake. "They stay there until dark, then roam around the edge of the timber and go out to the shoreline at the mouth of the cove." Casting or trolling deep-diving crankbaits is a good late-evening and nighttime fishing strategy. Walleye can be caught at night over lights during the summer. Fish on the dark side of the boat, away from the light. Jigging spoons and weight-forward spinners baited with nightcrawlers are popular lures.

Walleye also suspend out in the middle of the lake, close by schools of shad. Sand Island, just up Craig's Creek embayment from Holly Bay Marina, is a good place to start a search for suspended fish. Another good place to fish is the submerged hump just off the big island above the dam.

During the day, a live nightcrawler fished on a spinner rig is the presentation of choice. "I rig a nightcrawler on a double hook harness so it will trail behind a 1 1/2- or 2-ounce lead bottom bouncer," said Markesbery. "Ideally, you want the nightcrawler to be on a 2- to 4-foot leader." Considering the rocky lake's abundance of stumps and drift, though, 18- to 36-inch leaders are more practical. He injects air into the nightcrawler with a Lindy worm blower to make it float up, since walleye prefer their prey just off the bottom.

When walleye fishing in clear water, Markesbery spools his spinning reels in 6- or 8-pound test monofilament with two black finish size 4 Mustad Accupoint hooks snelled to the leader about 2 inches apart. "The hooks have short shanks and turned out eyelets," said Markesbery. "You don't need a big hook to catch a big walleye." A snell knot is used so the hooks will be in line on the leader, allowing the nightcrawler to drift naturally. To snell a hook, thread one end of the leader through the hook's eyelet, then wrap the line around the hook shank eight times," said Markesbery. "Bring the other end of the leader through the hook eyelet from the opposite side, and pull the line tight." Repeat the process for the front hook. Then thread four small, orange plastic beads on the leader ahead of the front hook. Next add a plastic spinner snap, which enables you to change blade colors or sizes without tying a new rig. Markesbery finishes his lure by adding another plastic bead.

"I prefer a No. 4 Colorado blade in silver finish because it imitates the flash of a baitfish," said Markesbery. In murky water, Markesbery sometimes switches to chartreuse blades or two-tone colored blades—chartreuse, red, or orange combinations—for added visibility. A snap swivel is used to connect the leader to the bottom bouncer to prevent the leader from twisting.

Markesbery likes to fish stair-step points, submerged humps, drop-offs, and river channel intersections. He especially likes points where there is a transition area between rock, sand, and mud. "On a stair-step point you'll often find the baitfish on one level and the walleye just below them," said Markesbery. "When the walleye feeds he swims up to take the bait, so you want your lure presentation a couple of feet above the fish." The ideal walleye point is one that stair-steps down to the deep water of a submerged creek or river channel. The series of drops become food shelves that attract shad, which in turn attract walleye.

Markesbery said the goal is to find walleye that are actively feeding. "For example, on a point you might mark some fish at 80 feet that are inactive, while the active, feeding fish may be up at 40 feet, or shallower. The active walleye will be up on a hump or point mingling with the shad."

In the summer, heavy boating traffic creates mudlines, which spell opportunity for walleye anglers. The cloud of suspended soil particles creates darker water rich in plankton, which draws baitfish. If you see a mudline, fish it by casting or trolling crankbaits. Markesbery suggested the Storm Deep Thunderstick, Rattlin' Fat Wart, and Rapala ShadRap. Proven color patterns include firetiger, rainbow trout, and black and silver.

Markesbery suggested fishing in the Craig's Creek embayment. He also likes the point at the mouth of Marsh Branch and the points at the mouth of Quaker Branch.

Largemouth Bass   The largemouth bass fishery is rated fair, and the outlook is for numerous 12- to 15-inch fish. The best fishing is in the Laurel River arm of the lake, which is more fertile.

On March 1, 1997, a 15-inch minimum size limit took effect. An angler opinion survey in 1995 showed strong support for the regulation change. The expected benefits are increased numbers of bass 15 inches and larger caught and harvested. About 45 percent of the black bass harvested from the lake are largemouth bass.

The best bass fishing of the year is in the upper lake during the spring and early summer. "It's especially good at night, when the bass move up on the flats," said Gerald Baker, a Laurel County native who has been fishing the lake frequently during the past thirteen years. "Be sure to fish those little timbered pockets off the main river." In late May and June, as surface water temperatures climb into the 70s and the spawn winds down, the bass in the lake transition from spring to summer patterns.

"Later, in the summer, I believe the main lake is better at night," said Baker. "Clear water and boat traffic forces you to fish at night during the summer." That is when Baker likes to fish stump beds on points and shallow ledges that drop off to deeper water. "Sometimes the fish are right up on the banks. If you cast 5 feet [out] from the shore, you might as well reel in and cast again."

A mix of lures and cover types seem to produce fish all spring. The wide variety of fish-holding structure includes flooded timber, blowdowns, big boulders, rocky points, and miles of chunk rock bank. When bass are not aggressive, fish plastic baits. Males finishing up their nest-guarding duties are especially vulnerable. They will occasionally chase a spinnerbait. A good spinnerbait pattern in late spring is casting beside flooded hemlock trees in timbered coves. "They like to suspend around the tree limbs," Baker said. "Just cast out the spinnerbait, let it fall 3 or 4 feet, then reel it in slow. If a bass is there, he'll nail it." In spring Baker fishes 1/4-ounce white and chartreuse spinnerbaits. At night he uses heavier 3/8-ounce black or brown spinnerbaits, rigged with black or brown pork chunks.

Some of the fastest action will come fishing lizards and worms off ledges in less than 10 feet of water. If the bait lands near a bass or comes close to its spawning bed, the bass will attack. Sight fishing, therefore, is very productive. Strikes can vary from a series of fast taps to big tugs. Pumpkinseed (pumpkin and pepper) is Baker's color preference for the 6-inch curlytail worms and 6-inch lizards he fishes. He rigs them Texas style, with a 1/8- to 1/16-ounce bullet sinker when fishing shallow.

There are also a lot of active bass found in logjams at the heads of coves. Logjams "happen when the wind blows floating trees into a cove or pocket. It's tough fishing." Baker has been known to tie up the boat and fish from the bank, or walk out onto a floating log to make a cast. "Logjams are good places to fish at night over a black light," he said. "That way you can watch the line for twitches, since most of the time they hit the worm on the fall."

Spotted Bass   The spotted bass fishery is rated good, and the outlook is for numerous 10- to 13-inch fish. The best fishing is in mid to lower sections of the lake on rocky banks. Spotted bass make up about 45 percent of the black bass population.

Smallmouth Bass   The smallmouth bass fishery is rated fair, and the outlook is for a stable but low population of 12- to 15-inch fish. A 15-inch minimum took effect on March 1, 1997.

The 1993 creel survey shows that smallmouth bass constitute about 10 percent of the black bass harvest. "We suspect that the smallmouth bass population may be improving," said Williams. "Fishermen are starting to catch more fish in the 3- to 5-pound range, and we're seeing more in our electrofishing samples." The creel survey was the first at the lake since the late 1970s. It came six years after 191,926 fingerling smallmouth bass were stocked during three successive years, beginning in 1985. "That averaged out to about 10 fish per acre over the three years," said Williams. Laurel River had a native population of smallmouth bass, according to pre-impoundment population studies.

The stockings in the late 1980s were part of a program to establish better populations of smallmouth bass in lakes which had adequate cool-water habitat, oxygen, and fertility levels. "The idea was not to create a put-grow-take fishery," said Ted Crowell, assistant director of the Division of Fisheries for the Kentucky Department of Fish and Wildlife Resources, but to bolster existing, self-sustaining populations.

Smallmouth bass are reproducing in Laurel River Lake. The proof is the fingerling smallmouth bass observed in electrofishing samples and those fish actually taken in cove rotenone studies, where small embayments are blocked off with nets and all the fish inside are killed to determine exact numbers and weights of the various species in the population.

"Smallmouth are more abundant in the lower half of the lake," said Williams. "We rarely get smallmouth above the Hightop boat ramp." The upper river section is a 2-mile stretch of water between the Hightop boat ramp and a shallow point marked by two buoys just upstream from where a big power line crosses the lake. There is not as much cool-water habitat in the upper lake. "In the summer, low [levels of dissolved] oxygen become a problem at the depths [where smallmouth want to be]."

Spruce Creek has historically produced some of the best smallmouth fishing on Laurel River Lake.

Fish jig and pork rind combinations and suspending crankbaits across the secondary points in March and April.

White Bass   The white bass fishery is rated good, and the outlook is for numerous 12- to 14-inch fish. "There's a big year class of 8- to 9-inch fish coming on," said fishery biologist John Williams. "We should have good fishing in about two years." Overall, though, white bass numbers have declined slightly in the 1990s.

Spring runs of white bass extend to the headwaters of Lynn Camp Creek, Craig's Creek, and the Laurel River (main river channel), where spawning migrations are halted at the Corbin City Dam, about a mile up the lake from the Laurel Bridge boat ramp, off Ky. 312. During the summer, try fishing the main lake channel and Sand Island, in the Craig's Creek embayment, just above Holly Bay Marina.

Bluegill   The bluegill fishery is rated fair to good, and the outlook is for numerous 6- to 7-inch fish. "We see very few large bluegill," said Williams, "but there are some bigger fish, if you know where to look for them." Fishing live crickets in timbered coves is a popular bluegill strategy that yields good catches in May and June.

Catfish   The catfish fishery is rated good, and the outlook is for numerous 1- to 3-pound fish. Both channel and flathead catfish are present, with fair potential for flatheads above 25 pounds. The best fishing is above the Flatwoods boat ramp to Corbin City Dam. Fishing pressure is low.

Crappie   The crappie fishery is rated poor, and the outlook is for very low numbers. Both white and black crappie are present, but the deep, steep-sided reservoir is difficult to sample using trap nets. "It's not good crappie habitat, and we can't find enough crappie to work up age and growth information." Most fish are of a decent size, with some 10- to 16-inch spring fish.

The lake's crappie population crashed in the late 1970s when record cold winters caused a severe shad die-off, said Williams. "Crappie never really recovered." But in recent years some good catches have been reported in the spring.

Fish the timbered coves in the Laurel River arm of the lake near the Flatwoods boat ramp. "Rogers Creek is especially good," said Williams. "Start out fishing in about 20 feet of water in the timber, then move up shallower until you find the fish."

Tailwater Fishing Opportunities

There is access on foot to the tailwaters from the dam, but there are no developed facilities, except for a parking area at the spillway, off Ky. 1193. During the spring, walleye often congregate in the tailwaters, offering excellent fishing opportunities amid rocks and flooded timber. There is a boat launching ramp at the mouth of the Laurel River, off Ky. 1277, about 1 1/2 miles from the dam.

MARTINS FORK LAKE

Bluegill ⊷	Smallmouth Bass ⊷
Catfish ⊷ ⊷	Spotted Bass ⊷ ⊷
Crappie ⊷	Walleye ⊷ ⊷ ⊷
Largemouth Bass ⊷ ⊷	Tailwaters ⊷ ⊷
Redeye Bass ⊷	

Location Martins Fork Lake is about 4 miles southwest of Cawood, in Harlan County, adjacent to Cranks Creek Wildlife Management Area. The dam, at river mile 15.6 of the Cumberland River, is a 97-foot-high concrete gravity structure, flanked by earthen fill and riprap. The lake, which flooded a flat valley on the Kentucky-Virginia border, was built to provide flood protection to the city of Harlan 13 miles downstream at the junction of Clover Fork of the Cumberland River. Built by the Nashville District of the U.S. Army Corps of Engineers at a cost of $20.3 million, Martins Fork Lake opened in 1979. The main access highway is Ky. 987.

Herb Smith Memorial Lake, known locally as Cranks Creek Lake or "The Old Lake," is connected to Martins Fork Lake by a wadeable stream. The 219-acre lake was built in 1963, and the dam was renovated in 1978. The lake's boat dock—Stone Mountain Boat Dock, is off Bay Branch Road, reached via Ky. 987 and Ky. 3099 (about four miles south of Cawood). There is no fee to launch a boat.

Herb Smith Memorial Lake, which has a large island (about 60 acres) in its center, has 9.6 miles of shoreline, a maximum depth of 60 feet, and an average depth of 29 feet. The reservoir supports largemouth, smallmouth, and spotted bass, bluegill, crappie, and channel catfish. Camping, bank fishing, and boat rentals are available. For information telephone the Stone Mountain Boat Dock at (606) 573-7352.

Size Martins Fork Lake is a 3.7-mile scenic reservoir. It has 340 surface acres at a summer pool elevation of 1,310 feet. It was impounded from Martins Fork of the Cumberland River, and the major tributary is Cranks Creek, which flows into the lake near its headwaters. There is a 10-foot drawdown to winter pool, elevation 1,300, which reduces the lake to 274 surface acres. Martins Fork Lake is both the smallest and the

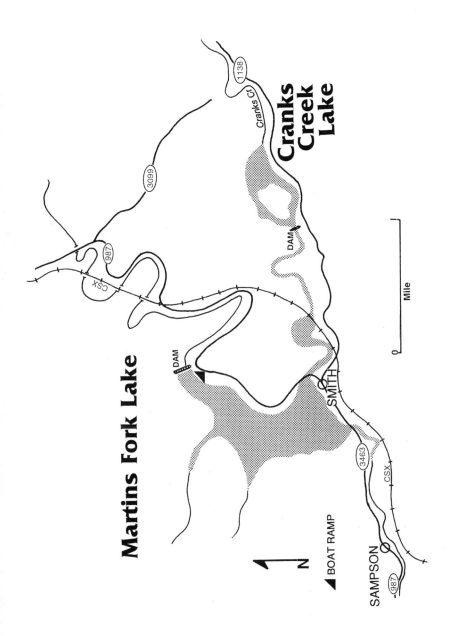

highest in elevation of the twenty-two lakes profiled in this book. Just above the dam, at its deepest point, the lake is about 45 feet deep.

Trophic State Index (TSI)   Martins Fork Lake has a TSI of 42, which ranks it as a mesotrophic lake (moderate fertility).

Lake Manager's Office   U.S. Army Corps of Engineers, Resource Manager's Office, Martins Fork Lake, 5965 Highway 987, Smith, KY 40867, telephone (606) 573-7655.

Managing Fishery Biologist   Kentucky Department of Fish and Wildlife Resources, Eastern Fishery District, Steve Reeser, District Biologist, 2744 Lake Road, Prestonsburg, KY 41653, telephone (606) 886-9575.

Lake Level/Fishing Report Line   The U.S. Army Corps of Engineers lake information line is (800) 261-5038. Another option is (800) 261-LAKE. Follow the recorded instructions to receive reports on the automated information line.

Marinas   There are no marinas.

Boat Launching Ramps   There is one boat launching ramp 1 mile above the dam, off Ky. 987.

Local Tourism Information   Harlan County Chamber of Commerce, Box 268, Harlan, KY 40831, telephone (606) 573-4717.

Fishing   Martins Fork Lake is a relatively shallow reservoir located in a wide valley. The lake was built on farmland, but since about 90 percent of the watershed is forested the lake is very clear most of the year, and low in alkalinity. Mining activity in the Cranks Creek watershed may be a contributing factor to the low pH of the lake water.

Martins Fork Lake has a very unique distinction. It is the only lake in Kentucky that has a population of redeye bass (*Micropterus coosae*), so it is the only lake in Kentucky where an angler has a chance to take four species of black bass: largemouth, smallmouth, spotted, and redeye. Other species present include walleye, bluegill, catfish, and crappie. Gizzard shad are the main forage fish. Threadfin shad were stocked in the past, but they succumbed to winter kill.

Fishing pressure has been growing steadily throughout the 1990s. A creel survey is planned for 1998 to assess fishing pressure and harvest, the first since the 1980s, when there was only a small weekend survey.

Anglers should keep in mind that both lakes (Martins Fork Lake and Herb Smith Memorial Lake) are restricted to ten-horsepower out-board motors. This regulation is strictly enforced. Boats with larger outboards may use trolling motors, but anglers must remove fuel tanks or leave the keys to their big motor at home to prove that they cannot run the big motor.

Walleye   The walleye fishery is rated good, and the outlook is for low numbers of 14- to 16-inch fish. Walleye have been stocked almost every year since 1979. The annual stocking is about 20,000 2-inch fry. "We don't know if natural reproduction is occurring," said Reeser.

Harlan County conservation officer Roy Harris said fishing pres-sure for walleye is very low and not many are caught. "The biggest one I've ever seen taken from the lake was a 28-incher." During the spring, fish jigs baited with live minnows in the upper lake (above Ky. 987) and near the mouth of Harris Branch. During the summer, fish spinner rigs baited with live nightcrawlers on the east shore of the lake, off the sand beach at Smith Recreation Area where creek channels intersect the main river channel.

Largemouth Bass   The largemouth bass fishery is rated fair, and the outlook is for low numbers of 10- to 12-inch fish. Largemouths weighing up to 7 pounds have been caught from the lake, but fishery biologist Steve Reeser believes heavy fishing pressure, the 12-inch mini-mum size limit, and nutrient-poor water are limiting factors to the bass fishery. Largemouth bass make up about 70 percent of the black bass in the lake.

"We're seeing a reduction in the number of larger bass," said Reeser. Illegal harvest of undersized fish may be one reason for the decline. "In our electrofishing data [sampling from 1986 to 1995] we're seeing more bass per hour, but the individual size has dropped." Largemouth bass growth rates at Martins Fork Lake are similar to those of Paintsville Lake.

Fish spinnerbaits in Crane Creek in the spring, Carolina-rigged plas-tic lizards in the summer on main lake flats, and jerk baits (suspending crankbaits) in the fall on the eastern shore of the lake. During the sum-mer the best fishing is at night, with some surface action in the morn-ings. Fish the Rebel Pop-R or other surface chugger baits.

Spotted Bass   The spotted bass fishery is rated fair, and the out-look is for low numbers of 8- to 10-inch fish. Spotted bass make up about 30 percent of the black bass in the lake. Fish rock banks on the lower lake with live minnows or 4-inch tube jigs.

Smallmouth Bass   The smallmouth bass fishery is rated poor, and the outlook is for low numbers of 10- to 12-inch fish. Most are below the 12-inch minimum size limit. Smallmouth bass make up only 1 percent of the black bass in the lake. Fish jig and pork rind combinations in the spring and crankbaits in the fall.

Redeye Bass The redeye bass fishery is rated poor, and the outlook is for low numbers of 8- to 9-inch fish. Few reach harvestable size, and the chance of catching a keeper fish is very low. Fish small crankbaits and live minnows.

Redeye bass were first identified in stream samples taken in the 1950s, prior to the lake's impoundment. A remnant population exists in the lake, and several specimens were observed in the fall of 1995 while gill netting for walleye, Reeser said. Redeye bass make up about 1 percent of the black bass in the lake. Since redeye bass are known to crossbreed with smallmouth bass, there is some concern that redeye bass could cause genetic problems that could lead to stunting. "But actually, the smallmouth bass population is so low, this concern is minimal," said Reeser.

Bluegill The bluegill fishery is rated poor, and the outlook is for low numbers of small fish. Most are 5- to 6-inchers, but during the spawn some 8- to 10-inchers are taken in the shallow upper lake. Fish red worms, wax worms, and crickets in shallow cover over brush.

Catfish The catfish fishery is rated fair, and the outlook is for low numbers of 10- to 14-inch fish. Channel catfish were initially stocked, and the population is now maintained by natural reproduction. Flatheads and bullheads are also taken. Fish cut bait, large minnows, and nightcrawlers in shallow coves and main lake flats.

Crappie The crappie fishery is rated poor, and the outlook is for low numbers of 6- to 8-inch fish. "In the spring there are a few big fish taken, 10- to 14-inchers," said Harris. Fish minnows over deeper structure and cast 1/16-ounce tube jigs to wood cover in coves in the spring.

Tailwater Fishing Opportunities

The tailwaters have been developed to create better access for bank anglers. This includes sidewalks with railings, steps, and a handicapped accessible fishing pier. Several species are available. Rainbow trout are stocked monthly (a total of 5,900 per year), except during August and September. Trout habitat extends for about 2 miles downstream, but it is marginal at best, with few, if any, holdover fish. Walleye are often caught from the tailwaters in the fall, during the seasonal drawdown, and in the early spring. "Walleye fishing usually starts in February," said Harris. "Walleye are caught on jigs, crankbaits, and chubs [minnows]." Some large channel catfish (up to 26 inches) are also taken.

NOLIN RIVER LAKE

Bluegill ⋈ ⋈ ⋈	Spotted Bass ⋈ ⋈ ⋈ ⋈
Catfish ⋈ ⋈ ⋈	Walleye ⋈ ⋈ ⋈ ⋈
Crappie ⋈ ⋈ ⋈ ⋈	White Bass ⋈ ⋈ ⋈ ⋈
Largemouth Bass ⋈ ⋈ ⋈	Tailwaters ⋈ ⋈ ⋈

Location   Nolin River Lake is about 85 miles south of Louisville in Edmonson, Grayson, Hardin, and Hart Counties. The dam is 7.8 miles upstream from the Nolin River's confluence with the Green River, and is off Ky. 728, about 10 miles north of Brownsville. The lake is just a short drive from Mammoth Cave National Park, one of Kentucky's most popular tourist attractions. The main access highways are the Western Kentucky Parkway, Ky. 259, Ky. 88, and Ky. 1827. Construction on Nolin River Lake started in January 1959 and was completed in March 1963.

Size   The 5,790-acre reservoir is 39 miles long and has 172 miles of shoreline at summer pool, elevation 515. The drawdown to winter pool, elevation 490, reduces its size to 2,890 acres. Nolin River Lake is 75 feet deep just above the dam, and the lower lake has an average depth of about 30 feet. Above Wax, the lake is much shallower, with an average depth of about 15 feet. The drainage area above the dam is 703 square miles.

Trophic State Index (TSI)   Nolin River Lake has a TSI of 43, which ranks it as a mesotrophic lake (moderate fertility).

Lake Manager's Office   U.S. Army Corps of Engineers, Resource Manager's Office, Nolin River Lake, 2150 Nolin Dam Road, Box 339, Bee Springs, KY 42207, telephone (502) 286-4511.

Managing Fishery Biologist   Kentucky Department of Fish and Wildlife Resources, Northwestern Fishery District, David Bell, District Biologist, 1398 Highway 81 North, Calhoun, KY 42327, telephone (502) 273-3117.

Lake Level/Fishing Report Line   There is no information line for Nolin River Lake.

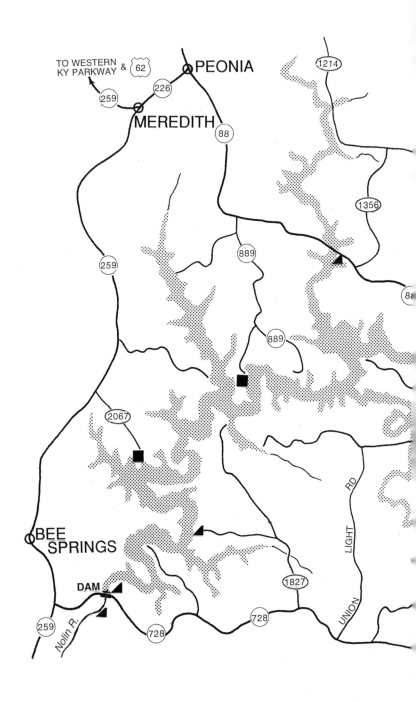

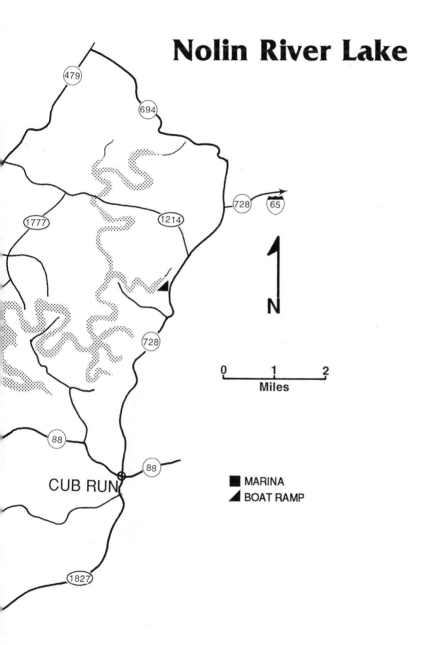

Nolin River Lake

■ MARINA
▲ BOAT RAMP

CUB RUN

Marinas   There are three marinas. *Wax Marina*, open seasonally (April 15 to October 15), is 15 miles south of Clarkson, off Ky. 88. The address and telephone number are Wax, KY 42787, (502) 242-7205. There is a $2 fee to launch at the boat ramp, $25 for an annual pass, with discounts available to senior citizens. *Moutadier Resort and Marina*, open seasonally (April 1 to November 1), is 12 miles south of Leitchfield, off Ky. 259. The address and telephone number are 1990 Moutadier Road, Leitchfield, KY 42754, (502) 286-4069. There is a $2 fee to launch at the boat ramp, $25 for an annual pass, with discounts available to senior citizens. *Ponderosa Boat Dock*, open seasonally (April 1 to November 1), is 13 miles south of Clarkson, off Ky. 88. The address and telephone number are 865 Ponderosa Road, Clarkson, KY 42726, (502) 242-7215.

Boat Launching Ramps   There are five boat launching ramps in addition to the ramps at the marinas. *The Nolin Lake State Park* (formerly Brier Creek) boat ramp is 7 miles northeast of the dam, off Ky. 1827. *Dam Area* boat ramp is on the south shore of the lake at the dam, off Ky. 728. There is a $2 fee to launch at the boat ramp, $25 for an annual pass, with discounts available to senior citizens. *Dog Creek* boat ramp is 10 miles northeast of the dam, off Union Light Road (Ky. 1015). There is a $2 fee to launch at the boat ramp, $25 for an annual pass, with discounts available to senior citizens. *Iberia* boat ramp is 5 miles southeast of Peonia, off Ky. 88. There is a $2 fee to launch at the boat ramp, $25 for an annual pass, with discounts available to senior citizens. *Bacon Creek* boat ramp is in the lake headwaters, off Ky. 728.

Local Tourism Information   Grayson County Tourism Commission, 122 East Main Street, Leitchfield, KY 42754, telephone (502) 259-2735 or toll free (800) 624-9951.

Fishing   Since it was impounded, Nolin River Lake has been considered a largemouth bass and crappie lake, but in recent years excellent walleye and white bass fisheries have developed. Other species which offer good fishing include spotted bass, catfish (channel and flatheads), and bluegill. Cover includes standing timber, stump beds, drift, fallen logs, rock piles and rock bluffs.

Nolin River Lake and neighboring Rough River Lake are a lot alike, but Nolin's main lake is larger and allows anglers to more easily escape pleasure boat traffic during the summer months. Since the late 1980s, recreation use, including fishing, has grown more at Nolin River Lake than at any U.S. Army Corps of Engineers lake in the Louisville District. "When Taylorsville Lake was built it took at lot of fishing pressure off Nolin, but that only lasted for about two years," said fishery biologist David Bell.

Forage at Nolin River Lake includes gizzard shad, threadfin shad, and log perch. "Threadfin were stocked up to the early 1990s," said Bell. "We did have some tremendous shad kills over the winter of 1995-96," and threadfin populations have all but disappeared.

Walleye The walleye fishery is rated excellent, and the outlook is for numerous 18- to 22-inch fish. About 300,000 fingerlings are stocked in Nolin every spring, usually in late May or early June. Beginning in late February, though, the walleye run is the main attraction. Fish white, chartreuse, or yellow jigs in the spring for river-run fish. "There's lots of fishing pressure in the 2 miles of river between Broad Ford and the Bacon Creek boat ramp." Actually, the walleye move up river from the lake as far as Wheeler's Mill, a distance of 10 to 12 miles. Bell knows this for certain because he has electrofished the headwaters to obtain about fifty brood fish for the state hatchery—ripe adults full of eggs and milt, ready to spawn.

"Walleye move up into the river as soon as we get that first rise [in water level], usually about the second or third week of February." In 1995, the walleye stayed in the river until early March, Bell said. When water temperatures exceed 60 degrees, white bass move up into the headwaters, too.

Later in the summer, crankbaits are hot, especially the Model A Bomber. "You can't beat the action." Also try fishing on cloudy, rainy days or at night. Bell said rocky points and mudflats seem to yield the most fish. He predicts that walleye fishing will improve as the years go by, especially during the summer months. Walleye as large as 11 1/4 pounds have been taken by the fishery crew, and Bell said he's heard of some 8- to 9-pounders being caught by anglers. "The walleye are shallower than most people believe," Bell said. "Normally, they're in 12 to 16 feet of water, just above the thermocline. . . . There's a lot of nice walleye in Nolin."

Crappie The crappie fishery is rated excellent, and the outlook is for numerous 9- to 12-inch fish. A 9-inch minimum size limit was adopted in 1992. Heavy rains and high lake levels during the springs of 1995, 1996, and 1997 helped crappie reproduction, hindered fishing, and are responsible for a stockpiling of high-quality crappie.

Generally speaking, Nolin River Lake seems to grow slightly bigger crappie than its neighboring reservoir, Rough River Lake. "Nolin usually has very heavy crappie fishing pressure," said Bell. "In a normal spring about 35 percent of the harvestable crappie are caught." It takes about two years for a crappie to reach the minimum size limit, and crappie up to 15 inches long are taken from the lake each year. Conoloway Creek is a top embayment for crappie. Crappie-holding cover includes deadfalls, shoreline stump beds, and standing timber. The best fishing in the spring is in the upper lake.

Both white and black crappie are present, with black crappie representing about 10 percent of the population. The black crappie are limited to the clear, rocky lower lake.

White Bass   The white bass fishery is rated excellent, and the outlook is for numerous 12- to 16-inch fish. "It's probably the best white bass fishery outside of Kentucky Lake and Lake Barkley," said Bell. "Adults are averaging 15 to 16 inches. . . . There's a good size range and fantastic numbers."

Nolin River Lake's white bass do not receive nearly as much fishing pressure as the lake's crappie and largemouth bass populations. "We did a tagging study, and less than 20 percent of the white bass tags were returned," said Bell. "It's an underutilized fishery. We know the white bass aren't being exploited." In 1991, 17,767 white bass were harvested, representing about 17 percent of the total weight harvested. By comparison, there was a 50 to 60 percent tag return on crappie and a 35 to 40 percent tag return on largemouth bass, meaning these species had a much higher harvest.

"The spring run is pretty substantial," Bell said. "White bass are caught from Cane Run [the first riffle on the Nolin River] upstream as far as Millerstown," which is about 11 miles away. Two popular spring fishing spots for white bass are the Broad Ford Bridge area and Bacon Creek.

In the mid-1990s, summer jump action really picked up on the main lake, especially in the mornings. "Largemouth bass are being caught in those jumps, too," said Bell. Most of the surface action is from the mouth of Dog Creek to Wax Creek. "There's a bunch of islands there, and white bass are pushing schools of shad up on the bars and points."

Fishing over lights at night for white bass has become quite popular, Bell said. "They start fishing at night with the full moon in June." Small slab spoons like the Hopkins or Little Cleo in a chrome or white finish, with the treble hook enhanced with white hair or silver tinsel and tied off with red thread, are highly productive. Fish around the light, vertically jigging the spoon in 12 to 20 feet of water. Most hits occur when the spoon is fluttering down through the water column. Sometimes anglers catch crappie and walleye while fishing over lights for white bass.

Largemouth Bass   The largemouth bass fishery is rated good, and the outlook is for numerous 12- to 15-inch fish. Nolin River Lake has a reputation for producing lunker largemouth bass, but heavy fishing pressure has impacted bass size and numbers since the early 1990s. "Fishing pressure doubled between 1986 and 1991," said Bell. "We're not seeing the numbers of 3- to 4-pound bass we did before." Bell said he thought the lake record largemouth bass weighed 11 pounds, 2 ounces and was caught at night on a buzzbait by Ray Merideth of Brownsville. About 60 percent of the black bass in Nolin River Lake are largemouth.

"The upper lake, beginning at Dog Creek, produces more largemouth bass," said Bell. "During the summer the best fishing is at night, but there is some jump action in July and August." Conoloway Creek is a good area for jumps. "I've seen the whole embayment erupt in small jumps," said Bell, "when bass are chasing shad fry." In the jumps, a good strategy is casting surface lures like the Rebel Pop-R.

A 15-inch minimum went into effect on bass at Barren River Lake on March 1, 1993, so many tournaments, and bass fishing pressure in general, shifted to Nolin. "The bass really got hammered," said Bell. "Anglers from Elizabethtown, Leitchfield, and Bowling Green were all hitting the lake hard." Therefore, on March 1, 1996, a 15-inch-and-1 limit was established on largemouth and smallmouth bass. That means the minimum size limit is 15 inches, but one fish under that size may be kept in the daily creel of six. "[The change in size limit] was as much social as biological," said Bell. "Anglers wanted it, and it's certainly not going to hurt."

Catfish   The catfish fishery is rated good, and the outlook is for numerous 1- to 3-pound fish. Both flathead and channel catfish are present. Nolin River Lake supports the region's premier flathead fishery. Occasionally, 20- to 30-pounders are taken in the shallow upper lake by fishing live bluegill or large shiners at night on the river channel flats. Fishing pressure is moderate.

Spotted Bass   The spotted bass fishery is rated excellent, and the outlook is for numerous 13- to 15-inch fish. "There's more spotted bass in the lower end because it's rocky, deep, and clear. . . . Spotted bass up to 15 to 16 inches long are being caught, and they're fat as footballs," said Bell. "The best section of the lake to fish is from Moutadier down to the dam." The spotted bass represent about 40 percent of the population.

Bluegill The bluegill fishery is rated good, and the outlook is for a stable population, with most fish in the 6- to 8-inch size range. "Nolin is one our better bluegill lakes," said Bell. "There's numbers of good-sized fish." Since the mid-1990s, bluegill average size seems to be increasing.

Tailwater Fishing Opportunities

With water temperatures staying in the 60s, the emphasis is on cool-water fisheries—mainly trout, muskie, and walleye. Laflin said each year about 18,600 rainbow trout are stocked. Brown trout have also been stocked in the past. "Some muskies are taken from the lower stretches," Laflin said.

High discharges of water through the dam in the spring of 1996 and 1997 have created a bonanza for walleye anglers. "I think a lot of walleye are going through the dam," said Bell. "Several walleye [tagged in the lake] have been caught in the tailwaters." The excellent walleye fishing extends downstream to Lock 3 on the Green River at Rochester, Kentucky, in Muhlenberg County. "This is virtually unknown except to local anglers."

There is not much current in the tailwaters. "It's more like a lake environment," said fishery biologist B.D. Laflin. "Most of the fishing is done in the 7.8-mile section from the dam to the mouth of the Green River." There is no fee to launch at the ramp below the dam, and the low flow does not hamper fishing for miles downstream.

Paintsville Lake

Catfish ⚬⚬
Crappie ⚬
Largemouth Bass ⚬⚬
Rainbow Trout ⚬⚬⚬

Smallmouth Bass ⚬
Spotted Bass ⚬⚬⚬⚬
Walleye ⚬⚬⚬
Tailwaters ⚬⚬⚬

Location   Paintsville Lake is a scenic mountain lake bordered by rock cliffs and vast forests of pine and hardwood trees. Lush stands of mountain laurel and rhododendron drape many of the shady, steep-sided hollows. The scenic reservoir, filled in 1983, is 116 miles east of Lexington in Johnson and Morgan Counties. The main access highways are the Mountain Parkway, Ky. 40, and Ky. 172.

Size   Paintsville Lake was impounded from Paint Creek, a tributary to the Big Sandy River. Maintained at elevation 709 year-round, the 18-mile lake has 1,139 surface acres of water. The lake is about 90 feet deep at the dam.

Trophic State Index (TSI)   Paintsville Lake has a TSI of 43, which ranks it as a mesotrophic lake (moderate fertility).

Lake Manager's Office   U.S. Army Corps of Engineers, Resource Manager's Office, Paintsville Lake, 807 Ky. 2275, Staffordsville, KY 41256, telephone (606) 297-6312.

Managing Fishery Biologist   Kentucky Department of Fish and Wildlife Resources, Eastern Fishery District, Steve Reeser, District Biologist, 2744 Lake Road, Prestonsburg, KY 41653, telephone (606) 886-9575.

Lake Level/Fishing Report Line   The U.S. Army Corps of Engineers lake information line is (606) 297-4111.

Marinas   There is one marina. *Paintsville Lake Marina*, open year-round, is 4 miles west of Paintsville, off Ky. 2275. The address and telephone number are Box 726, Paintsville, KY 41240, (606) 297-LAKE.

Boat Launching Ramps   There are three boat launching ramps. There is no fee to launch a boat at these three ramps. *Rocky Knob* boat ramp is adjacent to the marina, 4 miles west of Paintsville, off Ky. 2275. *Open*

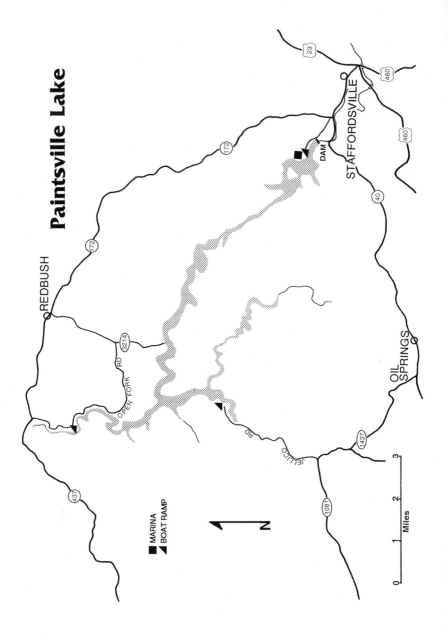

Paintsville Lake

MARINA
BOAT RAMP

Miles

Fork boat ramp is off Ky. 172 in Morgan County, at the upper end of the lake. *Big Mine Fork* boat ramp is on Jellico Road on the Little Paint embayment, off Ky. 1437 and Ky. 5041.

Local Tourism Information   Paintsville Tourism Commission, 304 Main Street, Paintsville, KY 41240, telephone (606) 789-1469 or toll free (800) 542-5790.

Fishing   Paintsville Lake is a highland reservoir built in a narrow gorge. Limited shallow water is a liability for some species, affecting reproduction. The rainbow trout and walleye fisheries attract a lot of attention, but the reservoir also supports largemouth bass, smallmouth bass, spotted bass, crappie, bluegill, and catfish. Gizzard shad are present in the lake.

The lake has several assets. There are two small islands across the lake from the Rocky Knob Recreation Area which are ringed with weed beds. There is also aquatic vegetation at the dam, along the riprap banks. Many of the coves are filled with flooded timber. Fish attractors are marked with buoys.

It also has several liabilities. The lake stays clear year-round and receives a lot of fishing pressure in the winter because of stable water conditions and good cool-water fisheries (rainbow trout and walleye). The narrow channel, lined with stumps and standing timber, makes many sections of the upper lake extremely hazardous to boaters. Idle speed areas in Little Paint Creek are marked by buoys.

Walleye   The walleye fishery is rated good, and the outlook is for numerous 15- to 18-inch fish. "Up until 1997, walleye fishing was a hit or miss situation," said Johnson County conservation officer Jeff Preston. "Walleye fishing has really improved." The fishery was established from an initial stocking of 270,000 fingerlings in 1984. Now, walleye over 10 pounds are present. However, there is no evidence that natural reproduction is occurring in the lake, so stockings have continued at a rate of about 60,000 a year to sustain the population.

Jigs and spinner rigs baited with nightcrawlers and fished close to the bottom are the top two walleye lures at Paintsville Lake. "Fluorescent green is a top color," said Preston. Local angler Dwight "Nightcrawler" Stambaugh catches fish on a homemade 1/8-ounce jig tipped with a live nightcrawler. Vertical jigging is his most productive fishing technique.

Rick Markesbery of Florence, Kentucky, extensively scouted and fished Paintsville Lake in 1994 and was the first angler to use spinner rigs to catch walleye there. "Trophy fish are present, but it's hard to find big concentrations of walleye," said Markesbery. He caught walleye from drop-offs in 25 feet of water off the islands across the lake from Rocky Knob Recreation Area.

"For spinner rigs [to be most effective] it's important to keep the lure close to the bottom and follow the bottom contour." To maximize this technique, the transducer of the fish finder should be mounted on the trolling motor shaft at the bow of the boat. "That way you can see the fish as you approach them. Turn off your trolling motor and drift over a spot that holds fish, otherwise you can spook them."

A walleye telemetry study, which tracked the movement of tagged fish for over a year, produced some useful information about walleye movements and preferred habitat. The object of the study was to help anglers locate walleye so they can catch them. "We wanted to know where the fish were other than in the coves in spring and around the islands at night," said fishery biologist Dan Wilson, who initiated the study in March 1993. The study involved twenty-five walleye collected from the lower 12 miles of the lake. Small transmitters were implanted in the abdomens of both male and female fish, ranging in weight from 2.6 pounds to 10.7 pounds. The following is an overview of the findings of the tracking study:

In early spring there is upstream movement, mimicking a spawning run.

In April and into May, until water temperatures reach into the 70s, about 80 percent of the walleye are suspended in flooded timber in coves, orientated to the shoreline. They seem to prefer pines and hemlocks over hardwoods. The thicker the cover, the better. Fifteen percent are located along the shoreline, and the remaining 5 percent are suspended in open water.

The average depth for all walleye during this time of year was 7 feet, or 5 feet in muddy water conditions.

Walleye movement picked up in the evening and ended in the early morning, but many fish moved less than 100 feet in one day. The most movement occurred in darkness. Some walleye moved from the timber to the mouths of coves or shoreline shallows on the main lake to feed at night.

June is a transition month for the thermal stratification of water. A warm-water layer develops at depths of 15 to 20 feet, with cooler water remaining at the lower levels. The zone between these two layers of water is called the thermocline. Over time, the deeper water begins to lose its dissolved oxygen, as bacteria consumes organic material that falls down through the water column.

The extreme lower lake is the exception, where good oxygen levels remain below the thermocline. As the water warms, walleye move deeper. Fishing is tough because walleye may move on a daily basis, adjusting to temperature changes, but timber in deeper water is the preferred habitat during this period of adjustment. During June and July there is a lot of movement at night into the main lake, with some fish moving as often as every two hours, within a 1- to 2-mile area.

In the summer, July through September, many walleye are located at the mouths of coves on the main lake, either holding off timber in about 30 feet of water or suspended over the bottom at a depth of 25 to 35 feet. The area from the island to the dam has cooler water than the upper lake, where walleye stay in the timber at depths of 13 to 15 feet. During the summer, walleye movement is greatest at night, but unlike in the spring, fish movement is away from the shoreline to deeper, open water structure. In October, walleye are unpredictable due the uncertain weather patterns. If the month is warm, walleye stay in their summer pattern.

Come November, when the weather turns cold and rainy, the lake begins to destratify and walleye begin to move up the lake. Only 47 percent of all fish are in standing timber. They tend to head for midlake channels, particularly in two areas—the junction of Little Paint and Open Fork, and within 2 miles of Upper Sandlick Branch.

Rainbow Trout   The rainbow trout fishery is rated fair to good, and the outlook is for numerous 10- to 14-inch fish. A seasonal fishery, the best fishing is from January through April. "As soon as the weather warms up, the fishing tapers off," said Preston. "The best fishing is in the winter. Very few trout are caught during the summer now."

Each year about 35,000 8- to 12-inch trout are stocked in January. "In 1998 we are considering changing the stocking regime, putting half of the trout in the lake in April," said district fishery biologist Steve Reeser. "That would ensure more summer fishing opportunities." Reeser said stocking all the trout in January makes them vulnerable. "They stay close to the banks and get caught pretty easily."

Factors that may limit the population's growth and survival include the lack of shad forage and the amount of cold-water habitat available. "The threadfin shad that were stocked winter killed, and gizzard shad numbers are limited," said Reeser. "I don't know if we can have big trout without shad." During the summer, trout are confined to the deep water in the lower quarter of the lake. Reeser said it is unclear now how long trout are surviving in the lake after being stocked. It is clear, however, that some holdover trout do exist since fish up to 20 inches have been taken by anglers. But sampling trout in a lake during the summer is very difficult since the fish are in deepest water available that is sufficiently oxygenated. Reeser said during the summer trout are usually near the thermocline (in 20 to 25 feet of water), but "they could be as deep as 45 feet, depending on dissolved oxygen levels."

Nightcrawlers, processed cheese spread, Berkley power baits, and kernel corn are top baits used when still-fishing during the winter or when fishing at night over lights during the summer and fall. Trout are also caught trolling small crankbaits during the winter months.

Largemouth Bass   The largemouth bass fishery is rated fair, and the outlook is for low numbers of keeper fish. Slow growth and heavy fishing pressure are the reasons there are few fish above the 15-inch minimum size limit. It is a shame the largemouth bass fishery is not better, because Paintsville Lake has a little bit of every kind of structure largemouth bass like—from grass beds and steep rock walls to shallow timbered flats.

Anglers must take different approaches to fishing as the year progresses. Tim McDonald, who has fished the lake since it was impounded, believes that in the spring a couple of timbered coves always seem to hold larger spawning bass—Gullett Branch and McKenzie Branch. "I think a lack of spawning areas in the lake has hurt the bass," McDonald said. Another good place to intercept a big bass is the submerged roadbed across the mouth of Osborne Branch.

Fish a Bomber Long A to bass sighted on or near spawning beds. "One of the hottest colors around the spawn is gold with a black back," McDonald said. "I get into a two- or three-jerk cadence, then let the lure float back up." As largemouth bass come off the nest, McDonald begins to fish deep pockets off the main channel where fish are tight to deadfalls and suspend under mountain laurel branches that shade the banks. To catch these bass he flips a 6-inch lizard, pegging the slip sinker to the lure with a piece of flat toothpick.

The grass beds in the lower lake along the islands hold bass throughout the warm months of the year since they are near the deep water of the main river channel. There is also a big grass bed along the riprap of the dam. The Rat-L-Trap crankbait, buzzbaits, and topwater chuggers like the Pop-R are excellent choices for fishing these grass beds at dawn. Then switch to Carolina-rigged lizards when the sun comes up over the horizon.

Preston said the submerged brush and standing timber in the Open Fork consistently holds lots of bass. Spinnerbaits and jig and pork rind combinations are fished in the upper lake where flooded timber lines creek and river channels.

Spotted Bass The spotted bass fishery is rated excellent, and the outlook is for numerous 10- to 14-inch fish. There is a stable population, with some very large fish (15- to 20-inchers). The best fishing is on rock structure in the lower half of the lake.

Smallmouth Bass The smallmouth bass fishery is rated poor, and the outlook is for low numbers of keeper fish (there is a 15-inch minimum size limit). The population is quite low and restricted to the extreme lower end of the lake, within 1 or 2 miles of the dam. Paintsville Lake stratifies thermally and has little cool-water habitat in the summer. Lack of cool water and competition from other black bass species are thought to be limiting factors to the population.

The smallmouth in the lake are the result of a remnant population in Paint Creek and six years of stocking, which ended in 1990. "The original plan was to stock smallmouth a few years to help establish a population," Wilson said. The stocking rate was about 25 fingerlings per acre. From 1984 through 1990, about 160,000 1 1/2- to 2-inch smallmouth bass were released in the lake.

The 1994 creel survey data showed that smallmouth bass make up less than 1 percent of all black bass caught during daylight. At night, the catch climbed to 6 percent. Despite the low population, there are some 18- to 20-inch fish taken by anglers.

Local angler Tim McDonald said two of the top smallmouth lures are 3/8-ounce spinnerbaits with willowleaf blades and 4-inch Texas-rigged lizards. "You want to find a bank where you can bounce your lure down a series of ledges," said McDonald. The rock wall across from the marina is a sleeper bank for smallmouth that most anglers overlook.

Catfish The channel catfish fishery is rated fair to good, and the outlook is for low to moderate numbers of 1- to 3-pound fish. Low numbers of channel catfish are being caught, but the lake contains some fish up to 12 pounds. The catfish are an overlooked species, and there is low fishing pressure. Anglers should concentrate their efforts in the shallow upper lake.

Crappie The crappie fishery is rated poor, and the outlook is for low numbers of small fish, but a few big crappie are caught in the spring. Both white and black crappie are present. Data from the 1994 creel survey showed that about 8,500 crappie were harvested, or about 2.3 pounds of crappie per acre. The average crappie harvested was a 9-incher.

"Only a small percentage of anglers are going after crappie," said Reeser. Most fishing is being done in the upper lake during the spring. Fish in brush or treetops along the bank near deep water.

Tailwater Fishing Opportunities

The tailwater facilities are excellent and are angler friendly. They include a concrete walkway, a paved fishing platform, and several hundred yards of riprap lining the banks of Paint Creek. The area is small and can be waded or fished from a float tube. Canoes and cartop johnboats are the best choices for floating the tailwaters, but there is no boat launching ramp immediately below the dam. A boat launching ramp in Paintsville (off the access road to the city water plant), where Paint Creek flows into the Levisa Fork of the Big Sandy River, is the take-out point for anglers floating the tailwaters.

Rainbow trout are stocked April through November, for an annual total of 18,000 fish. There is also a small stocking of brown trout. About 800 8- to 9-inch browns have been stocked annually in the tailwaters since 1994. "We stock them by canoe, using a float box. . . . Brown trout are more tolerant of higher water temperatures," said Reeser, "and reach a larger size quicker." Trout habitat extends for about 5 miles downstream. "There's some bigger rainbows [up to 20 inches] taken downstream from the tailwaters," said Reeser.

An occasional walleye is also taken from the tailwaters. In the spring of 1997 a 26-inch walleye was caught within the city limits of Paintsville, near the boat ramp at the mouth of Paint Creek.

ROUGH RIVER LAKE

Bluegill ⨀⨀⨀
Catfish ⨀⨀⨀
Crappie ⨀⨀⨀
Hybrid Striped Bass ⨀⨀⨀

Largemouth Bass ⨀⨀
Spotted Bass ⨀⨀
White Bass ⨀⨀
Tailwaters ⨀⨀

Location   Rough River Lake is a Y-shaped reservoir located about 70 miles southwest of Louisville, in Breckinridge, Hardin, and Grayson Counties. Construction on the lake began in November 1955 and was completed in June 1961. The dam is 89.3 miles above the Rough River's confluence with the Green River, and 6 miles above Falls of Rough, Kentucky. The main access highways are the Western Kentucky Parkway, Ky. 79, Ky. 259, and Ky. 737.

Size   At summer pool (elevation 495), the lake is 5,100 acres, has 220 miles of shoreline, is 39 miles long and is 65 feet deep just above the dam. The winter drawdown reduces the lake to 2,180 acres at elevation 470.

Trophic State Index (TSI)   Rough River Lake has a TSI of 48, which ranks it as a mesotrophic lake (moderate fertility).

Lake Manager's Office   U.S. Army Corps of Engineers, Rough River Lake, Resource Manager's Office, 14500 Falls of Rough Road, Falls of Rough, KY 40119, telephone (502) 257-2061.

Managing Fishery Biologist   Kentucky Department of Fish and Wildlife Resources, Northwestern Fishery District, David Bell, District Biologist, 1398 Highway 81 North, Calhoun, KY 42327, telephone (502) 273-3117.

Lake Level/Fishing Report Line   There is no lake information line.

Marinas   There are three marinas. *Bill's Marina*, open seasonally (April 1 to October 15), is 6 miles north of Leitchfield, off Ky. 737. The address and telephone number are 346 Peter Cave Ramp Road, Leitchfield, KY 42754, (502) 259-4859. There is no fee to launch. *Rough River Dam Marina*, open seasonally (April 1 to October 31, lake level permitting),

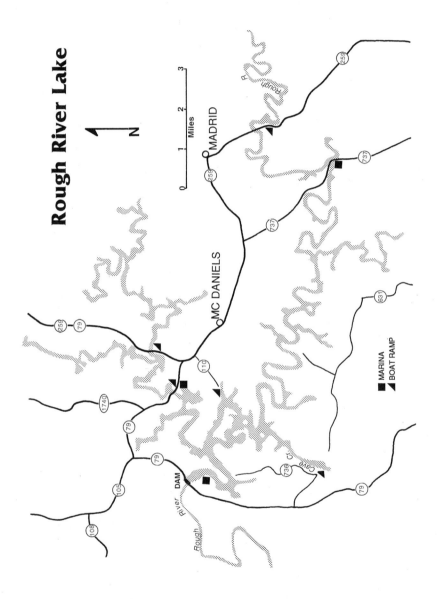

Rough River Lake

N

MADRID

MC DANIELS

DAM

■ MARINA
▲ BOAT RAMP

Miles
0 1 2 3

259
737
259
79
1740
79
79
105
108
110
736
631
79
259

Rough R.

Rough River

Cave Cr

is adjacent to Rough River Lake State Resort Park at the dam, off Ky. 79. The address and telephone number are 450 Lodge Road, Falls of Rough, KY 40119, (502) 257-2311. *Nick's Boat Dock*, open seasonally (April 1 to November 30), is 5 miles west of McDaniels, off Ky. 259. The address and telephone number are McDaniels, KY 40152, (502) 257-8955.

Boat Launching Ramps   There are five boat launching ramps on the lake in addition to the ramps at the marinas. At the first four listed there is a $2 fee to launch at the boat ramp, $25 for an annual pass, with discounts available to senior citizens. *Axtel* boat ramp is 4 miles east of the dam, off Ky. 79. *Cave Creek* boat ramp is 5 miles south of the dam, off Ky. 736. *Laurel Branch* boat ramp is 6 miles east of the dam, off Ky. 110. *North Fork* boat ramp is 7 miles east of the dam, off Ky. 259. *Everleigh* boat ramp is in the lake headwaters, 2 miles south of Madrid, off Ky. 259.

Local Tourism Information   Grayson County Tourism Commission, 122 E. Main Street, Leitchfield, KY 42754, telephone (502) 259-2735 or toll free (800) 624-9951.

Fishing   Rough River Lake has a standing crop that averages about 300 pounds of fish per acre. "The south fork, above Peter Cave, produces slightly higher numbers of bass and crappie, based on our electrofishing samples," said Bell. "We compared the north fork to the south fork for two years but didn't find real significant differences." The upper ends of the two forks are slightly more fertile than the lower lake.

Rough River Lake supports populations of largemouth bass, spotted bass, hybrid striped bass, catfish, crappie, white bass, and bluegill. There is also a remnant population of smallmouth bass, limited to the tributaries. The forage base is gizzard shad. Until 1995, threadfin shad were stocked, but populations have dwindled due to winter kills.

Because of its close proximity to metropolitan Louisville, Rough River Lake is a favorite with pleasure boaters. Some of the shoreline is developed with private vacation homes.

A few embayments (Little Clifty Creek, Cave Creek, and Tules Creek) have beautiful rock cliffs along the banks. There is an 80-acre island across the lake from Laurel Branch boat ramp. It is owned by the U.S. Army Corps of Engineers.

Crappie   The crappie fishery is rated good, and the outlook is for stable numbers of 9-inch fish. Crappie populations are coming on. "We sampled with trap nets last fall and found lots of 8- to 11-inch fish," said Bell. "The best I've seen at the lake." In the late 1980s and early 1990s, the crappie population fluctuated greatly and was dominated by 6- to 8-inch fish. On March 1, 1993, a 9-inch minimum was established. Crappie harvested in the spring of 1996 averaged about 9.2 to 9.5 inches, Bell said. White crappie are the dominant species. "Only 3 percent of the population is black crappie."

The best fishing in the spring occurs in the shallow tributaries, where fish stack up on timbered mud flats and in brush piles. Some top embayments for crappie are Tules Creek, Long Creek, and Georges Branch. "The Corps put in a lot of brush piles with the help of volunteers," said Bell. Crappie are native to Rough River, so there was no supplemental stocking after the lake was impounded.

White Bass   The white bass fishery is rated fair, and the outlook is for decreased numbers of 9- to 11-inch fish. In October 1995, disease killed thousands of 6- to 8-inch white bass. "We sent fish off [to the lab] to see what the cause of the fish kill was," said Bell. "They found bacteria, parasites, protozoans, you name it." Bell said he thought the outbreak was Mother Nature's way of thinning the populations. "We had a tremendous white bass spawn that spring. The fish were in bad shape." Lack of food for so many fish caused the white bass to be in a weakened condition, which encouraged diseases, Bell speculated.

Since its impoundment, Rough River Lake has supported white bass, but the fishery never became significant to anglers. "Historically, the lake has had a poor white bass population," said Bell. Poor spawning habitat (low flow and low water) may be a factor. "White bass represent about 3 percent of all fish harvested from Rough River Lake," said Bell. The most recent creel survey showed that 2,733 white bass were caught in 1993, up from 1,725 in 1988. Fishing pressure has been correspondingly low. "In early spring we've found some white bass up on shallow mudflats, but nobody is fishing for them."

The best fishing of the year is during the summer, when jump activity erupts off main lake points. Fish Long Lick Creek and Tules Creek. Look for lower densities but larger white bass in the future and much better fishing than in the past.

Hybrid Striped Bass   The hybrid striped bass fishery is rated fair to good, and the outlook is for keeper fish (15-inchers) becoming more numerous. "We're hoping that the hybrid striped bass will take the place of the white bass," said Bell. "They should do well; it's an ideal situation for them."

Hybrids were first stocked in 1995 at a rate of ten fingerlings (1 1/2-inchers) per acre, or 51,000 a year. "We're hoping [this new fishery] might take some pressure off [the hybrids] in Taylorsville Lake," said Bell. By August 1997, most of the hybrids should be keepers (15-inchers). The best strategy is trolling crankbaits and casting jigs and topwater lures in the jumps in June and July on the main lake.

Largemouth Bass   The largemouth bass fishery is rated fair, and the outlook is for a stable population but few keeper-sized fish. On March 1, 1996, a 15-inch minimum size limit took effect. One bass in the six-fish daily creel may be under 15 inches. "I believe the change [to a 15-1 limit] won't have that much impact overall," said Bell. "The average size of the bass will increase, but the opportunity to creel a smaller bass won't be taken away."

Rough River Lake has a reputation of producing largemouth bass up to 8 pounds. "It's a good bass lake, but it's difficult to fish," said Bell. "Locals, who know the lake and fish at night, catch some nice bass." Bass production and growth are good, Bell said. "The lake produces a lot of bass. That sort of equalizes the heavy fishing pressure." The average largemouth bass harvested prior to 1996 was a 12.8-incher. Largemouth bass are the dominate black bass species in the lake, making up 85 percent of the population.

Creel clerk Richard Mehlbauer said a rapidly falling lake level throughout April 1997 really made fishing tough. "There was lots of high, muddy water. In mid-April the lake was as high as 23 feet above summer pool." If there is a silver lining to high water, which frustrates anglers in the spring, it is bank erosion. "There was quite a bit of timber washed into the lake," said Mehlbauer

Spring and summer are prime seasons for largemouth. Mehlbauer said a real productive section of the lake in the spring is the bank from the mouth of Tules Creek to the North Fork boat ramp. In early spring, fish for largemouth bass in the shallow coves. "In late February through early April, you can find some awfully big bass in 3 feet of water or less," said Bell. During the summer months the best fishing is at night on rocky main lake points, where bass hold on stump beds. "The lake colors up real good in the summer," said Bell.

Spotted Bass   The spotted bass fishery is rated fair to good, and the outlook is for low numbers of high-quality fish. "There are a few 10- to 12-inch spotted bass, said Bell. "But, most fish are 8- to 10-inchers." "In recent years, spotted bass populations have been declining to about 15 percent of the black bass population," said Bell. "There's much more fishing pressure." Fish the rocky tributaries and the deep rock structure on the main lake, within a mile of the dam.

Catfish   The catfish fishery is rated good, and the outlook is for numerous high-quality fish. Both channel catfish and flatheads are present. The channel catfish is the dominate species. Catfish are an underutilized resource in the lake.

"In the 1993 creel survey the average channel catfish harvested was 15.9 inches," said Robert Rold, assistant fishery biologist in Kentucky's northwestern district. "That compares with the 14- to 16-inch average for channels taken from Barren, Green, and Nolin." A 16-inch channel catfish weighs about 2 1/2 pounds. Anglers took 2,418 channel and 195 flathead catfish that year. The average flathead harvested was a 21-incher that weighed about 3 1/2 pounds. "Fishing pressure is light to moderate," said Rold. "About 1.25 man-hours per surface acre of water."

The best fishing occurs in the upper lake, where depths are shallower and the water has some color. There is also potential for flatheads up to 30 pounds. "We find channel catfish on the mudflats near submerged creeks, and flatheads on the chunk rock banks and steep bluffs. The chunk rock provides the flatheads with lots of ambush points."

Both species are caught from riprap on the dam and where highway bridges cross the lake. "There's good fishing in late May and June when the channels come up onto riprap to spawn," said Rold. "We get quite a lot of bank fishing for catfish around campgrounds, private docks, and bridge crossings." Some areas suitable for bank fishing for catfish are Rough River Dam State Resort Park on Ky. 79, the Ky. 79 bridge over the North Fork of Rough River; the Ky. 79 bridge at the Axtel campground and boat launching ramp, and the Ky. 737 bridge at Bill' Marina.

Bluegill   The bluegill fishery is rated good, and the outlook is for a stable population of small fish. Most bluegills are less than 7 inches long, and fishing pressure is low.

Tailwater Fishing Opportunities

Several species are available. Walleye were stocked from 1976 to 1978, but the fishery never developed. Rainbow trout are stocked every month but November and December, for a total of about 11,600 fish annually. "We're starting to see [hybrid striped bass] showing up below the dam," said Bell. "I believe they're coming through during the drawdown."

There is no boat launching ramp in the tailwaters, but there is access for small johnboats (launched with a four-wheel drive vehicle), canoes, or float tubes. Access is limited downstream due to private property. The Ky. 110 bridge, about 8 miles below the dam, is a logical take-out point for canoe float trips.

Rough River Lake Dam.

TAYLORSVILLE LAKE

Bluegill ⊷ ⊷ ⊷	Largemouth Bass ⊷ ⊷ ⊷
Catfish ⊷ ⊷ ⊷ ⊷	White Bass ⊷ ⊷ ⊷
Crappie ⊷ ⊷	Tailwaters ⊷ ⊷
Hybrid Striped Bass ⊷ ⊷ ⊷	

Location   Taylorsville Lake is about 25 miles southeast of Louisville in Spencer, Anderson, and Nelson Counties. The lake was completed in the summer of 1982 and reached summer pool the following May. Impounded from the Salt River, the dam is 4 miles upstream of the city of Taylorsville and 60 miles from the Salt River's confluence with the Ohio River. The main access highways are Ky. 44, Ky. 248, Ky. 1066, and U.S. 62.

Size   Taylorsville Lake is 3,050 acres at summer pool (elevation 547). The winter drawdown is minimal, only 2 feet, reducing the acreage to 2,930. At summer pool, the lake is 18 miles long with 75 miles of shoreline. Taylorsville Lake is relatively narrow, only 2,000 feet wide at its widest point, and is 75 feet deep at the dam.

Trophic State Index (TSI)   Taylorsville has a TSI of 62, which ranks it as a eutrophic lake (high fertility).

Lake Manager's Office   U.S. Army Corps of Engineers, Resource Manager's Office, Taylorsville Lake, 2825 Overlook Road, Taylorsville Lake, KY 40071, telephone (502) 477-8882.

Managing Fishery Biologist   Kentucky Department of Fish and Wildlife Resources, Central Fishery District, Kerry Prather, District Biologist, 1 Game Farm Road, Frankfort, KY 40601, telephone (502) 564-5448.

Lake Level/Fishing Report Line   The U.S. Army Corps of Engineers lake information line is (502) 477-8606.

Marinas   There is one marina. *Taylorsville Lake Dock*, open seasonally (March 1 to October 31), is 5 miles east of Taylorsville, off Ky. 2239. The address and telephone number are 1240 Settler's Trace Road, Taylorsville, KY 40071, (502) 477-8766.

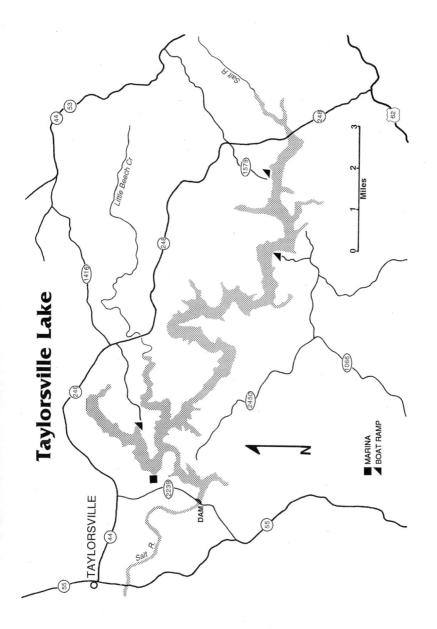

Taylorsville Lake

Salt R.

Little Beech Cr

TAYLORSVILLE

Salt R.

DAM

MARINA
BOAT RAMP

Miles

N

53
44
62
248
1579
1416
248
0066
248
2450
2239
44
55
55

Taylorsville Lake Dock.

Boat Launching Ramps   There are three boat launching ramps on the lake in addition to the ramp at the marina. There is no fee to launch a boat at any of the ramps on the lake. *Van Buren* boat ramp is 6 miles southwest of Mt. Eden, off Ky. 248. *Chowning Lane* boat ramp is 4 miles north of Chaplin, off Ky. 1066. *Possum Ridge* boat ramp is in Taylorsville Lake State Park, off Ky. 248.

Local Tourism Information   Taylorville/Spencer County Chamber of Commerce, 401 Main Street, Box 555, Taylorsville, KY 40071, telephone (502) 477-8369.

Fishing   Taylorsville Lake is the most fertile lake in Kentucky. This high fertility is due to the discharge of treated sewage effluent from Lawrenceburg and Harrodsburg and to the numerous cattle and dairy farms in the Salt River basin. Soon after its impoundment in 1983, biologists began to notice that fish reproduction at Taylorsville Lake was poor. The problem was traced to a heavy silt load that covered spawning areas, high levels of phosphates in the soil, and elevated levels of ammonia, which compromised water quality. Today, these environmental conditions have eased somewhat. Wave action has washed away much of the

A preimpoundment look at the dam at Taylorsville Lake from the visitors center.

silt, exposing rock substrate on banks, and better management of animal wastes on farms above the lake have led to improved water quality.

Taylorsville Lake supports populations of largemouth bass, hybrid striped bass, white bass, crappie, bluegill, and catfish. There is a small population of spotted bass and a very limited population of rock bass. The spotted bass are caught from the lower end of the lake, in the clear water around the dam. Once in a great while someone will catch a smallmouth bass that comes down into the lake from the Salt River, but the population is limited by the high trophic level of the reservoir. Zebra mussels were discovered on the hull of a houseboat docked on the lake.

Because of its closeness to metropolitan Louisville, Taylorsville Lake has a higher number of anglers per acre of water than any other major reservoir in Kentucky. Between April and October of 1995, anglers placed an astounding 564,120 hours of fishing pressure on the reservoir. Helping these anglers is a good deal of standing timber throughout the lake plus beds of pondweed scattered throughout Little Beech Creek.

Catfish   The catfish fishery is rated excellent, and the outlook is for numerous fish of all sizes. The channel catfish is the dominate species, with only a few flatheads present. Fish the timbered coves in the spring, the heads of creeks in the fall, and points next to the old river channel year-round.

Taylorsville Lake continues to offer some of the best fishing for channel catfish in Kentucky, despite growing fishing pressure. The catfish catch rose dramatically from 1,900 fish in 1989 to 9,500 in 1991, and 20,595 in 1992, when the fishery was "discovered." By 1995, the channel catfish had become the lake's third strongest species in terms of harvest and second strongest by weight (first strongest was crappie), accounting for 21 percent of the weight of all fish taken. The average channel catfish harvested was a 13.7-incher. "Channel catfish have really benefitted from the rainy years in the 1990s, which flushed a lot of silt out of the lake," said central district fishery biologist Kerry Prather. "Contrary to what people believe, they do best in lakes with clear, rocky bottoms."

When Taylorsville Lake opened, channel catfish populations had already received a boost. By the end of 1983, more than 57,000 2- to 8-inch fingerlings had been stocked to supplement existing native populations in the Salt River. Additionally, excess hatchery production was dumped in the lake in 1989. This excess amounted to 118,500 2- to 4-inchers. It is unknown to what extent the stockings contributed to the good fishing throughout the 1990s.

Taylorsville Lake is a natural habitat for catfish. There are lots of crevices from all the blown-down timber. The catfish need these crevices during spawning, which begins in June and continues through early July.

Fish with cut shad on flats near the old river channel for best results year-round. Jugs and trotlines are other fishing methods preferred by anglers. Roadbeds, ridges along the old river channels, and brushy flats are good fishing areas. "It's important to remember that catfish won't be below the thermocline, where dissolved oxygen levels are low," Prather said. He suggested fishing no deeper than 12 feet in the lower lake and no deeper than 6 feet in the upper lake.

Hybrid Striped Bass   The hybrid striped bass fishery is rated good, and the outlook is for stable numbers of fish over 15 inches in length. Taylorsville Lake has a five-fish daily creel limit on hybrids and white bass, with a 15-inch minimum. The hybrids were first stocked in 1989, and the lake is considered to have the state's third best hybrid fishery (behind Barren River Lake and Herrington Lake), despite extremely heavy fishing pressure in the early 1990s that cropped off a big surplus of adult fish. "The population hasn't recovered and probably never will," said Prather. "All that fishing with chicken livers really decimated the population." According to the 1995 creek survey, the average fish harvested is 17.1 inches and weighs about 2.6 pounds. "We're seeing hybrids up to 24 inches," said Prather.

Due to heavy fishing pressure, the stocking rate was bumped up to twenty fish per acre, Prather said. "Usually after that first year we go back down to ten fish per acre." Each year about 60,000 hybrids are stocked.

Trolling and casting crankbaits is a good way to catch hybrids spring through fall. "Red and chartreuse were the best colors in spring," said Ben Trail, of Louisville, who fishes the lake regularly. "During the summer it's orange, with a foil see-through body." His lure of choice is the Rat-L-Trap, a sinking, vibrating crankbait. "Shad is probably the best all-around color, but I think chrome has been overfished, and hybrids are wary of it," said Trail. Smaller lures are fished in the spring. Hybrids are feeding on 1 1/2- to 2-inch shad in June. Later in the year Trail will fish larger baits. He fishes a 3/16-ounce size in the summer, but occasionally an 1/8- or 1/4-ounce. "It depends on the time of year and the size of the shad."

Trail said hybrid fishing is particularly good in the spring when the lake is high. "I catch a lot of fish off flooded parking lots when the hybrids are in about 5 or 6 feet of water feeding on crayfish." He also fishes in Ashes Creek, trolling along the tree line.

Trolling speed and depth are as critical as fishing the proper structure. When he lets the lure out behind the boat, Trail counts out fifteen revolutions of the spool on his casting reel. "That's a good starting place," Trail said. "I will bring in line if the fish are shallower." The farther the lure is behind the boat, the deeper it runs. He trolls rather fast with his outboard motor. "In August you have to troll very slowly because the fish get lethargic during the dog days."

Trail prefers to fish with 8-pound test line and sets his reel's drag loose to avoid a break-off when he hooks into a big fish. He has caught hybrids from Taylorsville Lake weighing up to 8 pounds. Every now and then he catches a big hybrid right at dawn, but the best fishing is after 7:30 A.M., when the sun has climbed above the hills. "You can catch hybrids all day if you can stand the heat."

Trail uses a snap to attach his line to the lure. "I think it gives the lure freer action." Snaps also protect the line from the sharp edges of the wire split ring behind the nose of the Rat-L-Trap.

Points, flats, and submerged humps are the structure he trolls most often. Submerged humps tend to concentrate fish, especially if they are near the river channel and deep water. One area he trolls often during the summer months is a hump in midlake, off the main channel, where it is about 12 feet deep on top. Strikes come more often when he trolls toward deeper water from the shallow side of the lake. "All the fish are facing in about the same direction, and they're coming up to take the lure," Trail said. "They're in the deeper water, just below the hump." He often marks the hump with a small plastic buoy to keep from getting off line when trolling.

Largemouth Bass The largemouth bass fishery is rated good, and the outlook is for increasing numbers of 15- to 18-inch fish. It was a puzzle for nearly a decade, but problems with largemouth bass reproduction at Taylorsville Lake are in the past now. Today, the lake's largemouth bass fishery is considered one of the top five in Kentucky. At first, thousands of small bass had to be stocked in the lake each year to sustain the population. But reproductive success began to go up to acceptable levels in the early 1990s, so the stockings were discontinued after 1992.

"The lake was actually too fertile," said Prather. "The wrong kind of algae was being produced, blue-green instead of green algae, and that short-circuited the food chain." The lack of green algae impacted the amount of zooplankton that could be sustained. As a result, bass fry did not get adequate amounts of zooplankton to eat. The water quality problems were compounded by the drought in the late 1980s, but eased with a return to more normal rainfall levels in the early 1990s.

Taylorsville Lake continues to produce high-quality bass—healthy, football-shaped fish. "Bass have a tremendous growth rate, but there are very few large bass," said Prather. "The 8- to 10-pounders simply aren't there. Bass tend to live fast and die young. We don't see many bass over 6 pounds." A cove rotenone study in 1994 showed high poundages of largemouth bass—17.57 pounds per acre, which included 11.18 pounds of harvestable fish. The average weight of the keepers sampled was 1.53 pounds.

"Right now [1997] we're seeing larger numbers of 12- to 15-inch fish than ever before," said Prather. This bodes well for fishing in the late 1990s. There is a 15-inch minimum size limit on largemouth bass.

The best fishing in the spring is in the upper ends of shallow, timbered coves, where streams enter the lake. "We don't see that many bass [when electrofishing] on the main lake shoreline." Prather suggested fishing as far from boat ramps as possible.

Fishing for largemouth bass in Taylorsville Lake in early April. Photograph by Ron Garrison.

Flippin' is a good early season technique, beginning in late March, when bass move from deep water into heavy cover along the shore in coves, where shallow water is being warmed by the sun. Bass guide Brad Weakley said good colors in the spring are a black and blue jig, tipped with a black pork chunk, or a brown jig with a brown pork chunk if the water is muddy. He usually fishes a 3/8-ounce rattle jig.

Beech Creek and Little Beech Creek are excellent embayments to fish in March and April. Crooked Creek and Watts Creek, in the upper lake near Van Buren boat ramp, are also prime embayments in the spring. Seek out breaks in cover type, where a creek enters the lake, or a mud bank turns to rock. Deep water must be nearby.

Using slow-rolling spinnerbaits is also a good early season strategy on Taylorsville Lake. In May, Weakley often finds spotted bass on submerged roadbeds and gravel bars. He catches them on 4-inch tube jigs, in motor oil or smoke glitter color.

After the spawn, Weakly fishes Texas-rigged plastic worms and deep-diving crankbaits to try to entice finicky, suspended bass from flooded timber. "They're in deep water, below the mudline, living in an environment that's undisturbed by anglers and recreational boaters." The idea is to use as little weight as possible on plastic worms so they drift down through the water in a natural manner. "Also, when you use less weight you get hung up less," said Weakley. When fishing crankbaits, Weakley especially likes to concentrate on long, sloping points where a line of submerged timber extends from the shallows out into deep water and intersects a creek channel.

In the fall, largemouth bass return to their bank pattern, locating on rocks and in heavy cover. During the winter, though, bass move out to deep water in creek and river channels.

Crappie   The crappie fishery is rated fair, and the outlook is for increasing numbers of crappie. Beginning March 1, 1997, a 9-inch minimum size limit went into effect. "This should add numbers to the population," said Prather. "And cut down on the number of brood fish being taken." An angler opinion survey in 1995 found that 90 percent of crappie anglers interviewed were in favor of implementing a size limit on crappie at Taylorsville Lake.

Fishing pressure is heavy and growing. In 1995, 62,000 crappie were harvested from the lake, Prather said. "The average fish harvested was a 8.7-incher, but we saw fish up to 13 inches in the creel survey data." The daily creel limit on crappie had already been reduced in 1989 to fifteen because of heavy fishing pressure and poor reproduction. "Reproduction is on the increase and growth has improved greatly since then," said Prather. White crappie is the dominate species, but, Prather said, "We're seeing steady increases in black crappie, and we're finding fish in the upper lake, which is a bit surprising."

White Bass   The white bass fishery is rated good, and the outlook is for numerous 10- to 13-inch fish and increased numbers of fish over the 1996 population. The best fishing is in spring, when the white bass run starts at the headwaters of Taylorsville Lake. The run extends for about 10 miles up the Salt River in Anderson County. White bass first appeared in the lake in the early 1990s and ever since 1993 have been making a spring spawning run, starting in late March when water temperatures approach 50 degrees.

Anderson County conservation officer Steve Votaw said anglers can gain access to the Salt River at the Ky. 53 bridge at Glensboro, at the Anderson City Road bridge, off Ky. 44, and at the bridge on Dry Dock Road, off Ky. 44. Votaw said it is okay to fish where roadways cross the creek, but he reminded anglers that land along the river is private property. "You must get the landowner's permission to be fishing there [from the bank]."

Biologists admit they are puzzled about how white bass got established in Taylorsville Lake. Prather said the fish were illegally stocked in Taylorsville Lake and/or the Salt River by anglers. Aerated tanks were probably used to transport white bass from a nearby river or lake. White bass were not found in any of the fish samples taken from the Salt River before Taylorsville Lake was built, and Prather said there is no mention in the scientific literature of anything other than a remnant population of white bass in the entire Salt River basin.

Prather said white bass numbers appear to be increasing. There is a 9- to 12-inch size range, and most fish being harvested are 10-inchers. Votaw believes that someday the run "could be as good as the old days on Herrington Lake [the Dix River run]."

There is a 15-inch minimum and a daily creel limit of five fish on all white bass and hybrids caught from Taylorsvile Lake. In the Salt River, however, statewide regulations apply. That means there is no minimum size limit on white bass and a daily creel limit of thirty. The boundary between the lake and the river is defined as the first riffle, which is about a half mile upriver from the Ky. 248 bridge, near the Van Buren boat ramp.

Several lures are good for white bass. A white roostertail spinner is an excellent lure for white bass during the run. In the lake, anglers are casting crankbaits, slab spoons, jigs, and plunker and fly rigs. They are drifting live minnows at night on the main lake over lights.

Bluegill   The bluegill fishery is rated good, and the outlook is for good numbers of 6- to 7-inch fish. "We're getting decent growth, and fishing pressure is surprisingly high," said Prather. Big strings of bluegill are being taken on live bait from timbered coves. "We're not seeing lots of bluegills on the main lake banks."

Tailwater Fishing Opportunities

Just about any fish in Taylorsville Lake can be caught from the small tailwaters. "You're likely to see anything there," said Prather. "White crappie, hybrids, largemouth bass, spotted bass, sauger, even striped bass that come up the Salt River from the Ohio River." Fishing is best during high water.

Yatesville Lake

Bluegill ⚬⚬⚬⚬	Largemouth Bass ⚬⚬⚬
Catfish ⚬⚬⚬	Redear Sunfish ⚬⚬⚬
Crappie ⚬⚬⚬	Tailwaters ⚬⚬

Location Yatesville Lake, Kentucky's newest major reservoir, is 5 miles west of Louisa in Lawrence County. The backdrop is piney, forested hills. Impounded from Blaine Creek, which flows into the Big Sandy River about 25 miles upriver from Ashland, Yatesville Lake is within an easy drive of southern Ohio and the large urban area in nearby West Virginia. The main access highways are U.S. 23, Ky. 32, and Ky. 3. A state park is under development, with plans for a campground, picnic area, and sand beach.

Size The 2,242-acre lake first reached summer pool (elevation 630) in the spring of 1992. The drawdown to winter pool (elevation 624.8) reduces the surface acreage to 1,745. Yatesville Lake has 93.9 miles of shoreline and a maximum depth of 60 feet. The 20.6-mile lake's average depth is 17.7 feet. There are three islands. One island is just above the dam, the second is at the mouth of Twin Branch, and the third is at the former site of Carter Bridge.

Lots of timber was left standing in the lake bed, below elevation 633. Other lake structure includes two bridges in the lake bed that were demolished by soldiers from the Kentucky National Guard—the 140-foot single-lane DeLong Bridge on Ky. 1185 and Wellman Bridge on Ky. 32.

Trophic State Index (TSI) Yatesville Lake has a TSI of 43, which ranks it as a mesotrophic lake (moderate fertility).

Lake Manager's Office U.S. Army Corps of Engineers, Resource Manager's Office, Yatesville Lake, Box 1107, Louisa, KY 41230, telephone (606) 686-2412, fax (606) 686-3242.

Managing Fishery Biologist Kentucky Department of Fish and Wildlife Resources, Eastern Fishery District, Steve Reeser, District Biologist, 2744 Lake Road, Prestonsburg, KY 41653, telephone (606) 886-9575.

Yatesville Lake

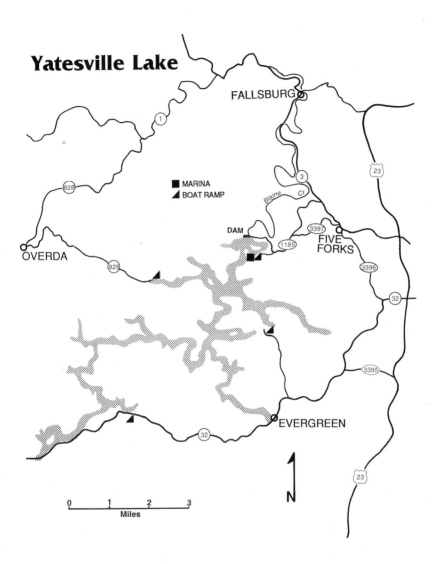

FALLSBURG

MARINA
BOAT RAMP

Blaine   Cr

OVERDA

DAM

FIVE
FORKS

EVERGREEN

0   1   2   3
Miles

N

Lake Level/Fishing Report Line   The U.S. Army Corps of Engineers lake information line is (606) 686-3161.

Marinas   *Yatesville Marina* is expected to be open for business in early 1998. It is adjacent to the Barker's Run boat ramp, 5 miles west of Louisa, off Ky. 1185.

Boat Launching Ramps   There are four boat launching ramps. There is no fee to launch at any of these ramps. *Barker's Run* boat ramp is near the dam, 5 miles west of Louisa, off Ky. 1185. *Rich Creek* boat ramp is in the upper lake, 10 miles west of Louisa, off Ky. 32. *Pleasant Ridge* boat ramp is 8 miles west of Louisa, off Ky. 32. *Twin Branch* is 10 miles southwest of Fallsburg, off Ky. 828.

Local Tourism Information   Ashland Area Convention and Visitors Bureau, 207 Fifteenth Street, Ashland, KY 41105, telephone (606) 329-1007.

Fishing   Yatesville Lake is shaping up as eastern Kentucky's best reservoir. The lake supports good to excellent populations of bluegill, largemouth bass, redear sunfish (shellcrackers), crappie, and catfish. A few smallmouth, old river fish, are still being caught at the head of the lake, but the population is very small and not expected to develop in the fertile waters. Gizzard shad were present in Blaine Creek preimpoundment studies, but for some reason no shad population has developed in the lake. However, there is adequate forage in the way of minnows, shiners, and small sunfish.

Yatesville Lake has classic structure—miles of submerged roadbeds, embayments filled with flooded willows and hardwoods, broad flats, and long, sloping points. The main lake tends to muddy up in the spring after heavy rains, but there are scattered patches of aquatic vegetation in some of the wooded coves fed by clear streams.

Unlike most major reservoirs in Kentucky, Yatesville Lake was built with fishing as the major consideration. After grading of the lake bed was finished, numerous fish attractors were built. "Large piles of trees were cabled down to tree stumps," said John E. McGinn, resource manager for the U.S. Army Corps of Engineers. "Twelve fish attractors are marked by buoys. In many coves, timber was left standing to benefit fishing."

The lake level was raised in stages over several months in early 1992 so that engineers could conduct routine safety tests on the dam. There were water quality considerations, too. McGinn said the last two of more than seventy oil wells in the lake bed were capped in January 1992.

Bob Kise fishes a brushpile marked by a fish attractor buoy.

Near the Barker boat ramp there is a paved fishing jetty with dusk-to-dawn lighting. It has metal handrails and is handicapped accessible. "It's about 25 feet deep off both sides [of the jetty], with riprap humps that come up to about 10 feet below the surface," McGinn said.

Results of the 1996 creel survey showed that 25 percent of the fishermen at the lake are nonresidents. Fishing pressure is increasing as the reputation of the lake grows.

Bluegill   The bluegill fishery is rated excellent, and the outlook is for high-quality fish up to 8 inches. Yatesville Lake offers Eastern Kentucky's best bluegill fishing. Rich farmland was covered by water when the reservoir was built, and the combination of high nutrient levels in the soil, good cover (standing timber and flooded bushes in coves), and the lack of gizzard shad has produced an outstanding bluegill fishery throughout the lake.

Bluegill are very popular with anglers. There was a supplemental stockings of bluegill in 1991-92 of about 340,000 1- to 1 1/2-inchers. According to the 1996 creel survey, 61 percent of the fish harvested were bluegill. Those bluegill represented 36.5 percent by weight of all fish harvested.

The best fishing is in the upper lake. Little Blaine and Rich Creeks are top areas for bluegill. Both embayments have lots of shoreline wood cover and fish attractors. Stringers of "hand-size or bigger" bluegills are taken from these embayments each May and June. Fish live crickets, red worms, and wax worms on poles or ultralight spinning tackle in the brushy shallows, or try foam spiders on a fly rod.

Largemouth Bass   The largemouth bass fishery is rated good, and the outlook is for an expanding population, with many fish in the 16- to 20-inch size range. Yatesville Lake is developing an excellent largemouth bass population, as is typical of new lakes. "There are really good catch rates and lots of bass stockpiled under the 15-inch size limit," said Steve Reeser, eastern district fishery biologist for the Kentucky Department of Fish and Wildlife Resources. "I predict the best fishing is yet to come. I think it will get progressively better." Bass over 7 pounds are being caught.

"Bass numbers are down and quality is up," said Reeser. "The bass I've seen are fat and in good condition." Spawning success has apparently been good, too, with 2 1/2- to 3-pound fish from the lake's first year class being caught. The 1996 creel survey showed that the average bass harvested was a 16.9-incher and that anglers caught 70,600 bass, released 1,500 fish over 15 inches in length, and harvested 963 keepers. About 68,000 undersized bass were released.

Local tournament angler Gary Nelson said the best bass fishing is in the mid to upper end of the lake, and in Little Blaine Creek. "Daniels Creek and Sans Branch are good in the spring."

Nelson said two top lures in March and April are jig and pork rind combinations and spinnerbaits (white or chartreuse and white). "Bass follow the channels. In timbered coves you'll find them staged on the creek channel drop-offs, prior to coming up shallow [to spawn]," said Nelson. Prespawn Nelson also fishes a Zoom fluke, a flat worm with a split tail. In February 1996, he caught a 6-pound, 9-ouncer that had moved up onto a submerged stump row after three days of warm weather.

Local bass angler Bob Kise also fishes plastic baits a lot, preferring the 4-inch Zoom finesse worm. "I fish a finesse worm year-round," said Kise, a member of the Louisa Bass Club. "It's a big fish lure in the spring, and you can catch bass in surprisingly shallow water." Kise hooks the 4-inch worm through the center and inserts a small piece (1/4- to 1/2-inch) of nail into its head. That makes the worm slowly sink with a spiraling action that drives bass crazy. Some of Kise's other favorite lures are 4-inch salty craws; 6-inch lizards, rigged Texas-style with a pegged 1/8-ounce slip sinker; and a variety of propeller surface lures.

Bob Kise with a largemouth bass caught on a 4-inch finesse worm.

Postspawn, in late May and June, bass move out to secondary points to rest up before heading back to creek channels. "Bass can be really aggressive," said Nelson. "I like floating a worm this time of year." His favorite colors are clear and pearl white.

In the fall, when the lake gets real clear, Nelson fishes jerk baits. He likes floating suspending crankbaits such as the Rattlin' Rogue or Rapala. "I also like floating a worm."

Stocking largemouth bass gave the lake a jump start. In March 1991, while the lake was about 10 feet below summer pool, 14,285 7- to 11-inch largemouth bass were placed in the lake. Later, in August, 171,000 2-inch bass and 8,200 4-inch bass were also stocked. So soon after the lake filled there were at least three year classes of subadult bass, and adult fish from Blaine Creek that were up to 17 inches long. This gave the lake a tremendous boost in reproductive potential.

Crappie   The crappie fishery is rated good, and the outlook is for good numbers of 9-inch fish. Keeper-size crappie were caught beginning in 1995, and the population is still expanding. "Crappie have been a real surprise," said Reeser. "Crappie were never stocked, and the population has really taken off."

Reeser said preimpoundment studies of Blaine Creek, which is a tributary to the Big Sandy River, showed that white crappie were present in the drainage. "Yatesville Lake is a shallow, turbid lake. [Water] conditions are conducive to them." The first ever creel survey on the lake in 1996 found that crappie anglers had a 92 percent success rate, topped only by bluegill anglers, who caught fish on 97 percent of the trips they made. "In new lakes the best fishing occurs in the first five to ten years, and we're in that period now."

Yatesville Lake has abundant crappie cover, shallow coves with plenty of flooded shoreline brush and standing timber. At winter pool, the reduced acreage makes some areas difficult to reach by boat. "Shallow water warms up fast, and this is where a lot of crappie seem to be in early spring." Fish the upper ends of creeks beginning in March. "We've had some good reports of stringers of 10- to 12-inch crappie being caught in the spring of 1996," said Reese. "Mostly by bank fishermen in the upper lake."

Redear Sunfish (Shellcrackers)   The redear sunfish fishery is rated good, and the outlook is for a very small population of 7-inch fish. According to Kentucky Department of Fish and Wildlife Resources stocking records, 241,000 shellcrackers were stocked in 1992. All the fish stocked were 1- to 1 1/2-inch fingerlings. "Shellcrackers are showing up in the creel survey data and our samples," said Reeser. "Anglers are harvesting about 1.2 fish per acre." Fish on the bottom with red worms, wax worms, or crickets in shallow embayments of the upper lake.

Catfish The channel catfish fishery is rated good, and the outlook is for numerous fish up to 18 inches in length. Fishing pressure is low. "What we're seeing is numbers of 2- to 3-pound fish," said Reeser. "This fishery is really coming on." Fish the main channel flats with live nightcrawlers or prepared baits in the evenings and at night during the summer.

Tailwater Fishing Opportunities

Development of the tailwaters is in the planning stage. The U.S. Army Corps of Engineers is considering building a boat launching ramp and creating better access for bank anglers, including sidewalks, steps, and railings. Blaine Creek is rich in warm-water fish. There were fifty-one species sampled in preimpoundment surveys, including excellent game fish populations of crappie, spotted bass, smallmouth bass, and rock bass.

Mark Reeder, superintendent of Yatesville Lake State Park, checks on the construction progress of Yatesville Lake Marina.

ADDITIONAL INFORMATION

Law Enforcement on Kentucky's Major Lakes

Kentucky's major lakes are patrolled by employees of the Kentucky Department of Fish and Wildlife Resources, Division of Law Enforcement. They have full police powers to enforce wildlife and boating laws. Kentucky boating laws are detailed in the free brochure *Kentucky Sport Fishing and Boating Guide*, which includes such topics as registration, safe operation, idle speed, personal flotation devices, fire extinguishers, navigation lights, littering, and boating accident reporting requirements. For a copy of the *Kentucky Sport Fishing and Boating Guide* telephone toll free (800) 828-BOAT.

Anglers are reminded that Kentucky state law prohibits drinking alcoholic beverages in public places, including Kentucky's' major lakes and other waterways.

Nonresident anglers bringing boats to Kentucky to fish must have in their possession valid licensing and registration for the vessel. They must also have proper safety equipment, which includes life preservers for each person on board.

How to Report a Wildlife or Boating Law Violation

To report a violation of a wildlife or boating law call 1-800-25-ALERT. The line is open twenty-four hours a day. Callers need not identify themselves, and all information will be kept confidential. Operators can give callers the name and telephone number of local wildlife and boating officers, but they are not equipped to handle routine information requests or to transfer calls.

Illegal Fishing Methods

Fish may not be taken by blasting with explosives, shooting with firearms, or shocking with electricity, under state fish and wildlife regulations. The regulation is outlined in Kentucky Revised Statutes 150.460, section 4. The fine for conviction of illegally taking fish is $100 to $500, imprisonment for up to six months, or both, plus the cost of replacement of the fish.

In Kentucky, only rough fish such as carp, suckers, buffalo, and catfish may be taken during the February 1 to May 10 gigging and snagging season. Gigging and snàgging is legal in streams and in lakes of less than 500 surface acres during the night. In lakes of more than 500 surface acres, gigging and snagging is allowed only during daylight hours. Game fish may not be gigged or snagged under any circumstances.

Persons convicted of illegal gigging or snagging may be fined from $25 to $200, plus court costs. Equipment confiscated as evidence, including boats, may be kept at the court's discretion.

Poachers often use a spotlight to find game fish in shoreline shallows, then spear them with a long-handled gig. Walleye are particularly vulnerable. They are easy to see because their large eyes shine brightly. They are easily gigged while momentarily blinded by the strong light.

Scuba divers may take only rough fish with either handheld spears, or mechanically propelled spear guns on lakes of 1,000 surface acres or larger. Divers are required to have a sport fishing license, and the daily creel limit is fifteen fish.

Fishing Tips/How Weather Affects Fish/ Seasonal Patterns

Fishing is not just sunny days and clear skies. The reality is that weather extremes and changing seasons have a major impact on fish location and feeding habits. Spring, a time of cold water, sluggish fish, and unstable weather patterns, is the best example. Here are some fishing tips related to weather and the seasonal patterns of fish:

> Since fish are cold-blooded animals, their metabolism and feeding activity is largely determined by water temperature. Water temperatures in the 50s demand a much slower lure presentation since warm-water species such as largemouth bass will not move far to eat and will not chase prey. In warmer water (70s, and higher), fish are more active and must feed more often.
>
> The spring spawning period is the best fishing of the year. Prespawn (March), when water temperatures are warming, big female bass move into the shallows and feed heavily as they swell with eggs.
>
> Some species, walleye and white bass for example, make seasonal migrations or "runs" to spawning grounds in lake headwaters. Often, their upstream migrations into rivers are halted by dams, and resulting concentrations of fish provide excellent angling opportunities.
>
> Warm-water species like crappie move up onto shoreline shallows twice a year—spring and fall. During the hot summer months

and during the cold winter months, they migrate out to deeper water, usually creek or river channels. Remember that deep water is cooler in the summer and warmer in the winter.

In tailwaters, smallmouth bass tend to locate near current breaks, whereas largemouth and spotted bass are likely to be out in the center of the eddy. Warm-water species will avoid current when water temperatures are below 60 degrees, so fish on or close to the bottom in deep pools, in bank eddies around concrete walls, or in eddies around bridge abutments.

In the spring, seek out warmer water from runoff, where small streams enter a lake. Bass tend to locate in these areas after warm rains. Even water a couple of degrees warmer than the lake's temperature can make a big difference. Prespawn, look for lunkers in these spots.

Cold fronts drive fish tighter to cover, but not necessarily into deeper water. The bites may be off until warm weather returns, but it is hard for a bass tight to cover to pass up a slow-moving lure right in front of its nose.

Downsize lures when fishing in the midst of a cold front.

Fish black-, brown-, or orange-colored lures in stained water. Go for brighter colors in muddy water.

In the spring, fish crayfish-colored lures around wood cover in shallow water on mud banks. These are areas where crayfish first emerge from the mud when water temperatures begin rising in the spring.

When water levels rise, move up with the fish to newly flooded fields and forests. It is surprising how many big bass are caught off flooded parking lots, drainage ditches, roadbeds, and boat ramps in the spring. Muskie especially like to move into flooded shoreline grass when lakes are on the rise in the spring.

When water levels fall, move out into deeper water, since fish will locate on structure out there.

Look for color edges, where muddy and clear waters blend together, to pinpoint fish location. Bass and walleye use the muddy edges as cover to ambush unsuspecting forage, a stray minnow not paying attention. Once the tributary clears, bass will head back upstream to shallow headwaters.

In the spring, fish the southwest-facing banks. Prevailing winds create waves that push schools of baitfish into the shallows and dislodge crayfish and other bait from the shoreline rocks and drift.

On holiday weekends, when pleasure boat traffic is high, fish at night.

During the bass spawn, the key is finding active, aggressive fish who are not on the nest. Bass on the nest should not be bothered. Leave them alone to their parental duties. Besides, spawning bass are tough to catch.

Fish spinnerbaits in the spring. They are good for locating fish, and the depth of the retrieve can be varied. Suspending crankbaits are also an excellent choice because they can be fished at the level where the bass are holding, and the lure will stay in the strike zone longer. That presentation entices bass when they are sluggish in the early spring.

Catch-and-Release

Catch-and-release fishing, which gained acceptance in the 1960s, is tremendously important today because there are so many more anglers and because of mounting pressure on our fishery resources. Bass tournament anglers pioneered catch-and-release fishing, but many other groups have advocated it for years. Catch-and-release has been widely adopted by trout, muskie, and striped bass anglers, especially during the cold-weather months when thermal stress is not a concern,

Fishery managers admit that if game fish anglers did not release a portion of their catch, they would be hard pressed to provide enough fish to satisfy all segments of the angling community. Some good advice is to release a portion of your catch so it can live to reproduce and provide future recreational opportunities.

If catch-and-release fishing had a motto it would be "handle with care." It is important to properly handle a fish that you are going to release. This caution is required to prevent delayed mortality. Actually, it is best to handle the fish as little as possible. Here are some suggestions:

The larger a fish is, the more care is needed in protecting it from injury. Fish weighing more than 5 pounds must be supported with both hands. One hand should grasp the lip while the other supports the belly.

A big fish grasped only by the jaw can suffer internal injuries. Fish cannot withstand the pull of gravity out of water. Injuries can occur if the jaw is bent, a common method of displaying fish. The heavier the fish, the greater the chance for ligament damage or even a dislocated jaw. While jaw injuries often heal, they can cause disfigurement that may impair a fish's ability to feed.

An indication that a fish is bleeding internally is redness in its fins.

Landing a fish by hand is preferred over the use of a net. Keep the fish in the water while unhooking it if possible. Landing nets should be made of a soft material that will not injure the fish.

The leading cause of delayed mortality is secondary infections from injuries. If a fish is allowed to flop in the bottom of the boat, it will lose the coating of mucus on its skin that helps protect it against bacterial infections.

Fish should only be handled with wet hands. This prevents unnecessary removal of the fish's protective coating.

Commercially available saline solutions can be used to help reduce fish losses, and they are highly recommended during the summer. These solutions reduce stress in bass and help replace the mucus coating. An antibiotic is usually added to help ward off infection. But anglers are cautioned that they may not be safe if the fish are to be consumed, since some of the commercial chemicals on the market contain ingredients deemed poisonous to humans and do not have GRAS (generally recognized as safe) status.

On a deep-hooked fish, when the hook cannot be removed without damaging the gills, tongue, or throat, cut the line or as much of the hook as possible before releasing the fish.

Above 70 degrees, constant aeration of water in the livewell is essential to maintain the high levels of dissolved oxygen fish need to live.

Add ice to lower water temperatures in the livewell when it climbs above 70 degrees, but keep the ice in a plastic bag or use a refreezable ice pack since chemicals used to purify water for human use are harmful to fish.

The temperature of the water in the livewell should be kept about 5 degrees lower than the lake's surface water temperature. Excessive cooling can cause heat shock when the bass is released in the lake.

Anglers who want more than a photograph of their trophy fish, but who do not want to kill their catch, now have a reasonable alternative. It is the reproduction fish—a clone made from gel coat fiberglass. Reproduction fish look so good only your taxidermist will know for sure that it is not the real thing. It is the ultimate memento from that fishing trip of a lifetime—something that you can admire for years from the easy chair in your den.

Harry Whitehead, owner of Gunners Taxidermy in Lexington, said there are several reasons an angler might consider having a reproduction made. First, some fish species cannot be mounted by conventional methods. "Large trout don't mount well because their skin is too thick and oily. If the oil can't be neutralized, the mount will decay over time." By conventional taxidermy methods, the fish's skin, fins, and head are draped over a plastic form. "A reproduction mount is much better quality. It will last longer and look better for a longer time," Whitehead said. Second, reproduction fish mounts are very lifelike. "You can even see the growth rings on the scales. If there's a weakness, it's the lack of detail in the fish's gills and mouth parts."

The reproduction fish is made from a mixture of silicone and graphite. "It's the ideal material because nothing will stick to it," Whitehead said. "Every detail will be faithfully reproduced on the blank." The blank is hollow when it comes out of the mold, but it is usually injected with urethane foam, which the taxidermist paints.

Whitehead said reproduction fish cost about 40 to 50 percent more than conventional mounts. A conventional mount is about $6 to $7 an inch. For example, a 24-inch, 9-pound largemouth bass costs about $156 to mount by conventional methods. A reproduction would be about $228.

A photo of the fish and a couple of quick measurements (length and girth width) before the fish is released alive will help your taxidermist create a reproduction that is as detailed as possible, both in size and coloration.

How to Fillet Fish

Filleting is the fastest way to make quick work of a mess of fish, and by removing the skin and the flesh surrounding the rib bones you are cutting away most of the fat. Be sure to fillet your fish on a flat surface. It will make the job much easier. An electric knife, with twin blades and slow gears, is the best choice. Do not force the knife, let the moving blades do all the work.

The first step in filleting with an electric knife is to make a cut behind the gills right down to the backbone. Then turn the knife toward the fish's tail, letting the blade glide along its backbone. Stop cutting about a quarter inch from the fish's tail. Next, flip the fillet and run the blade between the fish's flesh and its skin, with the scales intact. To make the fillet boneless, cut away the rib cage.

Fishing guide Bobby Leidecker fillets a white bass.

Fish Recipes

It is hard to beat the flavor of fish that has been cleaned and put on ice minutes after being caught. A little planning and proper care go a long way toward helping fish retain that fresh-caught taste.

Fish should be cleaned or filleted as soon as possible after being caught. At the very least, the fish's viscera and gills should be removed. If your catch cannot be cleaned immediately, put it on ice in a cooler. Keeping fish cool is a key to retaining that fresh-caught flavor. Bacteria ruins fish flesh by breaking down protein, resulting is that offensive "fishy" odor that you do not find in fresh fish. Ice water retards this bacterial growth. As a rule of thumb, the weight of the ice in your cooler should be about twice that of the catch. Be sure to drain off the water from the melting ice to rid the fish flesh of excess bacteria.

Properly handled fish retains good flavor for about a week. If you must freeze your catch, place chunks of fish in an old milk carton or plastic dish and cover them with water. This helps keep the fish from drying out and getting freezer burn.

Proper cooking is another key to fresh-tasting fish. Here are three basic recipes:

Fried Fish (Bluegill, white bass, crappie, catfish)

Heat about an inch of vegetable oil in an iron skillet. Cut the fish fillets into chunks and coat them with beaten egg. Then coat the fish in a mixture of corn meal, flour, salt, and pepper. If you like spicy-tasting fish, try sprinkling the coated chunks with Tony Chachere's Creole Seasoning.

When the oil is just about to start smoking, dip the fish chunks into the hot oil. If the oil's temperature is right, the fillets will cook rather quickly, forming a crunchy crust that seals in the flavor. When the fish chunks turn golden brown on one side, turn them over and brown the other side. Drain the cooked fish on a bed of paper towels and sprinkle with lemon juice.

Baked Fish (Walleye, striped bass)

Baked fish is the healthy way to enjoy your catch since the oven's heat melts away the remaining fat from the fillet.

Put the fillets on a roasting dish, salt and pepper them lightly, add butter (or a low-fat substitute) and 2 tablespoons of white wine, and top with slices of Vidalia onion and lemon.

Bake at about 375 degrees for 15 to 20 minutes per pound of fish. Do not overcook the fillets, or you will dry them out.

Microwaving Fish (Walleye, striped bass)

Microwaving in a covered dish is a good alternative to baking if you want your fillets moist and more flavorful.

Salt and pepper the fish lightly, add butter (or a low-fat substitute) and 2 tablespoons of white wine, and top with slices of Vidalia onion and lemon, and microwave on high. The microwaving time should be based on the weight of the fish to be cooked. Consult your owner's manual for cooking suggestions.

Zebra Mussels

The Kentucky Department of Fish and Wildlife Resources is requesting that boaters and anglers report sightings of zebra mussels and help prevent their spread to our major lakes. The first verified sighting of zebra mussels in Kentucky occurred in November 1991 in the lower Ohio River near Paducah. Zebra mussels are established in Kentucky Lake, Lake Barkley, Dale Hollow Lake, and Taylorsville Lake. Veligers, the larval stage of the mussels, have been sampled in Green River Lake, and there is concern that zebra mussels will become established in the Green River below the dam, a section of river that has the most diverse mussel populations in Kentucky.

Research has shown that zebra mussels can outcompete native species, leading to their decline and disappearance. A female zebra mussel can produce 30,000 to 1 million eggs per year. Adults grow in dense clusters, as many as 100,000 or more in a square meter.

Zebra mussels became established in the Great Lakes in 1986 and have since populated most of the connected drainages, including the Ohio, Mississippi, Cumberland, and Tennessee Rivers. In 1993 research biologists verified that the zebra mussel has even spread to the lower Mississippi River, to waters where it was thought the exotic nuisance species could not survive because of high temperatures.

The thumbnail-size, brown or yellow-striped mollusks are thought to have been brought to North America from Europe in the ballast of freighters. Expansion of their range continues, with uncertain effects on native aquatic life. They filter large volumes of water, consume plankton that is food for young-of-the-year game fish species, and encrust bottom structure, which could affect spawning substrate.

Anglers can help stop the spread of zebra mussels and protect their boats by observing these precautions:

Inspect your boat, motor, livewells, and boat trailer for zebra mussels. Remove any that are attached and destroy them by placing them in a jar filled with rubbing alcohol.

Flush the outboard, bilge, and livewell with uncontaminated water to remove larvae.

Zebra mussels can live out of the water for up to ten days but cannot tolerate prolonged heat. Hot salt water (140 degrees) is lethal, but a more practical remedy is to dry-dock your boat on its trailer for several days in the hot sun.

To report the presence of zebra mussels in Kentucky waters telephone (502) 564-3596.

Sun Protection

Anglers who spend a lot of time in the sun risk more than a bad sunburn. Overexposure to the sun is the cause of at least 90 percent of all skin cancers, including malignant melanoma, the most life-threatening form of skin cancer, which can spread rapidly throughout the body. Sun exposure has a cumulative effect on the skin and forces the aging process, causing wrinkles and dry skin, which weakens your skin's elasticity. See a dermatologist if moles or patches of rough skin on your face or hands become discolored. Here are some suggestions for avoiding overexposure to the sun:

Stay off the lake from 10:00 A.M. to 3:00 P.M., when the sun's rays are hottest (the fishing isn't any good that time of day anyway).

Wear a wide-brimmed fishing hat that covers your ears and neck. A ball cap does not provide enough protection.

Cover bare skin with clothing and use sunscreens on exposed areas, especially your hands and face.

Be particularly careful in the spring when the warm rays of the sun are most inviting.

Fishing Map Outlets

Fishing Hot Spots, Inc., of Rhinelander, Wisconsin, produces high-quality fishing maps for lakes in thirty-three states and Canada. Each map sells for $8.95. Add $1.50 for postage and handling on mail orders. The

Kentucky reservoir maps available include Barren River Lake, Cave Run Lake, Dale Hollow Lake, Green River Lake, Kentucky Lake, Lake Barkley, Lake Cumberland, Laurel River Lake, Nolin River Lake, Rough River Lake, and Taylorsville Lake. The 24 by 36-inch maps are printed on a paperlike plastic material that is waterproof and tearproof. The maps float and can be written on with pencil, pen, or crayon. Each map details fishing hot spots, has tips from local experts, and shows boat launching ramps, marinas, water depth, and structure. For mail orders, write to Fishing Hot Spots, Inc., 1999 River Street, Box 1167, Rhinelander, WI 54501, or telephone toll free (800) ALL-MAPS, or fax (715) 369-5590. A free catalogue is available to callers, and credit cards are accepted.

Kentucky Department of Travel Development

The best source for information on state parks, lakes, and privately owned resorts and marinas in Kentucky is the Department of Travel Development. Information may be obtained by writing to Kentucky Department of Travel Development, Capital Plaza Tower, Twenty-second Floor, Frankfort, KY 40601, or by calling toll free (800) 225-8747. Office hours are 8 A.M. to 4:30 P.M., Monday through Friday. Be sure to request information on the specific lake you want to visit.

Fishing guide Rick Holt shows off a morning's catch of striped bass from Lake Cumberland.

INDEX

alcoholic beverages, 263
alewife, 7, 187
all-tackle world record fish. *See* world
record fish, all-tackle *and* International Game Fish Association
Angler Awards Program, 4-5

Barren River Lake, 57; boat launching
ramps, 59; fishing overview, 59-60;
lake level/fishing report hotline, 57;
lake manager's office, 57; location,
57; managing fishery biologist, 57;
map, 58; marinas, 57, 59; size, 57;
tailwaters, 64-65; tourism information, 59; trophic state index, 57
bigmouth buffalo, 8
bluegill. *See* sunfish species
bluntnose minnow, 7
brook silverside, 7
brown trout, 43-44; at Dale Hollow
Lake tailwaters, 104; at Herrington
Lake tailwaters, 152-54; at Lake
Cumberland tailwaters, 196-97; at
Laurel River Lake, 210; at Paintsville Lake tailwaters, 236; state
record, 43-44
Buckhorn Lake, 66; boat launching
ramps, 66-68; fishing overview, 68;
lake level/fishing report hotline, 66;
lake manager's office, 66; location,
66; managing fishery biologist, 66;
map, 67; marinas, 66; size, 66;
tailwaters, 72-73; tourism information, 68; trophic state index, 66
bucktail spinners, 84

Carolina rig, 20, 22, 162
carp, 8
Carr Creek Lake, 74; boat launching
ramps, 76; fishing overview, 76; lake
level/fishing report hotline, 74; lake
manager's office, 74; location, 74;
managing fishery biologist, 74; map,
75; marinas, 74, 76; size, 74;
tailwaters, 79; tourism information,
76; trophic state index, 74
cast nets, 9
catch-and-release, 266-68
catfish, 9; at Barren River Lake, 61-62;
blue catfish, 13; at Buckhorn Lake,
72; bullhead catfish, 13; at Carr
Creek Lake, 78-79; at Cave Run
Lake, 86; channel catfish, 12; at
Dewey Lake, 107; at Fishtrap Lake,
114-15; flathead catfish, 12-13; at
Grayson Lake, 119-20; at Greenbo
Lake, 126; at Green River Lake,
138-39; at Herrington Lake, 151; at
Kentucky Lake, 164; at Kentucky
Lake tailwaters, 169; at Lake
Barkley, 177; at Lake Barkley
tailwaters, 179; at Lake Cumberland, 195; at Lake Malone, 204; at
Laurel River Lake, 215; at Martins
Fork Lake, 220; at Nolin River
Lake, 227; at Paintsville Lake, 235-
36; at Rough River Lake, 242; state
record, 12, 13; at Taylorsville Lake,
247-48; white catfish, 78-79; at
Yatesville Lake, 261
Cave Run Lake, 80; boat launching
ramps, 82; fishing overview, 82; lake
level/fishing report hotline, 80; lake
manager's office, 80; location, 80;
managing fishery biologist, 80; map,
81; marinas, 80, 82; size, 80;
tailwaters, 88-90; tourism information, 82; trophic state index, 80
commercial fishing, 8
crappie, 14; at Barren River Lake, 62;

ART LANDER JR. has fished Kentucky's major lakes since childhood. A native Kentuckian, Lander grew up in St. Matthews, a suburb in eastern Jefferson County. During college he worked as a summer fishery aide for the Kentucky Department of Fish and Wildlife Resources. He started writing about fishing, hunting, and outdoor recreation after graduation from Western Kentucky University with a B.A. in mass communications in 1972.

He worked in the tourism industry in the early 1970s, was a freelance writer/ photographer in the late 1970s and early 1980s, and worked as an information officer for the Kentucky Department of Fish and Wildlife Resources for two years. Lander has been a staff writer for the *Lexington Herald-Leader* since June 1986, writing the Sunday outdoors page. In 1991 he won the Best Outdoor Page Award, the top newspaper award presented by the Outdoor Writers Association of America.

Since 1985, Lander and his family have lived on a 107-acre farm in Henry County. He is married to folk artist Bonnie Brannin Lander. They have three children—Laura, 11; John, 9, and Maggie, 5. Lander enjoys fly fishing for bass and hunting deer and wild turkey. In his spare time he builds and shoots caplock and flintlock muzzle-loading rifles.